FOR THE PEOPLE

Visions of Governance in the 21st Century

Why People Don't Trust Government
Joseph S. Nye Jr., Philip Zelikow, and David King, editors
(1997)

Governance in a Globalizing World
Joseph S. Nye Jr. and John D. Donahue, editors
(2000)

Governance amid Bigger, Better Markets
John D. Donahue and Joseph S. Nye Jr., editors
(2001)

Governance.com: Democracy in the Information Age
Elaine Ciulla Kamarck and Joseph S. Nye Jr., editors
(2002)

Market-Based Governance:
Supply Side, Demand Side, Upside, and Downside
John D. Donahue and Joseph S. Nye Jr., editors
(2002)

FOR THE PEOPLE

Can We Fix Public Service?

John D. Donahue

Joseph S. Nye Jr.

Editors

VISIONS OF GOVERNANCE
IN THE 21ST CENTURY
Cambridge, Massachusetts

BROOKINGS INSTITUTION PRESS
Washington, D.C.

Copyright © 2003
Visions of Governance in the 21st Century

All rights reserved. No part of this publication may be reproduced or transmitted in any form or by any means without permission in writing from the Brookings Institution Press, 1775 Massachusetts Avenue, N.W., Washington, D.C. 20036 (fax: 202/797-6195 or e-mail: permissions@brook.edu).

Library of Congress Cataloging-in-Publication data

For the people : can we fix public service? / John D. Donahue, Joseph S. Nye, editors.
　　p.　　cm.
Includes bibliographical references and index.
　ISBN 0-8157-1896-9 (cloth)—ISBN 0-8157-1897-7 (pbk)
　1. Public administration—United States.　2. Administrative agencies—United States—Management.　3. Organizational change—United States.　4. Civil service—United States.　5. Political leadership—United States.　I. Donahue, John D.　II. Nye, Joseph S.
JK421.F593 2003
352.6'3'0973—dc21　　　　　　　　　　　　　　　　2003006184

9 8 7 6 5 4 3 2 1

The paper used in this publication meets minimum requirements of the American National Standard for Information Sciences—Permanence of Paper for Printed Library Materials: ANSI Z39.48-1992.

Typeset in Adobe Garamond

Composition by R. Lynn Rivenbark
Macon, Georgia

Printed by R. R. Donnelley
Harrisonburg, Virginia

Contents

Acknowledgments

THE VISIONS PROJECT has come full cycle. It was launched in 1996 by a new dean at Harvard's professional school of government to trace the changing contours of the world in which the Kennedy School's graduates would work. In seven years of scholarship and practical engagement it crossed the millennial divide, amending its banner from Visions of Governance *for* to Visions of Governance *in* the Twenty-First Century. During its transit from anticipating to accommodating the new century it tracked the diffusion of public missions away from the central state and into more complex networks of authority and accountability embracing multiple levels of government as well as private actors. In the five books Visions has produced directly, and at least as many more the project sparked or supported, it identified and examined pivotal challenges in the context and mission of modern governance. Prominent among these are the erosion of trust in government; the metamorphosis of "globalization" from a hyperbolic cliché to an intricately concrete reality; the unfolding consequences of the information revolution; and the protean role of growingly sophisticated but imperfectly channeled market forces.

As the project matured a key realization crystallized: Mastering these challenges depends—not exclusively, but overwhelmingly—on the talents, training, motivation, ethos, and organization of the people who do the work of governance. It comes down to the people. This is not particularly surprising, of course. It could be waved off as a self-serving conclusion, for scholars at a professional school of government, were the logic not so plain and the evidence not so compelling. This sixth and final Visions book both brings to closure a cycle of research and hints at new directions in teaching and practice for public service.

With the closing of the circle it is fitting to acknowledge the debts incurred not just in the production of this book, but throughout the enterprise. David C. King, Philip D. Zelikow, and Elaine Ciulla Kamarck helped lead Visions of Governance in the crucial early years, shaping its trajectory in both obvious and subtle ways.

The work of the project would not have been possible without the financial generosity and, in many cases, the astute advice of the Christian A. Johnson Endeavor Foundation, the Daniel and Joanna S. Rose Fund, the Herbert S. Winokur Fund for Public Policy, the Parker Gilbert Montgomery Endowment, Kenneth G. Lipper, the Henry J. Kaiser Family Foundation, the Xerox Foundation, the Carnegie Corporation of New York, Oracle Corporation, the Pew Charitable Trusts, the Stratford Foundation, the Ash Fund for Research on Democratic Governance, and the Smith Richardson Foundation.

The roster of authors who have written Visions of Governance book chapters and working papers is long and distinguished, including Graham T. Allison, Drew E. Altman, Arthur Isak Applbaum, Robert D. Behn, John M. Benson, Linda J. Bilmes, Robert J. Blendon, Iris Bohnet, Derek Bok, George J. Borjas, Mario Brossard, Mollyann Brodie, L. David Brown, Sheila Burke, L. Jean Camp, Ashton B. Carter, William C. Clark, Cary Coglianese, Richard Darman, Georges de Menil, Akash Deep, John M. Deutsch, Susan C. Eaton, Karen Eggleston, Jane A. Fountain, Jeffrey Frankel, Peter Frumkin, Archon Fung, William A. Galston, David Gergen, Stephen Goldsmith, José A. Gómez-Ibáñez, Anna Greenberg, Merilee S. Grindle, Lim Siong Guan, David M. Hart, William W. Hogan, Deborah Hurley, Ronald Inglehart, Matt James, Elaine Ciulla Kamarck, Nancy Katz, Barbara Kellerman, Steven Kelman, Robert O. Keohane, Alex Keyssar, Sanjeev Khagram, David C. King, Robert Z. Lawrence, David Lazer, Jane Mansbridge, Ernest R. May, Viktor Mayer-Schönberger, Jerry Mechling, John R. Meyer, Mark H. Moore, Richard Morin, Jeffrey R. Neal, Richard E. Neustadt, Joseph P. Newhouse, Pippa Norris, Gary

Orren, Paul E. Peterson, Susan J. Pharr, Dani Rodrik, Neal M. Rosendorf,
Tony Saich, Guido Schaefer, Frederick Schauer, Robert N. Stavins, John
Thomas, Dennis Thompson, Kenneth Winston, Virginia J. Wise, Richard
J. Zeckhauser, and Philip D. Zelikow.
Other participants, from Harvard and beyond, have worked through
Visions seminars, symposia, and working groups to inspire, critique,
reshape, and refine the written products, including Alan Altshuler, Francis
Bator, Michael Blake, Nolan Bowie, Kim Campbell, Carol Chetkovich,
Richard Cooper, Pepper Culpepper, Mickey Edwards, Jeffrey Eisenach,
David Ellwood, Richard Falkenrath, Marshall Ganz, Henry Louis Gates,
Ed Glaeser, Robert Glauber, Mary Ann Glendon, Jerry Grossman,
Ricardo Hausmann, Stanley Hoffmann, Samuel Huntington, Ira Jackson,
Sheila Jasanoff, Christopher Jencks, Alexander Jones, Calestous Juma,
Linda Kaboolian, Marvin Kalb, Joseph Kalt, Rod Kramer, Edwardo Loyo,
Taeku Lee, Dutch Leonard, Jeffrey Liebman, Richard Light, Florencio
Lopez de Silanes, Tom Loveless, Brian S. Mandell, Harvey Mansfield,
Theodore R. Marmor, Thomas McCraw, Shelley Metzenbaum, Andrew
Moravcsik, W. Russell Neuman, Bonnie Newman, Katherine Newman,
Kalypso Nicolaïdis, Anthony Oettinger, Richard Parker, Thomas
Patterson, Roger Porter, David Pryor, Robert Putnam, Iqbal Quadir,
Hannah Riley, Barbara Roberts, John Ruggie, Jeffrey Sachs, Michael
Sandel, Holly Taylor Sargent, F. M. Scherer, Philip R. Sharp, Miles Shore,
Theda Skocpol, Anne-Marie Slaughter, Monica Duffy Toft, Raymond
Vernon, Jane Wales, John White, Shirley Williams, Julie Boatright
Wilson, William Julius Wilson, Daniel Yankelovich, Peter Zimmerman,
and Jonathan Zittrain.
One hard truth about research—even well-funded work, rigorously con-
ceived and conducted, refined through collegial discussion, and presented
with care—is that it's not much good unless it's published, and published
well. Our relationship with the Brookings Institution Press has been a
pleasant and productive partnership, generating five books in four years.
We applaud the professionalism and acknowledge the wise counsel of
Christopher Kelaher (who first saw the merits of this series), Holly
Hammond, Katherine Kimball, Janet Schilling Mowery, Janet Walker, and
Susan Woollen.
This wide-ranging undertaking has relied over the years on the skills of
many Kennedy School staff members, both junior and senior. We owe

particular thanks to Janet Fletcher Hauswirth, Jeanne Marasca, Sarah Peterson, Sara Porter, Alex Scacco, Kristian Schneeman, Patience Terry, Lori Carr Trevino, Joan Goodman Williamson, Todd Wilson, and Robin Worth.

Lynn Akin warrants our special thanks. For the past five years Lynn has been the managerial and logistical mainstay for Visions of Governance. Her judgment, initiative, and relentless good cheer have been essential to our work, up to and emphatically including every detail of this book's preparation.

JOHN D. DONAHUE
JOSEPH S. NYE JR.

Cambridge, Massachusetts
May 2003

For the People

1

JOSEPH S. NYE JR.
JOHN D. DONAHUE

Introduction

AMERICANS HAVE BEEN ambivalent about government from the start. The Framers cherished liberty more than efficiency and designed our institutions accordingly.[1] Their goal, as it is sometimes said, was to make it impossible for King George to govern America—if necessary, at the expense of making it close to impossible for anyone else to govern. While the founding generation revered public service, they viewed it not as a separate profession but as the right and the duty of leading citizens at large. The proper preparation for public service was thus no different from the education that elites chose for their sons whatever their ambitions—a general grounding in the classics or, later, apprenticeship in law.

"Public business must be done by someone," John Adams wrote to his son in 1789; better that it be done by those well endowed with wisdom and integrity. But Adams warned that public service must be an avocation, not an occupation. The true public servant "must make it a rule never to become dependent on public employment for subsistence. Let him have a trade, a profession, a farm, a shop, something where he can honestly live, and then he may engage in public affairs, if invited, upon independent principles."[2]

Adams himself, to be sure, flagrantly violated his own maxim; from young manhood onward he was intensely and almost exclusively devoted to public life. Many other revolutionary-era leaders were full-time public

[margin note:] Compare to Weber

servants with a sideline in farming, law, or silversmithing, rather than the reverse. But it is nonetheless true that government employment was a decidedly modest occupational category in America's early decades. Aside from George Washington's army—which nearly everyone viewed as a temporary, if vital, aberration—government was mostly small, overwhelmingly local, and technically and administratively simple. The relative handful of appointive state and federal offices were regarded as spoils of battle, to be allocated by electoral victors to allies endowed with loyalty (to be sure) and good character (to be hoped) but seldom with any specialized skills.

This model gradually became less workable as a national economy emerged, technical and social complexity increased, and the Civil War and its aftermath sparked a surge in the scale and duties of the federal government. As the downside of the spoils system became apparent, Congress passed the Pendleton Act of 1883, creating a structured, merit-based federal civil service. Many states followed suit. Yet while the notion of a professional military career solidified with the establishment of West Point in 1802, the concept of a career in civilian public service developed only late in the nineteenth century, and the growth of federal government employment is largely a twentieth-century phenomenon. Although the Progressive Era led to significant increases in government regulation, as late as 1929 the federal government represented only 3 percent of America's economy. It was the military and social mobilization of the twentieth century that produced a federal government accounting for over 18 percent of gross domestic product, with state and local government adding roughly another 10 percent.[3] At the century's end nearly one out of every seven workers was employed by government.[4] While these percentages are low compared to other developed countries—and well under the peak of more than one-fifth of the work force a quarter century earlier—they are high by historical standards.

In the waning decades of the twentieth century Americans expressed growing dissatisfaction with government and public servants. Opinion polls in the early 1960s found that three-quarters of respondents held a great deal of confidence in the federal government. By the end of the century this had slipped to little more than one-quarter. State and local government scored slightly better in absolute levels of confidence but showed the same slide in citizens' esteem. Government employees, from teachers to postal workers to FBI agents, were increasingly portrayed in a negative light in popular culture. It became entirely unremarkable for politicians—even incumbents—to campaign against "the government." Educated young people, including graduates of schools of public policy and administration, became less likely to enter government service. Politicians and public officials from across the ideological spectrum grew concerned about a human capital crisis in government.

When the Visions of Governance project got under way in 1996, the first area of inquiry was the loss of confidence in government.[5] We found a variety of causes, some clearly related to the public sector's actual performance but many not. Declining esteem for the public sector was driven in part by changes in the news and entertainment media. Most people report forming their views of government from the media rather than from their direct experience. For example, according to one study in the 1970s (when the sharpest declines in trust occurred), two-thirds of the people who had direct dealings with federal and state bureaucrats reported that they were satisfied with their treatment even while disapproving of government in the abstract. If the conventional wisdom conveyed by political campaigns, news reports, and entertainment media is that government is a gang that can't shoot straight, then it is not surprising that polls mirror this conventional wisdom. And it is illuminating that the anomalous instances of agencies that bucked the trend of declining confidence, such as the military and the postal service, were the ones permitted to deploy advertising campaigns to present themselves in a positive light.

Moreover government was not alone in the loss of public confidence. Business, universities, the press, and many other institutions suffered a similar loss of esteem. In many ways this is both inevitable and healthy. As cultures mature, citizens tend to become more questioning of authority and more skeptical of institutions in general. Particularly in the United States, confidence in government may well have been artificially inflated in the 1950s and early 1960s as a result of its success in World War II, so that the subsequent slump can be seen as a reversion to the long-term American norm.

Yet it would be a mistake to let government off the hook completely. For one thing, the decline in confidence is not merely an American phenomenon. Polls show similar trends in most developed societies, including ones with strong state traditions, like France and Japan. And the polls are echoed in changes in behavior. Once the brightest university graduates in France sought entrance to the École Nationale d'Administration, and the top graduates of Tokyo University rushed to join the civil service, but the public sector is losing its perch at the pinnacle of the job market in both of these countries. Nor did the revolt against government start with the presidency of Ronald Reagan. The sense that government had become insular and aloof, bureaucratic and unwieldy (with a corresponding enthusiasm for markets as suppler and more flexible instruments) became widespread in the last quarter of the century. In fact, as Elaine Kamarck relates in chapter 8 of this volume, the reaction against government bureaucracy started earlier and went further in countries like Great Britain and New Zealand.

The perception of government as bureaucratic and inflexible undermines the willingness of young people to enter traditional public service. Money is part of the problem, too. As George Borjas demonstrates in chapter 3 of this book, government tends to pay less skilled workers better wages than they would earn in the private sector. But government compensation is relatively meager for skilled workers, reducing the incentive for the most talented people to enter or remain in government service. While the pattern of relative compensation is fairly clear, its implications are not. Talented young people are motivated not only—indeed, not primarily—by money but also by the desire to make a difference. This does not necessarily make government's recruitment problem easier, however. As the Brookings Institution political scientist Paul Light puts it, skepticism about government careers is not merely a matter of "show me the money" but also of "show me the work."[6] To the extent that the work is highly bureaucratized, hostile to initiative, rule bound, and rigged into rigid career ladders, it is less appealing to young people today. Added to this is the blow to morale inflicted by politicians' and the media's ingrained habit of casual contempt for government workers. It is not surprising that many public-spirited young Americans view the nonprofit sector more favorably as a setting for doing good without the rigidities and indignities of government work.

At first glance the September 11, 2001, terrorist attacks seem to have reversed some of these effects. The atrocities themselves remind us that the common good is no empty abstraction and that markets cannot solve all problems. Beyond that, the indelible memory of New York police, firemen, and rescue workers climbing the stairs of the World Trade Center while others were streaming down created a vivid, visceral image of what public service can mean. It is not surprising that applications for government work increased or that polls showed a rise in confidence in government to levels not seen since 1964. But September 11 did not put an end to the underlying problems that plague government and public service. Americans predictably rally around public leaders and public institutions in a crisis but (just as predictably) lapse back to prior attitudes and behaviors as the crisis ebbs. Polls about confidence in government and interest in public service dipped back downward within a year of the attacks. This is not surprising. Even a shock as stunning as September 11 can have only a limited impact on deeply etched public perceptions. Nor does the dramatically demonstrated importance of public tasks guarantee that government will be able to perform them well. Our work in the Visions of Governance in the Twenty-First Century project identified three long-term trends that are changing the context of government in this century. These interrelated forces include marketization (the elaboration and extension of market principles and institutions), globalization (the development of transcontinental interdependence that shrinks the effects of distance), and the information revolution (the dramatic decline in the costs of computing and communications).[7] Although these trends are not the only forces at work, they are acting to diffuse a degree of power, responsibility, and even legitimacy held by central governments. If one imagines the terrain of collective activity extending vertically from local to national to supranational and horizontally across the private, public, and nonprofit sectors, one can map the changing pattern of governance across a nine-cell matrix (table 1-1).

Governance—the authoritative organization of collective choice and action—thus extends beyond formal government. Private rules and standards can produce, undercut, or reshape public goods; witness the benefits of certified accounting when it operates as advertised, for example, and the havoc it wreaks when it goes bad. Nonprofit institutions can aggregate and assert political preferences, pursue on their own almost any specialized definition of the public good, or contract to provide government services across traditional boundaries. Central governments remain key actors, but they increasingly have to share the stage with other levels of government as well as other sectors.

Although formal government remains at the center of governance, its role is progressively diminished, and dissatisfaction with conventional bureaucracy is forcing a change in how it plays that role. The new public management and related reform themes stress performance measurement, outsourcing, and an enhanced reliance on indirect action rather than direct production of services by government agencies. The result is a need for different skills in government work, not only the capacity to discern public value through policy analysis and deploy government workers to deliver services directly but also the ability to structure and supervise contracts and negotiate with a broad range of actors in different sectors.

Table 1-1. *Trends in Governance in the Twenty-First Century*

Collective activity	For-profit sector	Public sector	Nonprofit sector
Supranational	Transnational organizations	Intergovernmental organizations	Nongovernmental organizations
National	National corporations	Federal agencies	National nonprofit groups
Local	Local businesses	State and local government	Local nonprofit groups

Public service in the era of distributed governance depends less on traditional aptitudes for direct administration and more on professional skills that can be roughly summarized this way:

—Appraisal. Calibrating the dimensions of a governance challenge and the defects of the status quo.

—Analysis. Appreciating, in a sophisticated way, the forces at work in a policy arena and identifying the incentives and predicting the behavior of the actors within it.

—Assignment. Selecting the institutional players to be tasked with a particular responsibility (to the extent the organizational constellation is malleable).

—Architecture. Designing a structure of information flows, financial relationships, and accountability arrangements with the best odds of focusing the energies of public and private participants on real sources of collective value.

—Assessment. Evaluating the enterprise, to whatever level of precision permitted by the available data and the degree of normative clarity and consensus that exists.

—Adjustment. Deploying formal or informal authority, guided by analysis and assessment, to fine-tune the structure, targeting, or operations of the endeavor.

The concept of public service is thus evolving to encompass the creation of shared benefits by actors outside formal government. If one defines leadership as the work of articulating and advancing shared goals, then public leadership is exercised by anyone who does this work for a community as a whole (as opposed to a self-selected subset of members, customers, or investors). Public leaders are defined by their activity (creating collective value) and not by their location in the traditional public sector. This is not to suggest that leadership is becoming an undifferentiated commodity that works in the same way, and to equal effect, in any setting. Often successful leaders in one group, time, or sector prove to be unsuccessful when the context changes. Yet a recurrent phrase in current work on leadership is "leadership without walls"—the ability to operate across different contexts, sectors, times, and institutions. One of the key issues for the future of public service broadly defined is how to prepare people for this type of work.

As Alexander Keyssar and Ernest R. May point out in chapter 12 of this volume, the United States has only recently embraced the mission of training people for public service, even as conventionally and narrowly defined. Only in the early twentieth century did the idea of training in public administration develop. Later in the century this was enriched by training in public policy and public management. Economics supplemented and, in some cases, supplanted administration and law as the dominant discipline for such training. The 250 or so schools and programs that comprise the National Association of Schools of Public Affair and Administration vary widely in their approaches and serve different segments of the market, from local to regional to national. But they are far from constituting a monopoly in the preparation of public servants. Recruits come from a wide range of backgrounds, though (as John Donahue demonstrates in chapter 4 of this book) top leaders, at least in the federal sector, still tend to spend much of their careers in government. Perhaps what is needed most is not a resolution to the old internal debate about how best to prepare people for government work but rather a broader, more ambitious discussion about the education of public leaders for work that is anchored in but not limited to formal government. This is a conversation that includes not only schools of public policy and administration but also schools of law, business, and other professions.

Just as war is too important to be left to the generals, so public service may be too vital to restrict to government professionals. But, like Moliere's bourgeois gentleman who discovered he had been writing prose all his life, we may have been practicing this craft without discerning its principles. The United States has never had a tradition of an elite civil service, relying instead on a veneer of federal appointees serving short stints at senior levels. This often results in rapid turnover and loss of expertise at the top. But, as Derek Bok argues in chapter 14 of this book, this pattern provides for a more rapid infusion of new ideas and for greater democratic accountability than is true of the elite services of Europe and Japan. For the benefits of this model of public service to outweigh the costs, he suggests, these "amateurs" must be both educated in relevant skills and encultured in the ethic of public service.

John Adams no doubt would endorse Bok's prescription. Indeed restoring and revising public service for the twenty-first century is a twofold challenge. Some public leaders will follow Adams's advice and serve episodically in government while pursuing mostly private work. Others will follow Adams's example and dedicate their careers to the public sector. We need to structure our rules and institutions—in government, in the private sector, and in academia—to affirm both paths and to equip budding leaders to follow them.

The diffusion of public leadership does not mean its diminution; quite the contrary. Government itself remains a distinctive and indispensable— even if not exclusive—arena for the exercise of public leadership. What we are witnessing, in short, is not the end of public service but its evolution. The evidence and arguments assembled in the chapters to come make it hard to deny that many aspects of public service are strained, bent, even broken. But they also offer grounds for optimism. The imperatives of public work and the systems allocating talent to tasks have been badly misaligned before. This is not the first time public service has been broken, and we are not the first generation challenged to fix it. From the Pendleton Act to the Progressive reforms to the first wave of professional training for government, our predecessors developed ways to better align the efforts undertaken "by the people" with the work to be done "for the people." The problems today are different, to be sure, and doubtless the remedies will be, too. But it is not reckless to expect that, guided by analysis like that assembled here, we will prove able to improvise fixes that fit the challenges of public service in the twenty-first century.

Notes

1. To be precise the champions of efficiency among the Framers lost most of the arguments on institutional design, as Robert Behn describes in chapter 11 of this book.

2. John Adams, letter to Thomas Boylston Adams, September 2, 1789, excerpted in David McCullough, *John Adams* (Simon and Schuster, 2001), p. 415.

3. Office of Management and Budget, *Budget of the United States Government, Fiscal Year 2003*, historical tables.

4. Bureau of Economic Analysis, Department of Commerce, *Survey of Current Business*, National Income and Product Account Table 6.5, various issues. About 3.5 percent of the work force was employed at the federal level (including the armed services and postal service), while another 12 percent worked for state and local government.

5. See Joseph S. Nye, Philip Zelikow, and David King, eds., *Why People Don't Trust Government* (Harvard University Press, 1998).

6. Paul C. Light, *The New Public Service* (Brookings, 1999), p. 3.

7. On these large trends shaping the challenge of governance, see the previous four books in the Visions series published by Brookings: Joseph S. Nye Jr. and John D. Donahue, eds., *Governance in a Globalizing World* (2000); John D. Donahue and Joseph S. Nye Jr., eds., *Governance amid Bigger, Better Markets* (2001); Elaine Ciulla Kamarck and Joseph S. Nye Jr., eds., *Governance.com: Democracy in the Information Age* (2001); and John D. Donahue and Joseph S. Nye Jr., eds., *Market-Based Governance: Supply Side, Demand Side, Upside, and Downside* (2002).

PART I

DIAGNOSIS
What's Wrong with Public Service Today?

2

DAVID GERGEN
BARBARA KELLERMAN

Public Leaders:
Riding a New Tiger

No one can say with certainty what the practice of public leadership will look like in the future, but we do know that it will be different and more demanding than in the past. Walls are coming down everywhere, information is exploding, diversity is increasing, resources are constrained, constituents are expecting better results for less money—and these are just the known changes. The rapidly unfolding events of the past few years—a bursting economic bubble, scandals in corporate suites, and now a widening war on terrorism—suggest that we are in for a period of unpredictability, even fragility, that will challenge the imagination of public institutions at all levels of government. After his tumultuous years in the White House, Harry Truman reflected in his memoirs, "Being a President is like riding a tiger. A man has to keep on riding or be swallowed."[1] Public leaders of the future will be riding a tiger, too.

To succeed, public officials will need to be well educated and broadly gauged. It will not be sufficient to master a single discipline; a city administrator will need to be a good organizer but must also be entrepreneurial. Nor will it be sufficient to know a single language; a school superintendent will need to speak Spanish as well as English. The chief executive officer of a public hospital must learn how to integrate information technologies into services for patients and doctors. The state director of natural resources will work out ever-closer relationships with nonprofits and corporate vice presidents for social responsibility. Men and women elected to office, from city hall to the White House, will be expected to understand cultures in lands they barely heard of growing up.

Moreover, those entrusted with power in public institutions must learn to exercise it differently than in the past. One institution after another has already learned that it can no longer pass out a manual of instructions and expect high performance: Every public servant must have the flexibility and latitude to respond nimbly to changing circumstances. An army lieutenant may take his troops into combat in January, start enforcing police laws in February, and begin rebuilding a community in March. The command-and-control approach of a General Patton is now out in the military, just as it has disappeared in other public institutions and in corporate America. Power must be allowed to move down within organizations, so that those at lower levels can act quickly on their own, unhampered by bureaucratic rigidities. As we are learning, the best leader is one who assembles the best team—and then becomes a leader of leaders. That is not to say that the person at the top must hand all decisionmaking to others below; that person must still set a direction, determine goals, and mobilize others. But success will no longer come by issuing edicts and micromanaging; it will come through inspiration and persuasion.

Where will we find the men and women to undertake such responsibilities? It won't be easy: The best of the younger generation are idealistic and want to achieve social change, but they are wary of careers in public service and disillusioned about politics. For those who do volunteer to serve, how can we best prepare them to serve well? That answer is also elusive: A student who specializes in economics may become an excellent budget director but a lousy governor, while a graduate with a more generalized education may lack the analytical skills to make sophisticated policy decisions. Clearly balances must be sought.

There are important implications here for universities seeking to prepare young people for service in the public arena. In chapter 12 of this volume Alexander Keyssar and Ernest R. May trace the slow and uneven path the United States has followed in preparing its citizenry for governance. For much of the nineteenth century, in Tocqueville's phrase, society paid little attention to the art of administration but lived "from hand to mouth, like an army in the field." In the late nineteenth and twentieth centuries universities began focusing on public administration as a field of study and instruction. Many students enrolled. That emphasis gave way in the 1960s and early 1970s to a focus on public policy, as confidence grew in the power of economics to solve public policy problems. But rather quickly the focus changed again, this time to what was called public management, as schools promised to train students in the implementation as well as the design of policies. That is the past that Keyssar and May describe. Now there are signs that another shift could be under way—toward a heavier emphasis on public leadership. Various universities, including Harvard, Yale, Stanford, and Duke, have launched leadership initiatives; faculties, while still abounding with skeptics, are showing increased interest; and students are responding enthusiastically. (The authors of this chapter direct the Center for Public Leadership at Harvard's Kennedy School of Government.)

A shift toward training in public leadership will not mean a radical change. Obviously students in universities, especially public policy institutions, must still learn traditional disciplines. Moreover, it is a rash scholar in leadership who claims that the field has developed firm intellectual foundations; the field remains relatively young and will require far more research and scholarship. But it is equally clear that it would be enormously constructive if large numbers of young people were being trained to become responsible, effective, moral leaders. Public policy institutes must do more than prepare their best graduates to be GS-15s; they must also prepare students to become assistant secretaries, cabinet officers, members of Congress, not to mention mayors, governors, and so on. Moreover, those graduates who do rise to the highest levels of civil service these days must do more than administer; they must also lead. Thus an increasing emphasis upon learning the theories and practices of public leadership seems well warranted.

In the meantime let us unpack more fully our central theme: that times are changing quickly in the public arena and that the practice of public leadership must change, too. In the leadership field, scholars keep in mind a trinity: the close connection between context, followers, and leaders. Context often shapes the kind of leader a society needs: Even as the storm approached in the late 1930s, for example, England thought of Winston Churchill as a finished politician; when the storm broke, he became the man of the hour. Similarly the character of followers shapes those who lead. Garry Wills writes that the American Revolution was more successful than the French Revolution in achieving a liberal society because people living in the colonies were more accustomed to living in freedom.[2] What can be said about the evolution of context, followers, and leaders in the United States in future years? We foresee significant changes in all three.

Contexts Are Changing

It has been said that since the fall of the Berlin Wall, indeed since the bloodless and astonishingly swift collapse of the Soviet empire, the world is a different place. Much the same was said after the attacks of September 11, 2001: that everything changed, as the strong sense of territorial safety and security that had been a hallmark of the American experience suffered a mortal blow. How deep the changes truly are remains to be seen. What is clear is that the beginning of the twenty-first century is characterized by a series of contextual changes (listed below) that will inevitably affect the way leaders and followers behave.

Security Concerns Are Returning

For a half century, stretching from World War II to the end of the cold war, national security concerns colored policymaking at all levels of government, especially the federal. But for a while, after the Berlin Wall fell, the country sensed that peace was at hand, and public leaders turned inward. Since those illusions were shattered, on September 11, the context for leadership is changing again and is likely to be reshaped for some years to come: The need for defense spending and homeland security will likely trump other concerns, such as social justice, health care reform, and possibly the reform of Social Security. Local officials will be forced to maintain high levels of protective security without federal funds to pay for them. Even when the economy begins growing at a brisker pace, leaders throughout public institutions are likely to face tight budgets and escalating demands. Moreover, as the United States injects itself more deeply into the Middle East and other regions, those involvements may touch off resentments that could bring increased threats to American interests here and abroad, while dampening prospects for international trade and investment. Indeed how can anyone speak with certainty about the international climate in coming years?

Globalization Is Increasing

The war on terrorism does not mean that the forces of globalization will disappear nor will the debate over its impact. Clashes could even intensify, and it will be virtually impossible for public leaders to shy away from the effects of globalized markets and politics. As President George W. Bush learned to his immediate chagrin, national boundaries still matter, but they are now porous in ways—literally and figuratively—that would have been unimaginable even a decade ago. Lands until recently thought remote by even the most sophisticated of political observers—Afghanistan is the obvious case in point—can become of key importance overnight. Large but somehow alien places—think of India and Pakistan—can threaten the health and welfare of those on continents far from their own. And, on an individual level, an Egyptian visiting the United States can wreak havoc. Without even addressing the importance of global monies and markets, it is easy enough to see that public leaders no longer have a choice: They simply must be up to speed about the world around them.

The Information Revolution Is Spreading

The public and nonprofit sectors have been much slower to embrace information technologies than the private sector, and they are now scrambling to catch up—a project that will go on for years.[3] Public-sector leaders are no longer immune from the impact of information overload or from the shifting centers of power brought on by the Internet. Technology can be a great equalizer, delivering power to the powerless and providing information to those formerly without access. Moreover the capacity of nonstate actors from around the world to connect and communicate in ways previously available only to nation-states can and does, in an age of terror, shape the ways in which governments and those who lead them behave.

Diversity Is Growing

In no small measure, because of more porous boundaries, American leaders are now required to play to publics far more heterogeneous than they were before. To be sure, this trend is not new. In particular since the civil rights and women's movements in the 1960s, various constituent groups in the American body politic, groups that had up to then been largely silent, have found their political voices. But the demographic changes just over the horizon are likely to have a massive impact upon public life. Already minorities have become the majority in nine of the nation's ten largest urban areas, and they are certain to press harder for a more equitable share of political power. Other interest groups, such as gay activists, will also insist on a more inclusive civic culture. All leaders, particularly those in the public arena, are required now to listen to the constituent voices in a way best thought of as new.

The Culture of Leadership Is Changing

The cultures of leadership and management have changed in recent decades, especially in the United States. Even into the 1960s and 1970s leaders and managers could freely command and control, but this kind of domination (by leaders) and subordination (by followers) is no longer considered acceptable. To be sure, when push comes to shove—when an employer, for example, feels obliged to dismiss some employees—leaders still lead and followers are still generally obliged to follow. But expectations on both sides have changed, with leaders adopting the language of cooperation, collaboration, and teamwork and followers expecting to participate, to be empowered, and to be members of teams. In fact even the word *follower* is somewhat frowned on, in favor of more politically palatable words such as *constituent* and *stakeholder*. While not fully authentic, for reasons implied above, the impact of this changing culture should not be underestimated. It yields a dynamic in which both leaders and followers behave differently.

Walls Are Falling between Public, Private, and Nonprofit Sectors

Since the beginnings of the republic, private citizens have been expected to pitch in from time to time, especially during a crisis. The legend of George Washington as a latter-day Cincinnatus was one of the most popular stories of the nineteenth century. But the predominant path for Americans has been to stay within a single craft or calling, rarely wandering into other domains. During the managerial revolution of the twentieth century, as experts and specialists rose to the fore, opinion makers like Walter Lippmann thought that people outside government should mostly stay there, because they did not know enough to run the affairs of the nation. Clearly the walls between and within sectors have started to tumble, as individuals frequently cross from one sector to another, and partnerships grow across sectors. Training and success in one field is increasingly seen as a springboard to another. Leaders of all three sectors are increasingly expected to act for the common good. Harvard MBAs have been elected president of the country and mayor of Los Angeles; United Nations' Secretary-General Kofi Annan, unable to secure sufficient funding from national governments, recruits corporations for the battle against HIV-AIDs; five alumni of Goldman Sachs now head up public-private bodies rebuilding New York City; the governor of Oklahoma is tapped to serve as national chair of a citizens committee to reform the Catholic Church; a former governor of Colorado runs public schools in Los Angeles, and a former antitrust chief runs public schools in New York City; states and cities privatize public services like prison management and school management, while CEOs forge links with public school systems; nonprofit organizations learn they can often succeed if they become entrepreneurial; U.S. senators leave Washington to run universities.

This trend is likely to accelerate in years ahead. Public institutions, held to short rations by taxpayers, will inevitably reach out more often to the private and nonprofit sectors for partnerships or more efficient means of delivering services; corporations, anxious to rebuild public trust and stave off more governmental regulation, will try to prove themselves as good corporate citizens, engaging in more generous forms of corporate social responsibility; nonprofits, learning how to solve problems in a single community, will find better ways to ramp up and achieve larger impact. Other forces will drive change, as well. Shorter job spans, accompanied by longer life spans, will not only mean that people hold as many as seven or eight different jobs over the course of a career, but they will also hop more frequently from one field to another. Recognizing, as Erik Erikson has written, that passages into middle and later life often spur people to give more back to society, it is especially likely that a burgeoning population of older Americans will seek out new ways to serve the common good. Moreover, as experience proves which experiments in public-private partnerships seem to work (and which fail), other communities are likely to embrace models revealed to be best practice.

Followers Will Change

Public leaders must not only cope with changing contexts, but they must also face changes in their constituencies: Most will demand higher standards of performance, in the following ways.

Constituents Will Demand a More Equitable Distribution of Power and Benefits

We have already felt an insistence from below that America's leaders be more inclusive, ensuring places at the table for many who have been left out in the past. The country's entire history, of course, has tended toward growing inclusion, as those at the bottom have successfully struggled for recognition. The growing political power of women and Hispanics, in particular, will ensure that this trend continues and indeed accelerates. Minorities such as gays, lesbians, and the transgendered are almost certain to win many of their battles, as well. One can see the face of change already in states across the Sun Belt, where Hispanics are claiming their rightful share of political power. While tensions often creep in to black-Hispanic relations, the infusion of more Hispanic leaders into public office from Florida to California will likely motivate African Americans to be more assertive in seeking their own share. The Hispanic surge will also force Republicans to be more inclusive, as they try to avoid another debacle like Proposition 187, which wrecked them in California.

Constituents Will Demand Higher Levels of Performance

Citizens are already asking that the government conduct business over the Internet, just as corporations do. If you can buy a vacation or a new car through the Internet, why not be able to pay your taxes, look up your Medicare benefits, or get a driver's license? Those demands will escalate in the future. Corporate America is now moving toward a new era of web services, tying together its business application systems so that a single customer representative can respond quickly to all of a customer's concerns. The current recession in the computer industry will not slow the pace of innovation. Consumers will become accustomed to ever-higher levels of service from corporations and will demand the same from the public sector. Governments, of course, are becoming more efficient through use of the Internet—former Mayor Rudy Giuliani claims a major role for New York City's information technology (IT) in reducing crime and responding to the emergencies of September 11—but in general most elements of the government have been slow to embrace IT. With the exception of the Defense Department, public leaders will be struggling to catch up with the private sector for years to come.

At the same time public officials may face demands for higher levels of service in protecting families and homes. Americans were forgiving of government for not foreseeing the attacks of September 11 but may be much less so if there are future terrorist strikes. The September attacks, along with the sniper episode in the suburbs of Washington in 2002, have demonstrated that governmental units will be expected to cooperate far more effectively across jurisdictional boundaries than ever before.

Constituents Will Be Less Willing to Follow the Leader

For a constellation of reasons, including political alienation, easy access to previously unavailable information, a media culture that tends to pull leaders down rather than build them up, increased mobility, attenuated family life, and an overall decline in respect for traditional authority, Americans are less inclined to comply than we once were. To be sure, the United States has never been a land in which followers were easy to gain. The revolutionary fervor that underpins our political institutions; the difficulties our structures impose even on presidential leadership; ideologies such as democracy, individualism, and egalitarianism; and capitalist markets all mitigate against leadership as easy work. But in this new time even traditional authority figures like fathers find that position alone does not carry much weight. Of the three basic resources leaders can draw on—power, authority, and influence—power and authority have been diminished. That leaves persuasion, and all the work it implies, as the twenty-first-century leader's most prominent challenge.

Leaders Must Change

The histories and habits of leaders are bound to shift with the shifting times. Twenty-first-century leaders will be born differently, educated differently, and behave differently. Listed below are changes that will be required of them.

Public Leaders Must Work across Every Imaginable Boundary

Work will be increasingly different than in the past, when neatly organized hierarchies prevailed at almost every level of government. A foretaste of this change is in the homeland security structure that President Bush and Congress have been wrestling over. As the Department of Homeland Security matures, its leaders will be expected to do more than manage their own operations at the nation's borders; they will be expected to achieve close collaboration among distinct agencies. To prepare for terrorist strikes they must also learn how to cooperate and coordinate with local and state officials and with others outside the public sector, especially business. To blunt the effects of an attack they must become sophisticated in science and technology. And to prevent terror assaults they must become critical analysts of a vast flow of information from the Central Intelligence Agency and the Federal Bureau of Investigation, a process that will demand that they become more international in orientation and learn how to connect the dots—something intelligence officers call fusion analysis. Greater international understanding is likely to be one of the single most significant shifts among national leaders of the future.

State and local government officials will be expected to have a greater range of experiences and talents, as well. Governors learned long ago that if they want to spur economic growth they have to travel overseas and invite companies to build or trade more extensively in their states. Even landlocked states like Utah and Oklahoma have become international in their orientation. States are pursuing economic gains through science and technology, as well; the states of the northeast, for example, have seen how much prosperity information technologies have brought to western states and would like to build an economic corridor of their own, based on the life sciences. Local officials are moving in the same direction: Mayors coming to Harvard are as eager to talk to Michael Porter, an authority on competitive strategy and economic development, as with experts in city governance.

Public Leaders Must Become More Transparent and More Effective in Persuasion

An element of secrecy has been acceptable for public institutions, and in the war on terrorism, just as in past wars, the public still favors it. The Bush administration maintains a high degree of secrecy. But the trend in institutions in the private and nonprofit sectors is toward greater transparency, and that trend is sure to grow in the public sector as well, in areas unrelated to terrorism. The public and the press (not to mention investors and Catholic parishioners) have had their fill of lies, double-dealing, and excessive spin. They are insisting on greater openness and accountability from powerful bodies. Some public leaders are discovering that greater transparency can be useful in building public confidence and in achieving greater managerial efficiency. In Baltimore, for example, Mayor Martin O'Malley has established a website for the city that gives residents up-to-the-minute information, neighborhood by neighborhood, on how city inspectors are faring in their work in areas such as sanitation inspections of local restaurants.[4] O'Malley believes that the city is building stronger bonds with its citizenry and holding itself to higher standards of performance with this and other e-government innovations. As public schools increasingly test students, parents will demand a high degree of transparency so they can see how their children—and their schools—are doing in relation to others.

The arts of persuasion, always key to democratic leadership, will become more important in future years. As Richard J. Murnane and Frank Levy write in *Teaching the New Basic Skills*, knowledge workers in every field will be expected to collect increasing amounts of information and then give meaning to it for others.[5] That will be especially true in the public sector, where the information flow from both home and abroad is becoming a tidal wave, far more than the average citizen can absorb. With the media commanding less authority, it will be up to public leaders to analyze and interpret information fragments in ways that are both meaningful and persuasive for the citizenry. Further, public leaders must learn how to speak to multiple audiences at the same time. In a nation with growing diversity and in a world where the United States has greater influence than any power since ancient Rome, a president who speaks to a business luncheon in Des Moines will find every sentence scrutinized through different prisms by people all over the globe. "With words we govern men," Disraeli said; in future we will learn how right he was.[6]

Public Leaders Will Be Expected to Deliver Continuous Innovations and Improvements

For years corporate CEOs have considered it imperative to renew their products and organizations on a continuing basis. The old cliché that one must keep pedaling the bicycle forward or fall off has applied with a vengeance to corporations in a competitive world. Those same imperatives will sweep over public institutions in future years. Major universities already find themselves in intense competition to attract the best students and faculty. University boards carefully compare their yield rates and the college board scores of the freshman class with those of rival schools. Rankings by journalistic organizations are almost as important to universities as credit ratings are for corporations.

So far most government bodies have not found themselves in intragovernmental competition. If anything, there is not yet enough performance-based management in the public sphere. But the bar is starting to be raised for public institutions. The testing and accountability movement in public education, for example, is catching hold nationwide, and teachers as well as principals and school superintendents will increasingly find that they must produce rising test scores in order to succeed in their jobs. Performance-based management is likely to spread for some years to come.

Public (and Nonprofit) Leaders Will Come to Closely Resemble Their Private Sector Counterparts, and Vice Versa

Political leaders will have to demonstrate managerial virtues such as competence and efficiency, and business leaders will have to demonstrate political skills such as listening, educating, mobilizing, and inspiring. All leaders will find themselves challenged by changes in the larger culture, including diversity, the need to balance family life and work, and demands for better access to quality education and health care. As the literature on public, private, and nonprofit leadership attests, our images of ideal leadership have merged. The traits and skills expected of leaders in one sector scarcely differ from those in the others. And the same challenges—mastering information, coping with complexity, understanding technology, managing change, mediating conflict, managing crises, making decisions under conditions of uncertainty, creating alliances, fostering diversity, addressing resistance and dissent, and finding time for analysis and reflection—are found in all sectors.

Preparing Tomorrow's Public Leaders

It is difficult to find a single phrase that adequately describes the kind of public leadership that will be needed in the first decades of the twenty-first century. We know that to be effective in this changing arena, men and women must be able to live and lead in multiple spheres with multiple audiences and multiple demands. We suggest that what is needed is 360-degree leadership. How do we prepare young people for this kind of public leadership, and where do we find them?

Many universities proclaim that one of their most important missions is to train young men and women to be the leaders of the next generation. If they are serious about that proposition, they must be serious about the study of leadership and leadership development. It would seem especially appropriate to build more leadership programs targeted toward service in the public and nonprofit sectors, with a close eye on how contexts and followers are changing and how leaders must change to meet new demands. Programs should intensify training for those who have often been at the margins in exercising leadership, including women, African Americans, and Hispanics. But responsibility for strengthening leadership studies does not fall solely upon university administrators; if anything, it falls more heavily upon scholars and practitioners in the field, for they must build and solidify the intellectual foundations.

A major challenge in the field is to understand more clearly how men and women mature into leaders. We know too little about what formative experiences and crucibles best shape them. Even though more attention is now being paid, leader learning remains a fledgling enterprise. Most scholars in the field believe that leadership can be taught and that its study can accelerate the development of future leaders. But we are still short on well-tested theories of leadership development. The military academies have addressed the issue more seriously than any other educational institutions and have been encouraged by the results. But even at the oldest, West Point, a recent faculty study concluded that the school did not have an overarching theory of how leaders develop. We would suggest that answers should be sought to an array of questions:

—Through longitudinal research, can we determine what combinations of training and experience make a positive difference in the development of leaders?

—What is most effective in encouraging character development, judgment, and a keen sense of ethics?

—What balance should be struck in the classroom between leadership theory, case studies, and experiential education?

—In addition to a general appreciation of leadership, what skill sets do emerging leaders need? A capacity to persuade? To negotiate well? To analyze with a discerning eye?

—Are students heading toward public careers best served by studying law, public policy, business, or some combination?

—The military draft was an important means for training emerging leaders. In its absence are there other ways women and men can assume responsibility early in life?

—Does a year or two of voluntary service in Americorps, the Peace Corps, or other organizations make a significant difference in shaping leaders?

—How can mentoring be most effective?

—Corporations now invest significant sums to help their executives gain self-awareness. What training should be offered to those heading into the public sector?

—What can we learn from bad leaders, the many people who have risen to the top and have been evil or incompetent? Where did their development go off track? Why do followers often go along with leaders who are clearly bad?

Even as we seek ways to prepare young people for public leadership, we must be equally attentive to the other challenge: How do we find them? Young people are less engaged in the public sphere today than at any time in recent memory. While more idealistic, they vote in appallingly low numbers, read little about public affairs, and are generally dismissive of politics. In the presidential election of 1972, 50 percent of eighteen-to-twenty-four-year-olds voted. That number has steadily declined. By 1996 it had fallen to 32 percent. Figures from the 2000 election show that it rose to 36.1 percent, but that is still far from where it was at its peak. Clearly the younger generation is turned off to public affairs at the very time the country needs a fresh infusion of strong, moral leadership. What is to be done?

Today's landscape finds a parallel in the America of the late nineteenth century. With the acceleration of the industrial revolution and the accumulation of power and wealth in the hands of corporate titans and party bosses, the United States needed more honest and talented leaders in positions of public responsibility during the final decades of the century. The civil service was rife with patronage, and educated men like Henry Adams thought that there was only one way to look at politicians: down.

It took a long time, but eventually changes came. During the 1880s Congress enacted civil service reform that tailored jobs to merit, and a few brave souls from patrician families decided that the best way to clean up public life was to get into the arena themselves. To the dismay of friends and some of his family, as James MacGregor Burns and Susan Dunn write, a twenty-three-year-old Teddy Roosevelt left Harvard in 1880 determined to lift the quality of politics in New York City by jumping into the fray himself. "When TR's fashionable friends heard that he had been frequenting Morton Hall, the clubroom for the 21st District Republican organization, they laughed at him. Politics was 'low,' they sniffed, and the organizations were not controlled by gentlemen. These patricians deplored his association with Irish saloonkeepers and other brutes and rascals smoking their cigars among the spittoons and beer tables of the clubroom. . . . He aspired to be a hero in an age without heroes."[7]

President Charles Eliot of Harvard applauded men who got off the sidelines: "I have sometimes been sorry for you and your immediate coadjutors," he told E. L. Godkin, editor of *The Nation*, "because you had no chance to work immediately and positively for the remedying of some of the evils you exposed. The habitual critic gets a darker or less cheerful view of the social and political state than one does who is actively engaged in efforts to improve that state."[8] The spirit of leaders like Roosevelt and Eliot helped to inspire a new generation to take up the struggle for reform, and over time the Progressive movement did much to clean up politics and usher in higher standards for public service and public leadership.

To draw young people into the public arena today, we need a wave of new reforms and a dose of inspiration from the new Roosevelts and Eliots in our midst. Congress and the White House must overhaul the civil service once again, so that government becomes a more attractive, exciting place to work. Dead-end jobs and sclerotic bureaucracies must give way to flexible, high-performance organizations where talent can exercise responsibility. Pay scales must be more competitive and jobs structured so that professionals can go in and out of government more easily. Elective politics will never be entirely free from money and special interests, nor in a democracy should it be. Politicians however must find a road back to respectability and high purpose, once again stirring the passions of the young. Politics was once seen as noble and can be again. So too our universities must do more than deepen knowledge and teach skills; they must also touch souls. Formal leadership training is important, but the preparation of a new generation of public leaders must be the work of many who care.

Notes

1. Harry S Truman, *Memoirs,* vol. 2: *Years of Trial and Hope* (Doubleday, 1956), p. 1.
2. Garry Wills, *Certain Trumpets: The Call of Leaders* (Simon and Schuster, 1994), p. 15.
3. The Visions of Governance in the Twenty-First Century project, John F. Kennedy School of Government, hosted the following conferences in Bretton Woods, New Hampshire: The Information Revolution: Impacts on Governance, July 19–22, 1998; Governance in a Globalizing World, July 11–14, 1999; Governance Amid Bigger, Better Markets, July 30–August 2, 2000.

4. www.ci.baltimore.md.us/news/citistat/index.html [October 29, 2002].

5. Richard J. Murnane and Frank Levy, *Teaching the New Basic Skills: Principles for Educating Children to Thrive in a Changing Economy* (Free Press, 1996).

6. Benjamin Disraeli, Earl of Beaconsfield (1804–81), *Contarini Fleming* (Harper, 1832).

7. James MacGregor Burns and Susan Dunn, *The Three Roosevelts: Patrician Leaders Who Transformed America* (Atlantic Monthly Press, 2001), pp. 25, 27.

8. Ibid., p. 24.

3

GEORGE J. BORJAS

Wage Structures
and the Sorting of Workers
into the Public Sector

T HE PUBLIC SECTOR employs around 16 percent of the American
work force. Since the 1970s a flurry of research activity has attempted
to determine if public sector workers receive "equal pay for equal work"
when compared to their private sector counterparts.[1] The past two decades
have also seen wage inequality substantially increase among salaried workers, both between and within skill groups.[2] Although much of the debate
over public sector wages has emphasized the size of the pay differential
between the typical worker employed in the public sector and a statistically
comparable counterpart in the private sector, this emphasis is myopic.
Given the changes in the wage structure that have occurred over the past
twenty years, it is unlikely that the wage structures in the private and public sectors have evolved in similar ways.

Differential changes in the wage structures of the public and private
sectors can be expected to alter behavior. Suppose, as is actually the case,
that wage dispersion has been rising at a faster rate in private sector jobs
than in public sector jobs. The relative change in the wage structure
would then suggest that private sector workers who belong to highly
skilled groups (such as college graduates) or who have relatively high earnings within a particular skill group will have reduced incentives to enter

I am grateful to Jack Donahue and Jerry Mechling for comments and suggestions.

the public sector. Conversely public sector workers who belong to highly skilled groups or who have relatively high incomes within a particular skill group will have increased incentives to leave the public sector and enter private sector jobs. In short the relative changes in the wage structures will probably influence labor supply decisions and alter the sorting of workers between the two sectors.

This chapter uses data drawn from the U.S. decennial censuses and from the Current Population Survey (CPS) to document changes in the wage structures that occurred in the private and public sectors between 1960 and 2000.[3] The evidence suggests that relative wage inequality was rising in the public sector before 1970 but that there has been substantial relative wage compression in that sector since the 1970s. The data further indicate that, as a result of the relative compression of public sector wages since 1970, high-skill private sector workers became increasingly less likely to quit their jobs to enter the public sector, and high-skill public sector workers became increasingly more likely to switch to the private sector.

Trends in Employment and Pay Levels

It is instructive to begin by describing some general trends in public sector employment and pay over the past few decades. I use two main sources of data for much of the study. The first is a 1 percent sample drawn from the Public Use Microdata Samples (PUMS) of the Census Bureau for the years 1960 through 1990. The second is the Annual Demographic Supplement (often termed the March Supplement) of the Current Population Survey for the years 1977 through 2001.

I restrict the analysis to workers who are between eighteen and sixty-four years old and are not self-employed. A particular worker is classified as employed in the private or public sector based on the information provided in the "class of work" variable in these data sets. Beginning with the 1970 census the class of work variable also indicates if a public sector worker is employed by the federal, state, or local government.

Employment

Figure 3-1 illustrates the trend in the fraction of the work force employed by the public sector over the 1960–2000 period.[4] Although the time-series presented in the figure uses data drawn from two sources (census and

Figure 3-1. *Share of Labor Force Employed in Public Sector, 1960–2000*

Percent

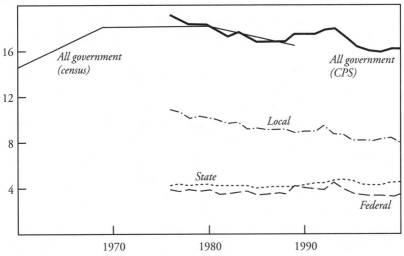

Sources: Bureau of the Census, Public Use Microdata Samples (PUMS), 1960–90; Bureau of the Census, *Annual Demographic Supplement, Current Population Survey,* 1977–2001.

CPS), the levels of public sector employment in the two data sets match quite well. In 1960 the public sector employs around 15 percent of the work force. That number peaks in the mid-1970s, when nearly 20 percent of workers are employed by the public sector. After that the share of public sector employment declines steadily; by 2000 it is around 16 percent.

Figure 3-1 also shows that much of the post-1980 decline in public sector employment can be attributed to what has been happening in local government. The (relative) number of persons employed by local governments falls substantially over that time. In 1976 about 11 percent of workers are employed by local governments. In 2000 that figure is 8 percent. In contrast the employment share of state and federal payrolls remains steady at around 4 percent through this period.

The Pay Gap

Many studies calculate the pay gap between comparable workers in the public and private sectors and examine variations in this gap over time and across levels of government. In this section I update this literature by documenting the long-run trends in the pay gap between 1960 and 2000.

To calculate the wage differential between public and private sector workers I use the sample restrictions typically used in the studies that document the evolution of the wage structure in the wage-and-salary sector.[5] I restrict the sample to full-time workers (persons who worked at least forty weeks a year and thirty-five hours a week in the calendar year before the survey). In addition I restrict the sample to those full-time workers who earned at least $67 a week in 1982 dollars (implying that their hourly income was at least half of the 1982 real minimum wage). Throughout the analysis I use the log of weekly wages as the dependent variable. (Using the logarithm, which puts the focus on proportionate rather than absolute differences, is standard in compensation studies.) Because there is a substantial wage differential between men and women in both the public and private sectors, I estimate the public sector pay gap separately for each gender. Initially I focus on measuring the pay gap between the public and private sectors overall, then later I discuss the pay differences among federal, state, and local governments.

The top panel of figure 3-2 illustrates the trend in the unadjusted log wage differential between the typical male public sector worker and the typical male private sector worker. The wage advantage enjoyed by men employed in the public sector rises steadily over four decades. In 1960 the typical man employed in the public sector earns, on average, about the same as the typical man employed in the private sector. The wage premium rises to around 5 percent by 1980, to 10 percent by 1990, and peaks at around 13 percent in 1995.

Of course the increasing pay difference may be attributed to differential changes in the human capital of the workers employed in the two sectors, particularly the increasingly higher level of educational attainment for workers in the public sector. It is important therefore to document the trend in the adjusted pay gap that exists between comparable workers employed in the public and private sectors.

I use a standard log wage regression to calculate the adjusted pay gap, where the regression controls for differences in educational attainment, age, race, and region of residence.[6] These regression models are estimated separately in each year, in each sector, and for each gender group. I then use the average characteristics of workers employed in the public sector over the entire 1976–2000 period (by gender) to predict the wage that this worker would have earned if employed in a particular sector in a particu-

Figure 3-2. *Public-Private Wage Differential, Men and Women, 1960–2000*

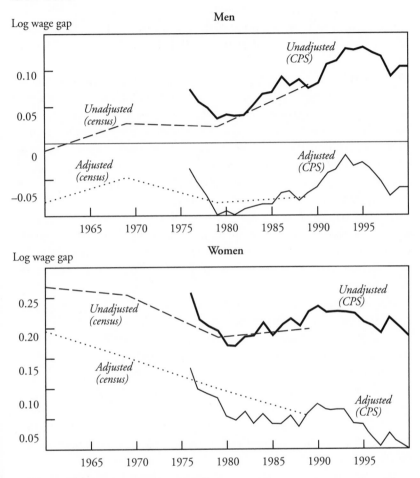

Sources: PUMS; *Annual Demographic Supplement.*

lar year. The adjusted pay gap is obtained by taking the appropriate differences of these predictions.

As the top panel of figure 3-2 shows, the calculation of the pay differential between the typical man employed in the public sector and his statistically comparable counterpart in the private sector reveals two interesting findings. First, the typical male public sector worker does not in fact enjoy a wage advantage over his statistically comparable counterpart in the private sector. In 2000, for instance, the typical male public sector worker earns 11 percent more than the typical private sector worker. But the typical male public sector worker earns 6 percent less than a statistically comparable male worker in the private sector. Second, there is remarkably little change in the adjusted pay gap between 1960 and 2000. It hovers between −5 and −10 percent throughout much of the four decades.

As the bottom panel of figure 3-2 shows, the trends in the adjusted and unadjusted pay gaps are quite different for women. Throughout much of these four decades, women employed in the public sector enjoy a large wage advantage over women in the private sector—in terms of both unadjusted and adjusted pay. In 1960, for example, women in the public sector earn around 27 percent more than women in the private sector, and the pay gap remains at 20 percent even after adjusting for differences in socioeconomic characteristics between workers in the two sectors. By 2000 the unadjusted pay gap falls slightly to around 20 percent. However, the monetary advantage suggested by the adjusted pay gap vanishes, so that the typical woman employed in the public sector earns just as much as her statistically comparable counterpart in the private sector. This decline in the pay advantage of women employed in the public sector partly reflects the significant improvement in economic opportunities for private sector female workers over the past few decades.

The two panels of figure 3-3 show the different trends in the adjusted pay gap (between the public and private sectors) across the various government sectors. The aggregate trends illustrated in the previous figures mask a great deal of variation in pay levels among the federal, state, and local governments. Figure 3-3 shows that, regardless of gender, workers in the federal sector enjoy a significant pay premium over comparable workers in the private sector, while workers employed by state and local governments suffer a significant wage disadvantage.

For men the adjusted pay gap between the federal and private sectors declines somewhat, from over 10 percent in the mid-1970s to around 3 percent by 2000. At the same time, however, men employed in state and local governments experience some improvement in their pay status. In 1980 these men have wage penalties of around 15 to 20 percent, but the size of the penalty falls to around 10 percent by 2000.

The significant decline in the adjusted wage premium accruing to the typical woman employed in the public sector (and documented in figure 3-2) can be attributed to a steep drop in wages for women employed by local governments. In 1976 the typical woman employed by a local gov-

Figure 3-3. *Adjusted Public-Private Wage Differential by Sector,*
Men and Women, 1977–2000

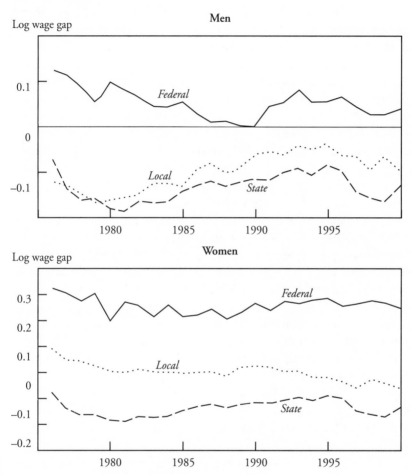

Sources: PUMS; *Annual Demographic Supplement.*

ernment earns around 10 percent more than a statistically comparable
woman in the private sector. By 2000 this 10 percent wage advantage
turns into a 10 percent wage disadvantage. It would be of interest to determine the factors that cause this shift in the economic opportunities available to women employed by local governments. After all, it is evident that
the factors lowering wages for women in local governments do not affect
women employed in other parts of the public sector.

Wage Structures in the Public and Private Sectors

Almost all the studies that analyze pay differences between the public and private sectors attempt to measure the pay gap between the typical worker in the public sector and a statistically comparable worker in the private sector. The magnitude of this pay gap for the typical worker is the focus in most policy discussions of pay comparability between the two sectors.

As I document in the previous section, the adjusted pay gap between the public and private sectors remains relatively constant for men but declines substantially for women in the past four decades. However, these trends occur against a background of historic changes in the U.S. wage structure. Wage inequality increased rapidly between wage and salaried workers in the past two decades. The labor market began to reward workers with higher levels of skills at much higher rates.

The implications of the trends in the adjusted pay gap for pay comparability policy discussions are unclear if the wage structures evolved in different ways in the public and private sectors. In other words, even though the adjusted pay gap for the typical man employed in the public sector may have been relatively constant over a forty-year period, differential changes in the wage structures imply that the pay gap facing men at different points of the wage distribution could have changed in substantially different ways. For instance if wage inequality increased at a faster rate in the private sector, the public sector would find it increasingly hard to attract and retain high-skill workers. Differences in the evolution of the wage structure between the private and public sectors—and not simply the magnitude of the adjusted pay gap for the typical worker—have important implications for the number and types of worker that the public sector can successfully recruit and retain.

To describe the secular trends in the wage structures of both private and public sector workers, I initially focus on the trends for the aggregate public sector. I also discuss the separate trends for federal, state, and local government workers in detail below.

A widely used measure of wage dispersion in the wage structure literature is the standard deviation of log weekly income. Figures 3-4 and 3-5 illustrate the trends in this measure of dispersion for men and women, respectively. Consider initially the evidence for male workers. The steep increase in wage dispersion for male workers employed in the private sector is familiar. Between 1960 and 2000 the standard deviation of their log weekly wage rises by almost 40 percent, from about 0.5 to almost 0.7, with

Figure 3-4. *Standard Deviations of Log Weekly Wage, Men, 1960–2000*

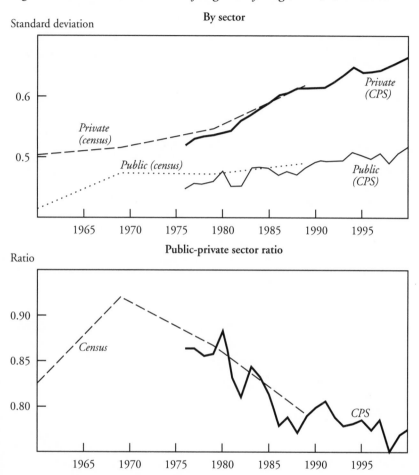

Sources: PUMS; *Annual Demographic Supplement.*

much of the increase occurring after 1980. Less familiar is the finding that public sector workers experience a much slower rate of increase in wage dispersion. In particular the standard deviation of the log wage for public sector workers increases only from about 0.4 to 0.5 between 1960 and 2000, and much of that increase occurs before 1970, at the time that employment in the public sector was expanding rapidly.

The bottom panel of figure 3-4 shows that, as a result of these trends, the ratio of standard deviations between the public and private sectors increases

Figure 3-5. *Standard Deviations of Log Weekly Wage, Women, 1960–2000*

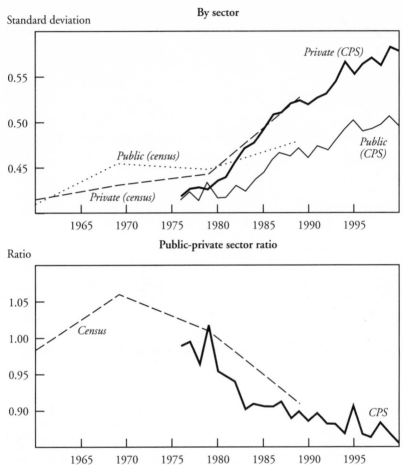

Standard deviation

By sector

Ratio

Public-private sector ratio

Sources: PUMS; *Annual Demographic Supplement.*

before 1970 and begins to decline thereafter. In 1970 the ratio stands at around 0.9. By the late 1990s the ratio falls to around 0.75. Because a higher rate of return to skills in a particular sector would increase wage inequality in that sector, the ratio of standard deviations between the two sectors can be roughly interpreted as a measure of the relative returns to skills in the public sector. The data clearly indicate that the relative returns to skills for men employed in the public sector decline steadily after 1970.

Figure 3-5 replicates the analysis for female workers. The results are quite similar. Wage dispersion for women employed in the public sector rises, relative to that in the private sector, before 1970 and declines steadily after that. In 1970, for example, the ratio of standard deviations stands at around 1.05. By 2000 the ratio is hovering at around 0.85.

Although the standard deviation of the log weekly wage is a commonly used measure of wage dispersion, it is a measure that is sensitive to outlying values in the wage distribution and particularly to the way that those outlying values are treated in the particular data set being analyzed. Census and CPS data typically truncate the earnings reported by persons with high income levels and instead assign all these high-income persons a "top code." For example, all persons who earned more than $75,000 in the 1980 census are coded as earning $75,000. To make matters worse, the truncation point for nominal earnings changes in a haphazard way over time. As a result the differential top-coding of earnings in different periods can influence the relative trend in the standard deviation of log weekly earnings, particularly if workers in one sector are more likely to be top-coded than workers in another sector.[7]

This technical problem can be avoided by using an alternative measure of wage dispersion, such as the wage gap between workers at the 90th percentile and the 10th percentile of the wage distribution. This measure of wage dispersion, often called the 90-10 wage gap, essentially discards earnings information for the top-coded observations.

The two panels of figure 3-6 illustrate the trend in the 90-10 wage gap for workers employed in the public and private sectors. As with the analysis of the standard deviation of log weekly wages, it is clearly evident that wage dispersion in the public sector, relative to that in the private sector, increases before 1970 and declines steadily after that. For example, the wage gap between the 90th percentile and the 10th percentile male worker in the private sector is about 1.3 log points in 1980 and increases to nearly 1.7 log points by 2000. In contrast, the 90-10 wage gap in the public sector increases only from about 1.1 to 1.3 over the same period.

There is a relative compression of wages in the public sector over the past three decades, even when one looks at the evolution of the wage structure within each level of government. To easily summarize the available evidence, I calculate the 90-10 wage gap in a particular level of the public sector as well as in the private sector and then take the difference between these two quantities to define the relative change in wage dispersion in the

Figure 3-6. *Trends in 90-10 Wage Differential, Men and Women, 1960–2000*

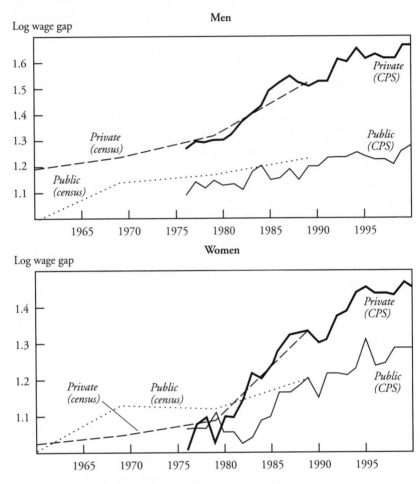

Sources: PUMS; *Annual Demographic Supplement.*

public sector. Figure 3-7 summarizes the evidence by illustrating the trends in the relative 90-10 wage gap for each sector for men and women. Although the within-sector trends are more "noisy" than the trends found for the aggregate public sector, the general pattern is unmistakable. For both men and women it is evident that relative wage dispersion in the public sector declines after the late 1970s. As an example the 90-10 wage gap for men employed in state government is around –0.1 log points smaller than

Figure 3-7. *Trends in Relative 90-10 Wage Differential by Sector, Men and Women, 1977–2000*

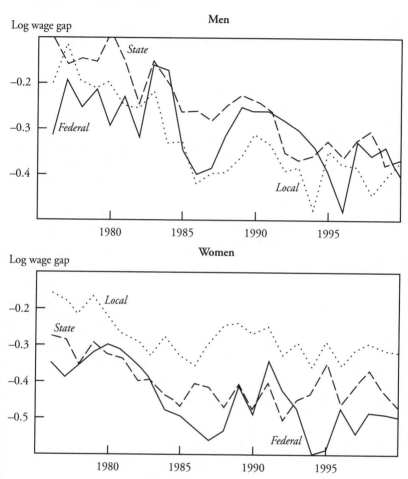

the respective gap for private sector workers in 1980. By 2000 this statistic falls to around –0.4 log points, indicating a substantial narrowing of the wage distribution in the state government sector relative to that of the private sector.

It is also of interest to investigate the channels through which wage inequality declines in the public sector relative to the private sector. For instance there is a substantial increase in wage differentials across education

Figure 3-8. *Relative Wages of College Graduates, Men and Women,*
1960–2000

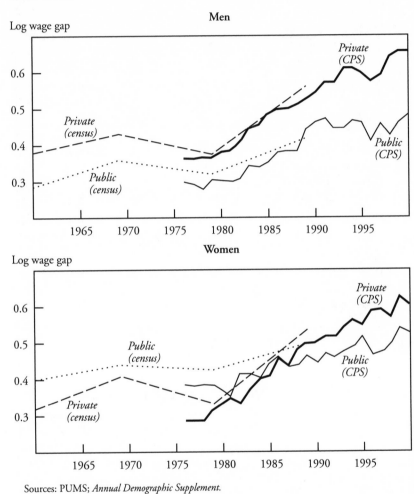

Sources: PUMS; *Annual Demographic Supplement.*

groups. The two panels of figure 3-8 show that the increase in educational
wage differentials occurs at a much faster rate in the private sector than in
the public sector.

The top panel of figure 3-8 shows a substantial rise in the wage gap
between male college graduates and high school graduates in the private
sector. In 1980 the typical male college graduate in the private sector earns
about 40 percent more than the typical high school graduate. By 2000 the

wage gap between these two groups increases to about 66 percent. In contrast, the typical college graduate in the public sector earns 31 percent more than the typical high school graduate in 1980, but this gap rises to about 49 percent by 2000. The bottom panel of figure 3-8 shows a similar widening of educational wage differentials for women in the private sector and a much smaller widening in the public sector. In sum, part of the relative compression of the wage distribution in the public sector can be directly attributed to the fact that the increase in the returns to schooling in public sector jobs do not keep pace with the rise observed in the private sector during the 1980s and 1990s.

Finally, wage inequality in the private sector rises relative to wage inequality in the public sector, even within narrowly defined skill groups. I measure within-group wage inequality by the mean-square error (that is, the standard deviation of the residual) from a regression of log weekly earnings on age, schooling, region of residence, and race. This regression is estimated separately for each sector, for each gender group, and in each calendar year. Figure 3-9 illustrates the trend in the ratio of the within-group adjusted standard deviations of the log weekly wage between the public and private sectors. The figure clearly shows that within-group relative inequality rises in the public sector before 1970 and falls steadily afterward.

In sum, analysis of the census and CPS data available since 1960 clearly indicates that there is a substantial difference in the way the wage structures of the public and private sectors evolved during this period. The much-documented increase in wage inequality, both across and within skill groups, is most evident among private sector workers. Income inequality, either across or within skill groups, did not rise as much in the public sector. Interestingly this was not always the case. Before the 1970s, at the time that public sector employment was expanding rapidly, wage inequality was rising at a much faster rate in the public than in the private sector.

The Sorting of Workers between Sectors

The very different rate of change in relative wages across and within skill groups in the public and private sectors during the 1980s and 1990s implies that the economic incentives for particular types of persons to enter or leave a sector also changed over the period.[8] One can measure how these incentive effects influence the allocation of workers by analyzing the movement

Figure 3-9. *Ratios of Mean-Square Errors, Public to Private Sectors, Men and Women, 1960–2000*

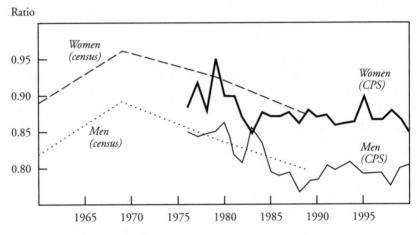

Sources: PUMS; *Annual Demographic Supplement.*

of workers between the private and public sectors and by examining how the skill composition of these "movers" responded to the relative compression of wages in the public sector.

I use the 1979–2001 CPS Outgoing Rotation Group (CPS-ORG) files to analyze the mobility between the two sectors.[9] Some workers in these files can be matched across two consecutive calendar years. These matched data can be used to determine if the person's class of work (that is, public or private sector) changes in the two-year period. As before, I restrict the analysis to workers aged eighteen to sixty-four.

Table 3-1 summarizes the transition rates among the various sectors for the entire 1979–2001 sample period.[10] During this period the year-to-year transition rate from the private sector to the public sector is only 2.5 percent, with most of these movers obtaining a job in the local sector. In contrast the mobility rate from the public sector to the private sector is 9.7 percent. The transition rate out of the public sector varies significantly across the various levels of government: It is 7.6 percent for federal workers, 11.2 percent for state workers, and 9.7 percent for local government workers. The data also reveal a significant amount of mobility between the state and local sectors but relatively little movement between the federal sector and other levels of government.

Table 3-1. *Public-Private Sector Transition Rates, 1979–2001*
Percent

Beginning employment sector		Ending employment sector			
		Public			
	Private	All	Federal	State	Local
Private	97.5	2.5	0.4	0.7	1.4
Public	9.7	90.3	...	...	...
Federal	7.6	...	88.9	1.6	1.9
State	11.2	...	1.2	78.3	9.3
Local	9.7	...	0.7	4.7	85.0

Sources: PUMS; *Annual Demographic Supplement*; Bureau of the Census, Current Population Survey Outgoing Rotation Group (CPS-ORG), 1979–2001.

For most of what follows I focus on transitions between the public and private sectors and ignore those transitions that occur within the public sector itself. I define the quit rate from public sector jobs as the fraction of workers employed in the public sector who become private sector workers in the following year. Similarly, I define the entry rate into the public sector as the fraction of workers initially in the private sector who move to a public sector job in the following year.

The top panel of figure 3-10 illustrates the year-to-year quit rates out of the public sector. It is evident that there is a significant increase in the quit rate out of the public sector beginning around 1990. In the late 1980s, for example, the quit rate out of public sector jobs is just below 9 percent. By 2000 this quit rate increases to almost 13 percent. In the federal sector the quit rate rises from 5.8 to 9.6 percent between 1990 and 2000, while in the local sector the increase is from 8.5 to 13.2 percent. The bottom of figure 3-10 illustrates the trend in year-to-year entry rates into the public sector. Not surprisingly, because they are mainly determined by employment demand in the public sector, these entry rates are more stable over time, hovering between 2 and 3 percent throughout the period.

As noted above, the characteristics of workers who entered and who left the public sector between 1979 and 2000 should have changed in response to the relative changes in the wage structure. I now turn to a more formal analysis of this hypothesis.

To simplify the analysis I restrict the study to the sample of marginal workers—that is, those workers who either left or entered the public sector

Figure 3-10. *Public Sector Quit and Entry Rates, 1979–2000*

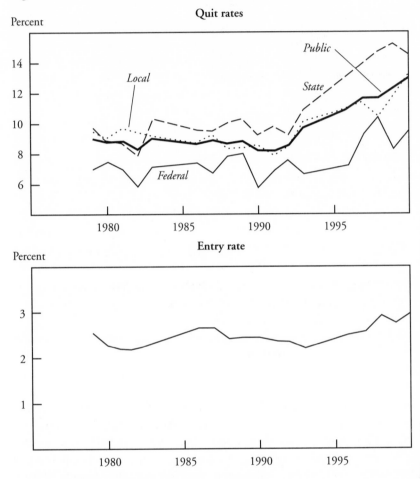

Sources: PUMS; *Annual Demographic Supplement*; CPS-ORG.

during any two-year period. The empirical analysis therefore ignores the largest group of workers, those who did not change sectors. This group of nonmovers either did not pay attention to the changing opportunities provided by the different evolutions of wage structures or found that, perhaps because of the high transaction costs involved in any move, they could not take advantage of the changing opportunities and stayed in their initial placement. By focusing on the sample of movers, the analysis should be able to isolate the impact of the relative compression of wages in the public sector on the sorting of workers across sectors, if any such impact actually exists.

The samples of marginal workers are constructed as follows. Consider the workers who are employed in the private sector in some calendar year t. By linking these workers in the CPS-ORG data across years t and $t + 1$, I observe the private sector earnings of workers who are about to enter the public sector. Similarly, by linking workers across years $t - 1$ and t, I observe the private sector earnings of workers who have just left the public sector. In short, in any given CPS-ORG cross-section I can measure the private sector earnings of two distinct groups of workers: those who are about to enter the public sector and those who have just left the public sector. The comparison of the private sector earnings of these two groups—and how the wage difference between these groups varies as the public sector wage structure becomes relatively more compressed—should provide a great deal of information about the impact of the changing wage structures on the sorting of workers across the two sectors.

I estimate the following regression model in the pooled sample of these marginal workers:

$$(3\text{-}1) \qquad \log w_{it} = X_{it}\, b_{0t} + \alpha\, Q_{it} + \beta\, \sigma_t + g\, (Q_{it} - \sigma_t) + \epsilon_{it},$$

where w_{it} gives the weekly wage of private sector worker i at time t; X is a vector of socioeconomic characteristics (described below); Q_{it} is a dummy variable set to unity if the worker has just quit the public sector and set to zero if the worker is about to enter the public sector; and σ is a measure of the relative dispersion in the public sector at time t.[11] For simplicity I use the sex-specific ratio of standard deviations between the public and private sectors as the measure of dispersion. Since the wage structure evolved somewhat differently for male and female workers, the variable σ_t takes on a different value for men and women at any given point in time. The parameter of interest in this regression model is the coefficient g, which indicates how the wage differential between workers who have just quit the public sector and workers who are about to enter the public sector varies with respect to the relative dispersion in the public sector. I argue that the wage differential between the "quitters" and the "entrants" should be larger when there is more compression in the public sector (that is, the quitters will tend to be high-skill workers, and high-skill workers will not want to enter the public sector). The coefficient γ therefore should be negative.

I estimate this regression model on the sample drawn from the CPS-ORG data by pooling all the marginal workers over all the years for which

Table 3-2. *Relative Wage Compression in the Public Sector and the Sorting of Workers, Three Regressions*[a]

	Model		
Dependent variable	1	2	3
Log weekly wage	−0.414 (0.126)	−0.289 (0.104)	−0.154 (0.117)
Worker is in the top tenth of wage distribution	−0.204 (0.048)	−0.190 (0.047)	−0.153 (0.045)
Worker is in the top third of wage distribution	−0.311 (0.097)	−0.266 (0.095)	−0.169 (0.093)
Control for socioeconomic characteristics	No	Yes	Yes
Control for period effects	No	No	Yes

Sources: PUMS; *Annual Demographic Supplement*; CPS-ORG.

a. All regression specifications include dummy variables indicating if the worker is in transit from federal or state government and a variable measuring the adjusted pay gap between the public and private sectors. The socioeconomic characteristics held constant in column 3 include a vector of variables indicating the worker's age, educational attainment, and region of residence, and a dummy variable indicating the worker's race and gender. Sample size is 34,454 observations. Standard errors are in parentheses.

the merging can be conducted. Table 3-2 presents the estimates of the coefficient γ. Consider the first row of the table, which corresponds to the regression model specified in equation 3-1. In the absence of any variables standardizing for differences in observable skills across workers, the first column of the table reports a statistically significant estimate of −0.414 for the coefficient γ.

It is instructive to interpret this coefficient in terms of a specific simulation of the model. I document earlier that the relative ratio of standard deviations between the public and private sectors declines by about 0.15 percentage points between 1976 and 1990. One can use the estimated coefficient of −0.414 to predict the impact of this observed decline in relative wage dispersion on the wage differential between the workers who have just quit the public sector and those who are about to enter the public sector. In particular the relative compression of the public sector wage distribution increases the wage differential between quitters and entrants by 6 percentage points (or −0.414 times −0.150). It is evident therefore that the impact of the wage structure on the relative quality of workers that the public sector attracts and retains is not only statistically significant but also numerically important.

The other columns of the first row of table 3-2 reveal the nature of this sorting effect in more detail. The second column addresses the possibility that the variable measuring the relative dispersion in the public sector wage structure is just standing in for a time trend. As I show earlier, relative dispersion in the public sector has declined steadily since 1970. It may well be that for some unrelated reason the wage gap between the quitters and the entrants was rising over time, and the regression coefficient γ is just capturing a spurious correlation. To net out this spurious effect, I add a vector of dummy variables indicating the calendar year of the observation to the regression model. This vector is not completely collinear with the relative dispersion variable (σ_t), because the dispersion variable takes on different values for men and women. By including these period effects, the coefficient γ now measures the impact of relative dispersion on the wage gap between quitters and entrants in any particular year. It is evident that the estimated effect remains negative and significant. In fact the estimated coefficient of -0.289 implies that the 0.15 percentage point drop in the relative dispersion of the public sector wage distribution increases the wage gap between those who have just quit the public sector and those who are about to enter it by about 4 percentage points.

The last column of the table introduces standardizing variables into the regression model, including the age, race, educational attainment, and region of residence of the worker. Even after adjusting for differences in these variables across workers, the data reveal a link between the sorting of workers and the wage structure (although the coefficient is not significant). There is a possibility however that the regression is overcontrolling by including these socioeconomic characteristics. After all, the different evolutions of the wage structures in the two sectors will lead different types of workers (such as the more educated) to choose different sectors.

The remaining rows of table 3-2 look at alternative measures of the impact of relative wage compression on worker quality. Instead of using the log weekly wage as the dependent variable in the regression model, the dependent variable indicates if the worker is in the top tenth or the top third of the private sector wage distribution. Table 3-2 clearly shows that there are significant sorting effects when worker quality is defined in terms of worker placement in the private sector wage distribution. Consider, for example, the difference in the probability that quitters and entrants are in the top third of the wage distribution. This difference is sensitive to the relative compression of wages in the public sector. The 0.15 percentage point decline in the relative dispersion of the public sector implies about a 5 percentage point increase in the difference between the probability that a quitter and an entrant are in the top third of the wage distribution.

The sorting evidence presented in table 3-2 aggregates all levels of government into a single group, the public sector, and nets out any sectoral effects on the wage gap between quitters and entrants by including dummy variables indicating if the marginal worker is in the federal, state, or local government. Table 3-3 reports the results when the regression model is estimated separately for marginal workers in each sector of government.[12] Each of the three samples being considered therefore contains workers who either have just quit or are about to enter a particular level of government (for example, state government). The relative dispersion variable (σ_t) is now defined in terms of the ratio of standard deviations between the particular government sector and the private sector. Since the measure of within-sector relative dispersion is noisier because of the smaller samples, it is not surprising that the standard errors of the estimated sorting effect tend to be higher than in the analysis that pools observations across government sectors. Nevertheless the data are roughly consistent with the hypothesis that the relative compression of wages in each level of government in the public sector adversely affects the quality of the work force in that sector.

In the state government sector, for example, the relative measure of dispersion drops by 0.1 percentage point between 1976 and 2000. The estimate of the coefficient γ in table 3-3 (in the absence of any controlling variables) is -0.835. This coefficient implies that the observed compression of wages in the state government sector (relative to the private sector) generates an 8 percentage point increase in the wage gap between workers who just left the state government sector and workers who are about to enter it, an effect that is both numerically and statistically significant. The evidence tends to be weakest for federal workers, where most of the estimated coefficients are negative but not statistically significant.

Summary

This chapter documents that the wage distributions in the public and private sectors evolved in different ways in the past four decades. In general terms the pay gap between the typical public sector worker and a comparable private sector worker was relatively constant for men between 1960 and 2000 but declined substantially for women. Equally important, before

Table 3-3. *Wage Structure and the Sorting of Workers,*
by Government Sector, Three Regressions[a]

Sector and dependent variable	Model		
	1	2	3
Federal government			
Log weekly wage	−0.069	−0.090	0.031
	(0.307)	(0.304)	(0.293)
Worker in top third of distribution	−0.181	−0.251	−0.107
	(0.162)	(0.182)	(0.167)
State government			
Log weekly wage	−0.835	−0.510	−0.135
	(0.365)	(0.379)	(0.425)
Worker in top third of distribution	−0.467	−0.552	−0.336
	(0.237)	(0.249)	(0.305)
Local government			
Log weekly wage	−0.131	−0.063	0.014
	(0.129)	(0.109)	(0.109)
Worker in top third of distribution	−0.104	−0.082	−0.100
	(0.090)	(0.088)	(0.084)
Controls			
Period effects	No	Yes	Yes
Socioeconomic characteristics	No	No	Yes

Sources: PUMS; *Annual Demographic Supplement*; CPS-ORG.

a. All regression specifications include a variable measuring the adjusted pay gap between the particular government sector and the private sector. The socioeconomic characteristics held constant in column 3 include a vector of variables indicating the worker's age, educational attainment, and region of residence and a dummy variable indicating the worker's race and gender. Sample size is 5,480 observations for the federal government, 9,972 for state government, and 19,002 for local government. Standard errors are in parentheses.

1970, at the time when public sector employment was rising rapidly, wage dispersion in the public sector was increasing relative to wage dispersion in the private sector. Beginning in the 1970s, however, this situation reversed, and there has been a significant relative compression of the wage distribution in the public sector during the past two decades.

The differential shifts in the wage structures of the two sectors will likely affect labor supply behavior by altering the sorting of workers between the sectors. As long as the correlation between economic performance in the public and private sectors is strong and positive (so that the same persons tend to be relatively successful regardless of where they work), these labor supply responses suggest that high-skill workers will increasingly want to be employed in the private sector.

This chapter uses data drawn from the Current Population Survey to investigate if such a supply response occurred. The evidence suggests that, as wage structures evolved, the relative skills of the "marginal" persons who moved across sectors also changed significantly. As the wage structure in the public sector became relatively more compressed, the public sector found it harder to attract and retain high-skill workers. In short, the substantial widening of wage inequality in the private sector and the relatively more stable wage distribution in the public sector created magnetic effects that altered the sorting of workers across sectors, with high-skill workers becoming more likely to end up in the private sector.

Although most studies of pay determination in the public sector focus on the earnings gap between the typical worker in the public sector and a statistical counterpart in the private sector, it is clear that the difference in the shape of the wage distributions between the two sectors plays a significant role in determining the public sector's ability to attract and retain a high-quality work force. The analysis suggests that future policy discussions of public sector wages need to pay more attention to the relative dispersion in the income opportunities offered to government workers.

Notes

1. See Joseph Gyourko and Joseph Tracy, "An Analysis of Public and Private Sector Wages Allowing for Endogenous Choices of Both Government and Union Status," *Journal of Labor Economics*, vol. 6, no. 2 (April 1988), pp. 229–53; Lawrence F. Katz and Alan B. Krueger, "Changes in the Structure of Wages in the Public and Private Sectors," *Research in Labor Economics*, vol. 12 (1991), pp. 137–72; Brent R. Moulton, "A Reexamination of the Federal-Private Wage Differential in the United States," *Journal of Labor Economics*, vol. 8, no. 2 (April 1990), pp. 270–93; and Sharon Smith, *Equal Pay in the Public Sector: Fact or Fantasy* (Princeton University, Industrial Relations Section, 1977). Many studies analyze various aspects of the labor market in the public sector. The interplay between political factors and market forces in setting public sector pay has been discussed by George J. Borjas, "Wage Determination in the Federal Government: The Role of Constituents and Bureaucrats," *Journal of Political Economy*, vol. 88, no. 6 (December 1980), pp. 1110–47; and Lee A. Craig, "The Political Economy of Public-Private Compensation Differentials: The Case of Federal Pensions," *Journal of Economic History*, vol. 55, no. 2 (June 1995), pp. 304–20. Employment discrimination and comparable worth remedies have been analyzed by George J. Borjas, "The Politics of Employment Discrimination in the Federal Bureaucracy," *Journal of Law and Economics*, vol. 25, no. 2 (October 1982), pp. 271–99; and Greg Hundley, "The Effects of Comparable Worth in the Public Sector on Public/Private

Occupational Relative Wages," *Journal of Human Resources*, vol. 28, no. 2 (Spring 1993), pp. 318–42. The determination of job queues and quit rates has been analyzed by Mathew Black, Robert Moffitt, and John T. Warner, "The Dynamics of Job Separation: The Case of Federal Employees," *Journal of Applied Econometrics*, vol. 5, no. 3 (July–August 1990), pp. 245–62; and Alan B. Krueger, "The Determinants of Queues for Federal Jobs," *Industrial and Labor Relations Review*, vol. 41, no. 4 (July 1988), pp. 567–81. Wage setting in particular local governments or federal agencies has been analyzed by William J. Moore and Robert J. Newman, "Government Wage Differentials in a Municipal Labor Market: The Case of Houston Metropolitan Transit Workers," *Industrial and Labor Relations Review*, vol. 45, no. 1 (October 1991), pp. 145–53; Jeffrey Perloff and Michael L. Wachter, "Wage Comparability in the U.S. Postal Service," *Industrial and Labor Relations Review*, vol. 38, no. 1 (October 1984), pp. 26–35. Detailed surveys of this literature can be found in Ronald G. Ehrenberg and Joshua L. Schwarz, "Public Sector Labor Markets," in Orley Ashenfelter and Richard Layard, eds., *Handbook of Labor Economics,* vol. 2 (Amsterdam: North-Holland, 1986), pp. 1219–68; and Robert G. Gregory and Jeff Borland, "Recent Developments in Public Sector Labor Markets," in Orley Ashenfelter and David Card, eds., *Handbook of Labor Economics*, vol. 3C (Amsterdam: North-Holland, 1999), pp. 3573–630.

2. The following document these important trends: Lawrence F. Katz and Kevin M. Murphy, "Changes in the Wage Structure, 1963–87: Supply and Demand Factors," *Quarterly Journal of Economics*, vol. 107, no. 1 (February 1992), pp. 35–78; and Kevin M. Murphy and Finis Welch, "The Structure of Wages," *Quarterly Journal of Economics*, vol. 107, no. 1 (February 1992), pp. 215–326.

3. My findings are closely related to the analysis of Lawrence F. Katz and Alan B. Krueger, "Changes in the Structure of Wages in the Public and Private Sectors," *Research in Labor Economics*, vol. 12 (1991), note 1. They also use CPS data between 1967 and 1987 to estimate both the size of the pay gap between public and private sector workers and to provide some evidence on the different evolutions of the wage structure in the two sectors. The present chapter updates many of the Katz-Krueger calculations through the year 2000 and extends the analysis by investigating the link between the skills of workers who move across sectors and the relative changes in the wage structures.

4. In both census and CPS data much of the employment information, such as earnings, refers to the calendar year before the survey. I typically use this timing convention when presenting the data throughout the chapter. The exception is the presentation of the 1960 census data. For expositional convenience the figures date this data point as of 1960 (when in fact it refers to 1959).

5. Lawrence F. Katz and David H. Autor, "Changes in the Wage Structure and Earnings Inequality," in Orley Ashenfelter and David Card, eds., *Handbook of Labor Economics*, vol. 3A (Amsterdam: North-Holland, 1999), pp. 1463–555.

6. The independent variables include a vector of dummy variables indicating the worker's age (18–24, 25–34, 35–44, 45–54, and 55–64), educational attainment (less than high school, high school, some college, and a college degree or more), region of residence (Northeast, North Central, South, or West), and a dummy variable indicating if the worker is black.

7. In the 1980 census for example top-coding affects 0.6 percent of male workers in the private sector, but only 0.1 percent of workers in the public sector.

8. Rebecca M. Blank, "An Analysis of Workers' Choice between Employment in the Public and Private Sectors," *Industrial and Labor Relations Review*, vol. 38, no. 2 (January 1985), pp. 211–24, presents an early analysis of how workers choose between the public and private sectors.

9. The sample size in the CPS-ORG is substantially larger than in the March CPS. Due to changes in survey design, workers cannot be matched between 1984 and 1985 or between 1994 and 1995. It is also difficult to match workers between the 1995 and 1996 surveys. The income data in the CPS-ORG refers to usual monthly income.

10. The transition rates are calculated in the sample of workers who worked in both years, so they do not capture transitions in and out of the labor force.

11. The regression model also includes a vector of dummy variables indicating if the marginal worker is in the federal, state, or local sector. In addition the regression includes a measure of the public-private sector wage differential, which clearly can affect the number of workers who move across sectors and thereby intensify or dilute the selection effect.

12. The measure of relative dispersion used in the regression models is the measure of compression that applies to the particular sector (that is, federal, state, or local government).

4

JOHN D. DONAHUE

In-and-Outers: Up or Down?

I S PUBLIC LEADERSHIP—as something other than just plain leader-ship—losing its distinctiveness? Of course we still need people who accept responsibility for defining and pursuing the public good; few dispute the enduring relevance of this broad definition of the term. Three popular lines of argument, however, challenge the permanence of distinctly public leadership as a specialized and essential social asset. The first contention is that government is ceding much of its franchise for creating public value. Maturing markets get ever closer to the theoretical ideal of maximum welfare through private exchange, by this argument, while nonprofits proliferate to cover a growing share of the tasks not yet within the market's reach. A proposition in line with this theme might be: Larry Page has contributed vastly more to Americans' access to information since he cofounded Google in 1998 than has James H. Billington in his fifteen years as librarian of Congress.

A second and related line of logic is that, even for the missions that remain the responsibility of government, the actual work is increasingly delegated to outside organizations. The leaders of these organizations

Brian Min provided research assistance for this chapter, and his energy and resourcefulness are gratefully acknowledged, as are comments on a prior draft from Joseph S. Nye Jr. and Herman B. Leonard.

accordingly do a growing share of the heavy lifting on collective endeavors. A representative proposition here: As states turn to companies like Lockheed Martin to deliver welfare services, Lockheed chairman Norm Augustine exercises more leverage over efforts against poverty than do many government officials.

A third theme is that government itself is ever more likely to be led by people whose experience and orientation are cross-sectoral rather than anchored in the public sector. A proposition here: Franklin D. Roosevelt entered the New York Senate in his twenties and never thereafter worked a day outside government. George W. Bush earned a master's of business administration degree and worked in business for nearly two decades before entering public service. FDR exemplifies the past of government leadership; "W" exemplifies the present and future.

The implications, if this broad challenge to traditional ideas of public service turns out to be sound, are undeniably consequential. The trend, however, is widely accepted but weakly demonstrated. There is more debate over what to do about the transmutation of public leadership than over whether it is occurring. This chapter aims to back up a bit, to test the facts of the case by assembling and assessing evidence germane to the third and most specific theme of fading public leadership. Are government leaders less and less a breed apart, more and more drawn from and shaped by the private sector?

In-and-Outers

Public and private leadership has never been neatly segregated, especially in the United States, and "in-and-outers" have long shuttled from law firm to cabinet post to foundation chair. In the mid-1980s (before the blurring line between public and private became quite so routine an observation), the political scientist Hugh Heclo examined the peculiar way we populate high public offices. "Americans have created a unique approach to staffing the top of government," he writes, "with an assortment of characters whose career stakes are tied neither to party politics nor to government administration."[1] Here is a reasonable working definition of the in-and-outer: an individual, especially a highly qualified one, whose career includes both public and private positions and for whom business or nonprofit work holds weight equal to or greater than that of government in his or her experience, professional orientation, and sense of self.

In-and-outers are indisputably a major presence in American government and one of the features distinguishing the United States from nations with traditions of specialized elite public service.[2] The issue is whether the public sector's reliance on in-and-outers is deepening, declining, or staying the same. If in-and-outers are becoming dominant in government's upper reaches, we can (for example) worry less about the quality of "permanent" government employees, focus rather more on broad-spectrum professional training than on preparation for work in any single sector, and concentrate on easing the flow of talent across sectoral boundaries.

The broad question about in-and-outers can be parsed into two slightly different variants. First, are cross-sectoral career histories increasingly common among key public officials? Second, is experience outside government increasingly prominent in government leaders' backgrounds? The ideal way to answer these questions, of course, would be to identify a large sample of senior officials from a wide range of public sector organizations over a very long period of time and collect detailed information on their career histories. Determining that current or recent officials switched sectors more often and spent more time outside government than did their counterparts ten, fifty, or a hundred years ago would bolster the hypothesis of diminishingly distinctive public leadership.

A less daunting alternative to a comprehensive study is to focus on a particular subset of American public leaders. The most telling subset for this purpose is presidential appointees in the federal executive branch. This group recommends itself for several reasons. First is its significance. There is room for honest disagreement about the importance of the executive branch relative to the legislature or judiciary, of the federal relative to state and local government, and of political appointees relative to career civil servants. But few would deny that presidential appointees are a reasonably interesting segment of the public work force.

Second is its sensitivity to changes in both the demand for and the supply of in-and-outers. The career civil service is notoriously resistant to lateral entry; senior officials generally start in the lower ranks and work their way up to the higher reaches of the general schedule or into the senior executive service. The two largest categories of public workers—teachers and soldiers—both have technical and cultural barriers to entry that limit sudden surges in imported personnel. While the presidential appointments process is by no means unconstrained—the president must be mindful of Senate confirmation and political obligations—the impediments to matching tasks with talent are lower than they are in other parts of the public sector. So any trend toward in-and-outers should show up soonest and strongest among presidential appointees.

The third reason for focussing on this group is empirical clarity and convenience. Presidential appointees comprise a well-defined and bounded group. The *United States Government Manual* unambiguously identifies each position and its incumbent in each fiscal year.[3] Biographical data on presidential appointees generally appears in the standard reference *Who's Who in America;*[4] indeed presidential appointment appears to be one of the automatic triggers for inclusion in *Who's Who.* The basics on the career backgrounds of most presidential appointees are also covered in the *Federal Staff Directory* and in agency reports or websites.[5] Compared to the hazards and burdens of tracking the careers of other categories of public leaders, examining presidential appointees is relatively straightforward.

Prior Empirical Work

The literature on the career backgrounds of presidential appointees is remarkably sparse and dated. The dustiness of one book is revealed by its title: *Men Who Govern.*[6] This Brookings study examines the characteristics and career histories of around a thousand appointees from 1922 through 1965. Two decades later the National Academy of Public Administration built on that study, extending the data on political appointees into the Reagan administration.[7] The career background information in these studies, however, is sadly thin. Both record the "primary occupation" of appointees, defined as the sector in which the official spent the largest part of his or her prior career. The records thus have no information about the proportions of a career spent in each sector or about the sequencing of jobs. The NAPA study, though not the Brookings study, also collected information about the job held by appointees just before joining the government. In both studies prior experience is coded in a binary way as public or private, with no separate category for nonprofit work. Universities, foundations, political parties, and labor unions are classed with law firms and lumber companies as private sector employers.

The conclusions suggested by these studies are correspondingly rickety, but they offer limited support for the claim that government increasingly relies on imported leaders. The share of appointees whose "primary occupation" was private rather than public was within a few points of 50 percent for most of the administrations from FDR to Ronald Reagan, with

three exceptions: FDR himself, who drew about 60 percent of his top people from the private sector, and Eisenhower and Kennedy, who drew about
70 percent. Truman's mix was about half-and-half, and Johnson, Nixon,
Ford, Carter, and Reagan returned to that rough balance.[8] The data on the
jobs appointees left to join the government (while covering a shorter
period, since NAPA but not Brookings recorded this item) is somewhat
more consistent with rising reliance on in-and-outers. The share of appointees hired away from private sector jobs was about 30 percent for
Johnson, rose to over 40 percent for Nixon, dropped back to around
30 percent for Ford, then rose to nearly half for Carter and over half for
Reagan.[9] So ignoring Ford—properly so, since he replaced Nixon midterm
and made few fresh high-level hires—we see a substantial climb in appointments from the private sector between the 1960s and the 1980s.

But these results are not very satisfying, both because of the coarse characterization of prior career experience and because the story ends in the
mid-1980s. A more up-to-date and nuanced picture is needed. A fully
developed version of this picture would examine a large sample of appointees from each administration over the past half century or so. I hope
some enterprising doctoral student undertakes such an effort, but here
again I retreat to the less grueling alternative of a strategically selected subset. What subset offers the biggest evidenciary bang for the data-collection
buck? A defensible approach for some kinds of trend research is to sample
at (say) five-year intervals, but in this case that would be hazardous. The
propensity for hiring from within or outside government almost surely
changes over the course of an administration and may differ between
Democratic and Republican administrations as well. So the accidents of
interval sampling would likely lead to blurred or biased results.

A better sampling rule is to examine the first year's appointments for an
administration marking a partisan shift. This offers the best odds for spot-
ting an increase in in-and-outers. In its first year after a period out of
power, an administration can call on the deepest bench of willing and able
candidates outside government. Later years' appointments tend to be
heavy with internal promotions—upgrades from assistant secretary to
undersecretary, for example, with the old job at Ford (whether the auto
company or the foundation) falling further into the past. And excluding
transitions between presidents of the same party eliminates the dampening effect on external hiring of follow-on administrations' tendency to
retain some holdovers (whether in the same or a different post within government). Applying these screens to postwar administrations yields seven

points of observation: Eisenhower (1953), Kennedy (1961), Nixon (1969), Carter (1977), Reagan (1981), Clinton (1993), and Bush (2001).

The Data

For each of these inaugural years following a switch in party control, a reference group was defined to include around fifty top officials:
  —the president and vice president[10]
  —the chief of staff, budget director, and other top White House aides[11]
  —all cabinet secretaries and deputy secretaries[12]
  —a random selection of undersecretaries and assistant secretaries.[13]
Only confirmed officials (for positions requiring Senate approval) were included in the reference group. If a position was vacant or held by an acting official, the post was simply dropped from the group.[14] We then sought biographical information for each official identified. In most cases such information was available in the contemporary edition of *Who's Who in America* or in one of the next two years' editions. If not, we turned to the *Federal Staff Directory*. If neither of these standard references covered an official, we sought a biography from his or her current or prior employer. In the few cases where we could not obtain a sufficiently detailed biography, the official was dropped from the reference group. This procedure yielded biographical profiles on a total of 339 officials, with the size of the reference group for each administration ranging from a low of forty-six to a high of fifty-three. This is not a full census, since even under Eisenhower the number of senior presidential appointees was well in excess of fifty, and the share of an administration's senior officials included in the reference group falls over time as top positions proliferate. But the proportion of an administration's cabinet, subcabinet, and equivalent posts studied is always one-quarter or higher, making sampling bias a minor concern.[15]

  For each official we recorded the starting year and ending year of every job held prior to the presidential appointment at issue. We coded each job as either public, private, or nonprofit, thus refining the dichotomous public-private breakdown employed in prior studies. Measuring the length of tenure in each job also permits a more precise characterization of prior careers than "predominantly" in one sector or another, since we can track the actual share of a career spent in each category.

In the vast majority of cases, the classification of a prior job was straight-forward, but on occasion a degree of judgment was required. For example we counted trade associations as private rather than nonprofit employers, even if they are technically not-for-profit, and then for consistency we classed labor unions the same way. A professorship at a state university was coded as a nonprofit job, since it seemed silly to treat Berkeley and Stanford differently when assessing appointees' prior careers. Managing a campaign or a political party was counted as public rather than, as would be technically accurate, nonprofit. Full-time military service was coded as public experience; reserve service concurrent with another job was not counted.

Findings

Is sector switching becoming more common among top federal officials? Yes, by and large, though the trend is not a clean one. Appointees in the Eisenhower administration crossed sector boundaries on average less than once in the course of their prior careers. About 40 percent never changed sectors, and another third moved just once. In the Clinton administration the average number of sector switches before presidential appointment exceeded two. More than one-third of the Clinton appointees had changed sectors three or more times; fewer than one-fifth had stayed in the public, private, or nonprofit sector. Clinton's deputy labor secretary, Tom Glynn, for example, started as a VISTA volunteer when he finished college in 1968. In the 1970s Glynn became a junior policy adviser to a Republican governor of Massachusetts, took time off to earn his doctorate, then went to Washington for a series of increasingly responsible staff jobs in cabinet agencies and the White House. In 1981 he was hired as a senior administrator at Brandeis University, moving on after two years for another stint in Massachusetts state government, though this time in a Democratic administration and as deputy commissioner for welfare. He was lured to the private sector in 1988, managing Boston's World Trade Center, then spent two years as chief executive officer of the sprawling Massachusetts Bay Transportation Authority before Brown University recruited him as head of finance and administration, the post he held when called to Washington.

The increasing rate of cross-sectoral job hopping is even more striking once differences in the amount of prior work experience is taken into

Table 4-1. *Average Number of Sector Switches of First-Year Appointees before Appointment*

Administration	Total	Per decade of career
Eisenhower (1953)	0.9	0.33
Kennedy (1961)	1.5	0.62
Nixon (1969)	1.3	0.46
Carter (1977)	1.4	0.60
Reagan (1981)	1.7	0.71
Clinton (1993)	2.1	0.90
Bush (2001)	1.6	0.62

Sources: *Who's Who in America* (New Providence, N.J.: Marquis Who's Who/Reed Elsevier); *Federal Staff Directory* (Washington: Congressional Quarterly Press).

account (table 4-1). In some administrations (Eisenhower, Nixon) the typical appointee had around twenty-eight years of work experience, while in others (Kennedy, Carter, Reagan, Clinton) the norm was several years less.[16] Factoring in the five years' difference in average work experience for Eisenhower versus Clinton appointees, for example, reveals that Eisenhower officials averaged one sector switch for every three decades of work, while the Clinton officials' pace was close to a switch each decade. Officials in the Bush administration were somewhat less footloose across sectors than their Clinton counterparts and even made slightly fewer switches than Reagan appointees. But the broad trend, from 1953 to 2001, seems generally upward and is consistent with the story of increasingly broad-spectrum career backgrounds for public leaders.

It is not enough to establish that top officials change jobs and switch sectors more often than their counterparts of a generation ago, however. Support for the "fading public leadership" account requires nongovernmental experience to be increasingly important in public leaders' backgrounds. And here the evidence from presidential appointees' biographies is surprisingly at odds with the idea that distinct categories of leadership are giving way to an undifferentiated pool. Table 4-2 tracks the average proportion of appointees' prior careers that was spent in each sector. It shows a wrenching shift between Eisenhower's first-year appointees (with government work accounting for an average of just 26 percent of preappointment experience) and Kennedy's first-year appointees (double the proportion, at 52 percent.) The striking point, though, is that the weight of public sector experience in top officials' careers consistently rises from the Carter admin-

Table 4-2. *First-Year Appointees' Prior Careers Spent in Each Sector*[a]
Percent

Administration	Public	Private	Nonprofit
Eisenhower (1953)	26	64	10
Kennedy (1961)	52	39	9
Nixon (1969)	41	47	12
Carter (1977)	42	38	21
Reagan (1981)	47	44	9
Clinton (1993)	49	33	17
Bush (2001)	55	32	14

Sources: *Who's Who in America; Federal Staff Directory.*
a. May not sum to 100 because of rounding.

istration on, reaching a peak of 55 percent in 2001 under George W. Bush. Business experience generally trends downward, with an uptick under Reagan. The average career share in the nonprofit sector displays no simple pattern, other than a spike in the Carter administration.

Slicing the data different ways provides more nuance to the story, revealing the following.

Sit-and-Stayers

People who might be called "sit-and-stayers"—who spent more than 90 percent of their prior careers in a single sector—are indeed becoming less common, which fits the conventional wisdom. Sit-and-stayers accounted for about 65 percent of Eisenhower's appointees, less than 20 percent of Clinton's, and between 30 and 40 percent for the other five administrations. But for every administration after Eisenhower, including the three Republican administrations, the largest share of sit-and-stayers were those anchored in government. In the George W. Bush administration, for example, 23 percent of appointees had overwhelmingly (90 percent or more) public sector resumes, compared to 6 percent nonprofit and just 4 percent business experience.

Mostly-Inners

Only around one-quarter of Eisenhower's appointees had spent half or more of their prior careers in the public sector. But, in every subsequent administration sampled, the share of "mostly-inners" exceeded 40 percent. Over 55 percent of George W. Bush's appointees had spent the majority of their prior careers in government, the highest share of mostly-inners of the seven administrations studied.

Never-Inners and Barely-Inners

Appointees with no public sector work history or with government experience summing to less than one-tenth of their careers were common under Eisenhower (53 percent of appointees) but otherwise accounted for fewer than one-fifth of appointees. For every group from the Reagan administration onward, these two categories have collectively claimed 15 percent of top appointees.

A cautious summary of these findings can be phrased like this: The relative importance of business and nonprofit work in the backgrounds of first-term presidential appointees displays no consistent pattern over the past half century, so that (at least for this sample, within this segment of the public sector) the hypothesis of growing reliance on nongovernmental expertise is not supported. A less cautious interpretation: For the past thirty years (since the Nixon administration), at the points in time and for the kinds of positions most open to the flow of talent from outside government, the relative importance of public sector experience is rising, not falling.

These findings can be interpreted in several ways, of course, including ways that are consistent with the claim that distinctly public leadership is losing ground. But the simplest account may be the strongest: Public leadership is different. It requires a portfolio of instincts, skills, and habits of mind distinguishable from the business or nonprofit leader's toolkit. Some people have a special taste and talent for this kind of work. It follows that reinforcing that taste and refining that talent endures as an eminently worthwhile enterprise.

Appendix 4A

Readers who harbor doubts about the validity of these data or who enjoy pondering the timeless treachery of numbers are offered this appendix on potential sources of bias and alternative explanations.

On the Reliability of the Data

Do the data summarized here offer a reasonably representative picture of trends in in-and-outers, or might they be biased? This is a legitimate question to pose regarding any attempt to extract inferences about a half-century of experience from 339 resumes. The data are certainly biased in one sense—the reference years (the first year of an administration marking a change in party control) are selected to be especially hospitable to the recruitment of top officials from outside government. This though is deliberate; some accidental biases are worth considering.

CHANGING RATES OF MILITARY SERVICE. I count a stint in the military as a public job, which some might argue is technically correct but distorts the story. Could shifts in the prevalence of military service bias the trends? This probably has something to do with the spike in average government experience under Kennedy—the bulk of Kennedy appointees had "public jobs" during World War II—but cannot explain the high levels under Clinton and Bush. Indeed, when Clinton and Bush appointees were young men, military service was no longer routine for the kind of people who become cabinet secretaries, so this factor somewhat suppresses the rising share of public sector experience.

INACCURATE RESUMES. My sources of biographical data—usually *Who's Who in America*—rely on self-reported information. Could presidential appointees have been lying about or otherwise distorting their prior careers in ways that generate a false impression of increasing public sector weight in the average appointee's career history? Distortion is always a risk with self-reported data. But note that *Who's Who* and the *Federal Staff Directory* are highly public references, making it hazardous for a public official to misrepresent his or her history. More to the point, in light of trends in the cultural status of government during this period, it seems improbable that officials' tendency to pare private sector experience from their resumes and exaggerate public sector experience would rise over time and peak in the Bush administration.

INCREASING CONFIRMATION PROBLEMS FOR OUTSIDER APPOINTMENTS. The Senate confirmation process has become slower and more troublesome over time. It could be that snags and lags in confirmation have become differentially problematic for nominees who have a lot of private sector experience, while government insiders (relatively speaking) sail through. Thus the design of the research—examining appointees in place during an administration's first year—would miss many "outsider" appointees who will eventually show up. (This is related to but different from the possibility that business-oriented candidates will refuse to serve or fail to be confirmed; here the arrival of outsiders is delayed but not blocked.) This is plausible, though it is not obvious that confirmation delays have more to do with nominees' private sector than governmental backgrounds. The only way to exclude this possible source of bias, though, is to replicate the analysis to cover later stages of each administration.

THE SHIFTING WEIGHT OF GOVERNMENT ECONOMY-WIDE. The public sector share of American employment has fluctuated over the post-war era. It climbed from a demobilization trough of under 15 percent to more than 20 percent in the late 1960s and early 1970s, then slid gradually back to around 15 percent.[17] Perhaps we are just seeing the echo of this surge. That is, in 1993 or 2001 cabinet secretaries (just like all the other fifty-somethings in America) were more likely to have government experience than people who had not been in the work force during the uptick in public employment. There may be something to this; the proportion of public work in top officials' career histories has a decent correlation (0.68) with the five-year average share of public employment economy-wide twenty years earlier. But most of the variation in overall public employment is accounted for by the military (which expanded in the Vietnam War and contracted thereafter) and by education (public school payrolls swelled to accommodate the baby boomers, then ebbed as the demographic bulge moved onward). Federal civilian employment has been a more or less steadily declining share of overall American employment since around the early 1950s. The ranks of top appointees include relatively few former teachers, and as noted, military service cannot explain the pattern. So it is unlikely that a cohort effect is masking some growing propensity for nongovernmental experience among presidential appointees.

THE CHANGING CABINET AND SUBCABINET PROPORTION. The rising number of cabinet and cabinet-equivalent positions over time, coupled with a roughly constant size for the reference groups studied, means that the proportion of undersecretaries and assistant secretaries is higher for earlier than for later administrations. If top officials are more likely than less senior appointees to have extensive government experience, this could distort the analysis and lead to an erroneous conclusion that public experience is rising among presidential appointees. As a prophylactic against this possibility, I analyze each year's cabinet and subcabinet populations

Table 4A-1. *First-Year Appointees' Prior Careers in Government*[a]
Percent

Administration	Constant-weight	Unadjusted
Eisenhower (1953)	27.4	25.9
Kennedy (1961)	52.5	51.8
Nixon (1969)	41.3	41.1
Carter (1977)	43.9	41.5
Reagan (1981)	49.1	46.8
Clinton (1993)	50.8	49.4
Bush (2001)	53.6	54.7

Sources: *Who's Who in America; Federal Staff Directory.*
a. Corrected for differences between most-senior and less-senior appointees, and unadjusted.

separately, and then apply a constant weight to each subpopulation (51 percent cabinet; 49 percent subcabinet), which eliminates the effect of the changing mix across administrations. This alternative method yields a picture that differs only slightly from that painted by the raw data. The main effect is to smooth out the trend of government experience growing in importance from 1969 to 2001.

In short, while this topic may benefit from a more comprehensive empirical examination, with a larger data set and more sophisticated methods, the simple approach employed here seems to be a reasonably robust rough cut.

Alternative Explanations

Even if the data's soundness is conceded, there may be accounts of these findings that save the story of increasingly cross-sectoral leadership. For example, the results could reflect a deeply dysfunctional presidential appointments process rather than a diminishing preference for leaders geared to the private sector. By this argument the best picks for cabinet and subcabinet posts are indeed people with plenty of experience outside government. But an increasingly excruciating appointments process—intrusive background checks, onerous financial disclosure requirements, rancorous Senate confirmation hearings—means that the best picks refuse to serve. So to a growing degree presidents have to settle for their second or third choices. These tend to be people with prior government experience who know the ropes and can better navigate the process or who simply have a demonstrated tolerance for its burdens and indignities. If and when the system gets fixed, we will see a surge of beyond-the-Beltway appointments.

It is hard to dispute that the tortuous process repels some potential appointees, and it is plausible that business-oriented candidates are differentially deterred. This factor probably exerts some downward pressure on the supply of appointees from the business and nonprofit worlds, but whether the effect is trivial or profound remains unclear. The only ways to know for sure are either to conduct detailed and candid interviews with the last several presidential personnel directors to see how many chief executive officers and foundation heads turned them down or to fix the appointments process and see what happens. In the meantime, the weight to accord this factor is a matter of judgment. My own instinct is that differential filtering of business-oriented candidates has a real but minor impact on an administration's composition.[18]

Another alternative account could focus on the surprising result that the first MBA president seems to have the most insider-heavy of the seven administrations and declare the George W. Bush presidency an anomaly. By this argument 2001 is improperly classified as the first year of a fresh party in power; it is better thought of as the thirteenth year, albeit after a hiatus, of the Reagan-Bush regime. It is not surprising to find a surfeit of government experience in what is essentially a restoration; this is an idiosyncrasy with no implications for the broader shift toward business-oriented in-and-outers. There may be something to this. All public sector experience for four of the forty-seven Bush officials studied took place between 1980 and 1992.[19] On the other hand, eighteen of the forty-seven had worked for government outside this twelve-year period. Nor can the restoration hypothesis explain the slow but steady growth in prevailing levels of government experience from Nixon to Carter to Reagan to Clinton.

Anne-Marie Slaughter has offered an elegant explanation for the apparent increase over time in appointees with a preponderance of government experience: two-career couples.[20] The exigencies of a spouse's career may not have dissuaded a Detroit auto executive from heeding Ike's call to service in 1953. But today many, perhaps most, potential appointees can be expected to have a working spouse, and the intimate negotiations sparked by a prospective move to Washington could culminate in candidates declining to serve. Families already established inside the Beltway face no such complexities. This could account for some of the pattern, though it would be surprising if it were the only factor.[21] Another partial explanation may be the vertiginous rise in private sector versus public sector compensation. Fifty years ago the pay of presidential appointees was, if less than princely, in the same general league as what a successful professional could expect in private life. Today's salary for a cabinet member, while several multiples of the average family income, is roughly equivalent to starting pay for graduates of top law or business schools and a small fraction of a law partner's or CEO's compensation. The prospect of moderating a family's consumption levels or drawing down savings probably deters some prospective appointees.[22]

Another interpretation of these findings that preserves the fading-public-leadership story would argue that the federal government's prominence within the public sector is eroding, as resources, authority, and popular legitimacy shift to the states and cities. The resurgence of national security concerns after the events of September 11, 2001, may undercut this assertion, but it has been a valid generalization for most of the past generation or so.[23] While the advertised transformation of leadership may not be apparent at the national level, the argument continues, it is occurring at the increasingly important state and local levels. I have little information and hence no strong position on whether state and local leaders (unlike presidential appointees) are increasingly drawn from business and nonprofits. The claim is entirely plausible, but then the corresponding claim about top federal officials was plausible, too, and turns out to be wrong.

Notes

1. Hugh Heclo, "The In-and-Outer System: A Critical Assessment," in G. Calvin MacKenzie, ed., *The In-and-Outers: Presidential Appointees and Transient Government in Washington* (Johns Hopkins University Press, 1987), p. 195.
2. See Derek Bok, "Government Personnel Policy in Competitive Perspective," chapter 14 of this volume.
3. The *United States Government Manual* is published annually by the Office of the Federal Register of the National Archives and Records Administration and distributed in print form by the Government Printing Office as well as electronically.
4. *Who's Who in America* (New Providence, N.J.: Marquis Who's Who/Reed Elsevier). Editions are published annually.
5. *Federal Staff Directory* (Washington: Congressional Quarterly Press). Multiple editions are published each year.
6. David T. Stanley, Dean E. Mann, and Jameson Doig, *Men Who Govern: A Biographical Profile of Federal Political Executives* (Brookings, 1967).

7. The NAPA study is described and its results summarized in MacKenzie, *The In-and-Outers*.

8. Ibid., table 1.8, p. 19.

9. Ibid., table 1.7, p. 17.

10. One could argue that these officials are elected, not appointed, and hence should be excluded. But the career trajectories of the people at the top of the team seem highly relevant to the search for a shifting definition of public leadership.

11. The difference in the number of individuals studied across reference years is mainly a function of the changing size of the senior White House staff as new organizations (such as the National Economic Council) are established.

12. In the results presented below, deputy secretaries are included with secretaries and top White House staff in the subgroup of senior appointees labeled, not quite accurately, as the cabinet group.

13. The selection process involved randomly choosing a starting agency for each reference year, randomly choosing a letter of the alphabet by which to choose the name of the first assistant secretary or undersecretary for that year's reference group, then going through the list of subcabinet officials in the administration and selecting each *n*th official, with *n* being the number of subcabinet officials in the administration divided by the number needed for the reference group, or 50 minus the number of cabinet and cabinet-equivalent officials.

14. In the case of undersecretaries and assistant secretaries, we replaced the missing position with a substitute, using the same random selection procedure. In the case of cabinet positions (where we included all, not just a sample, in the reference group), a vacancy meant a smaller reference group. This caused a relatively minor loss in information; only 7 out of 140 cabinet-and-equivalent positions over the period could not be examined.

15. I am grateful to Richard Light for advice on this point. Note that the total of Senate-approved presidential appointees is much higher—roughly 2,000—but includes a large number of commission and board members, diplomats, U.S. attorneys, and other officials beyond the White House staff, cabinet, and subcabinet members at issue here.

16. To some extent the variation in the length of prior career reflected differences in age, but another major factor is the broad increase in professional training prior to the start of a career.

17. These percentages are calculated from data in Bureau of Economic Analysis, Department of Commerce, *Survey of Current Business*, National Income and Product Account Tables 6.5B and 6.5C, various issues.

18. This judgment is based in part on the admittedly casual empiricism of my brief experience in presidential personnel during the Clinton transition, where I found little evidence of a general reluctance to serve. Never before or since have my phone calls been so promptly returned. That said, other administrations, drawing on different pools of potential personnel, may encounter more systematic resistance.

19. These four are Secretary of Labor Elaine Chao, Deputy Secretary of Transportation Michael P. Jackson, and two Treasury Department officials, Assistant Secretary for Economic Policy Richard Clarida and Assistant Secretary for Financial Institutions Sheila Bair.

20. Dr. Slaughter made this observation at a Visions of Governance seminar at the Kennedy School, January 28, 2002.

21. The simplest test for this account would be to track officials by prior address, not prior career, to see if geographic inertia is increasing.

22. This effect is likely exacerbated by rising living costs in the Washington area. Today, to a far greater degree than in Eisenhower's time, housing prices in Washington and its suburbs are bid up both by lawyers, lobbyists, and other professionals who orbit the federal government and by prosperous employees of the region's growing high-tech industry.

23. I have discussed this trend in John D. Donahue, *Disunited States: What's at Stake as Washington Fades and the States Take the Lead* (Basic Books, 1997).

5

PIPPA NORRIS

Is There Still a
Public Service Ethos?
Work Values, Experience, and
Job Satisfaction among
Government Workers

Jim Hacker, Minister for the Department of Administrative Affairs: "Who else is in this department?"

Sir Humphrey Appleby: "Well briefly, sir, I am the Permanent Under Secretary of State, known as the Permanent Secretary. Woolley here is your Principal Private Secretary. I too have a Principal Private Secretary, and he is the Principal Private Secretary to the Permanent Secretary. Directly responsible to me are 10 Deputy Secretaries, 87 Under Secretaries, and 219 Assistant Secretaries. Directly responsible to the Principal Private Secretary are plain Private Secretaries, and the Prime Minister will be appointing 2 Parliamentary Under Secretaries, and you will be appointing your own Parliamentary Private Secretary."

Jim Hacker: "Do they all type?"

"OPEN GOVERNMENT," *yes minister,* VOL. I, BBC, 1980

IN RECENT DECADES many countries have sought to strengthen the quality, efficiency, and responsiveness of government services. In the United States these initiatives have surfaced with different guises, rationales, and doctrines under successive administrations. During the mid-1970s the concern was the reduction of bureaucratic red tape and paperwork; during the 1980s it was downsizing the state, expanding the nonprofit voluntary sector, and importing business school techniques into the "new public management"; during the 1990s the theme became "reinventing government" so it "works better and costs less"; and the latest manifestation after the events of September 11, 2001, is the reorganization of agencies under the Department of Homeland Security.[1]

Concern about government performance is shared by many other Western governments that have perhaps gone even farther down this road through the process of privatization, marketization, and the import of corporate management techniques, as well as through the growth of distributed governance and joined-up agencies in the core executive.[2] Post-Communist and Latin American societies have often gone through "shock therapy" designed to shrink the state, while administrative reforms in many poorer African states have emphasized investment in the human capital of public sector workers by improving the skills, training, pay, and conditions of government employees.[3]

One fundamental concern surrounding attempts to improve public sector organizations is how far governments can succeed in recruiting, retaining, and rewarding well-motivated workers who are committed to achieving the goals of the organization. Indeed Robert Behn identified this as one of the three big questions that scholars of public management should be attempting to answer, specifically "how public managers can motivate public employees (and citizens too) to pursue important public purposes with intelligence and energy."[4] Getting the right people in the job, energizing them to work effectively for the organization's overall goals, and rewarding them for good performance have long been regarded as vital parts of any lasting reform of the civil service and arguably a far more effective long-term strategy, motivational theories suggest, than structural reorganizations or technocratic solutions.[5]

It remains difficult to prove that factors such as work motivation, job rewards, and employee talent actually matter to organizational performance. It could be that employees form a contented and satisfied work force, enjoying exceptionally generous benefits and perks, and yet the organization fails to achieve its primary goals. Indeed, in a "lean and mean" model, some level of dissatisfaction among the work force could be interpreted as a sign that they are working hard and may be boosting productivity. Alternatively the structure and function of the organization may facilitate efficient achievement of its aims, almost irrespective of patterns of recruitment, rather like the army boot camp model that strips down recruits and rebuilds them.

Nevertheless a common assumption in personnel management, social psychology, and public administration is that recruiting and matching the right people to the right job, then using suitable carrots and sticks to motivate good job performance, facilitates efficient service delivery. Attempts to build an effective public sector seem unlikely to succeed if, as popular stereotypes suggest, government bureaucrats are attracted by a protected world of job security, regular paychecks, and safe pensions rather than by dedication to the public good; if the civil service is full of cautious, rule-following, and risk-averse pen-pushers rather than aggressive, go-getting innovators; and if the old-fashioned, hierarchical, hidebound organizational culture of the civil service rewards longevity and promotes go-with-the-flow loyalists rather than creative leadership, excellent performance, diverse perspectives, and imaginative problem solving.[6] There is a perception, at least in the United States, that civil service work is less satisfying than private sector work, which could cause problems in recruiting government employees of the right caliber and skills.[7] Despite the importance of understanding patterns of recruitment, retention, and rewards in government work, a comprehensive literature review by Bradley Wright concludes that studies in public management have established few consistent results or clear-cut conclusions.[8] The present study seeks to analyze whether distinctive work orientations are evident among government workers and, in particular, whether public and private sector employees in many countries differ from each other in their motivational values, employment experiences, and job satisfaction.

Theoretical Framework

The primary aim of studies of job satisfaction and work motivation has been the pragmatic one of learning how to energize employees to get things done and thereby get the organization to work better and cost less. An extensive literature has examined the motivation of employees in different environments, drawing upon organizational studies, occupational and industrial psychology, the sociology of the workplace, economics, public administration, and management studies.[9] Motivational theories flowing from these disciplines have generally recognized the importance of two antecedent variables that are purported to determine job satisfaction, as illustrated in figure 5-1, namely, the motivational values that people bring to the job, including their prior needs, expectations, and priorities, and their subsequent experience of employment in the organization. As in previous studies, job satisfaction is understood here as a relative concept reflecting the congruence between prior motivational values and subsequent employ-

Figure 5-1. *Model of Job Satisfaction*

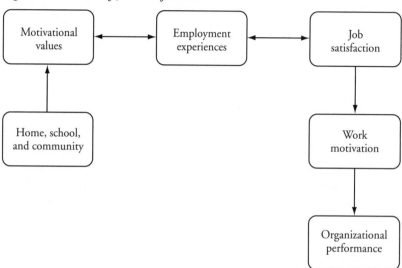

Source: Adapted from Bradley E. Wright, "Public Sector Work Motivation: A Review of the Current Literature and a Revised Conceptual Model," *Journal of Public Administration Research and Theory,* vol. 11, no. 4 (2001), pp. 559–86.

ment experiences.[10] In turn job satisfaction is expected to influence a more general work motivation, although this is usually inferred rather than observed, and a motivated work force is expected to contribute positively toward the performance of organizational goals.

Motivational values concern the basic priorities, needs, and values that people are seeking to fulfill from their work. Opportunities in the labor force offer a range of different rewards, which can be classified analytically into three major types: Material benefits include matters such as pay and work-related pension or other financial benefits, opportunities for career promotion, good working conditions, flexible hours, job autonomy, convenience of workplace location, and job security. Social benefits include occupational status and social prestige, opportunities for work-related travel, the acquisition of new skills and qualifications, intellectual stimulation, and access to social networks and social capital. Idealistic rewards include the opportunity to help people, to contribute toward society, to make the world a better place, to exercise creative or artistic talents, and to promote particular lifestyles, social ideals, or beliefs. Values represent basic orientations, whether toward personal, social or political goals and priorities, which in turn influence attitudes and shape behavior.

Socialization theory suggests that, like other basic values, motivational goals toward work are acquired through formative experiences in the family and home, in school, and in the local community during childhood and adolescence. Studies of socialization processes have commonly found that even young children can articulate a fairly developed sense of what they want to do when they grow up and that these goals evolve as they enter adulthood. Decisions to select one career pathway over another involve tradeoffs, or ranked priorities, among competing goals, such as the importance given to pay or job security. Such value priorities have been found to shape patterns of recruitment and job choices, including the careers that graduates pursue upon first leaving college.[11] The double arrow in figure 5-1 suggests that motivational values shape the initial decision to enter particular jobs in the labor force but that subsequent employment experiences may modify these initial priorities.

This model assumes that motivational work values help shape the initial decision to enter the public or private sector, if each is commonly associated with certain distinctive rewards. Hence those seeking to serve the community and help people might be drawn to become teachers, nurses, or social workers; those attracted by job security and good pensions might decide to enter the civil service or local government; and managers in the private sector might give higher priority to material benefits, such as generous salaries or company cars. Some evidence has been found to support these propositions. For example, Karl and Sutton report that public sector employees lend greater emphasis to interesting work, while private sector workers give higher priority to good wages.[12] Other studies have found little consistent evidence that each sector is strongly associated with different values. Understanding the details of motivation is important when considering whether governments are offering the right package of benefits to recruit and retain the right workers from a heterogeneous labor force.[13]

Employment experiences represent the actual rewards and benefits that people believe they receive from work, and these can also be expected to differ systematically between public and private sector organizations.[14] In particular, financial rewards may be lower in the civil service than in equivalent managerial positions in the corporate world, and evidence suggests that this disparity may have grown, as pay and conditions for senior public sector officials have been deteriorating in many countries in recent years.[15] Government agencies are not subject to the financial discipline of the marketplace, which makes it more difficult to relate job promotions and pay raises to simple monetary indicators of performance, like sales and profitability, although at the same time this situation has traditionally offered civil servants greater job security and work-related pension benefits.

On the negative side, work in the public sector can be expected to offer managers less autonomy and independence. Government agencies are required to meet certain standards of public service—especially those of democratic accountability, probity, transparency, equity, and responsiveness—which do not limit decisions to the same degree in the corporate world. Because of these requirements, traditional Weberian public sector organizations have usually imposed greater procedural constraints on the actions of their employees—for example, in the allocation of government benefits according to standardized rules that limit local officials' discretion. There are many reasons, therefore, to believe that public and private sector employees experience different benefits from work. Beyond the basic public-private dichotomy, of course, the rewards of work are also shaped by many other factors, including occupational status and rank, the function and size of the organization, the managerial culture, and the organizational structure.

The difference between people's motivational values and their actual experience of the rewards and benefits of work contributes toward job satisfaction, understood as a relative concept. If initial expectations match the experienced benefits fairly closely, then we would expect to find high job satisfaction. If, however, people pursue a certain job only to find that it fails to deliver the expected benefits, then they can either adapt their initial expectations to the actual conditions they experience, or they can become disillusioned and demoralized and look for greener pastures. Job satisfaction involves many components, and the definition used here is a minimalist one that simplifies many complex issues. Nevertheless it does tap in to a common way of understanding the rewards people derive from the workplace. It is often assumed that public sector workers experience less satisfaction than those in equivalent positions in the private sector—for example, if senior civil servants have lower pay, fewer perks, poorer working conditions, or more bureaucratic constraints than corporate managers, they must be less content—yet the evidence supporting these claims remains mixed.[16] Even if "objective" conditions of work in the public and private sectors differ, this does not necessarily mean that these will generate differences in job satisfaction, because the essential point is the match between expectations and conditions.

Evidence

Many previous studies have used selective samples within particular organizations and types of jobs, such as studies of health workers or local officials in employment or housing agencies. Studies limited to public sector employees, moreover, such as the senior managers in the federal bureaucracy, tell us little unless we can compare them with equivalent private sector workers. Interviews and other qualitative studies provide rich insights into people's work experience but have a limited ability to leverage generalizations that hold across different sectors, types of organizations, and occupational strata. Surveys of the school-leaving or college populations can help us understand the initial decision to pursue a particular career path but, unless longitudinal panel surveys are used, such methods are blind to subsequent employment experiences and job satisfaction and to how initial motivational values are modified by experience in the work force. Surveys limited to one particular nation make it difficult to generalize across different types of culture and state structures, such as the substantial contrasts between the civil service in Westminster, Washington, Paris, and Stockholm.

For all these reasons, this study draws on surveys with samples representative of the general population, including the working and nonworking public, in many countries. The International Social Survey Programme (ISSP) survey on work orientations conducted in 1997 covers a wide range of nations, including Bangladesh, Bulgaria, Canada, Cyprus, the Czech Republic, Denmark, France, Germany (western and eastern), Great Britain, Hungary, Israel, Italy, Japan, the Netherlands, New Zealand, Norway, the Philippines, Poland, Portugal, Russia, Slovenia, Spain, Sweden, Switzerland, and the United States.[17] The comparative framework therefore includes many of the most affluent countries in the world, although with sharply different traditions of public sector employment. Within postindustrial societies, Norway and Sweden exemplify smaller affluent welfare states with extensive public services, while the size of the public sector has historically been smaller in Japan and the United States. The surveys also include a wide range of post-Communist states in eastern and central Europe, as well as Asian societies. Countries are classified into five major world regions sharing similar cultural backgrounds and political traditions, as illustrated in table 5-1. The ISSP survey provides a wide range of measures; we have selected the ones focused on attitudes toward motivational values, employment experiences, and job satisfaction. The logistic regres-

Table 5-1. *Classification of Nations into Regions*

Anglo-America (N = 4,462)	Scandinavia (N = 4,586)	Western Europe (N = 12,915)	Central and Eastern Europe (N = 8,014)	Asia (N = 3,200)
Great Britain	Denmark	Cyprus	Bulgaria	Bangladesh
Canada	Norway	France	Czech Republic	Japan
United States	Sweden	Israel	Eastern Germany	Philippines
New Zealand		Italy	Hungary	
		Netherlands	Poland	
		Portugal	Russia	
		Spain	Slovenia	
		Switzerland		
		Western Germany		

Source: Work Orientations II, International Social Survey Programme (ISSP), 1997 (www.issp.org/surveys.htm).

sion models use standard social controls for factors that have commonly been found to influence both motivational values and employment experiences, including age, gender, education, and subjective social class.

Motivational Values

The first issue concerns why people seek careers in public service and whether they are different from those opting to work in private business. To explore this we use one simple item in the survey that asked people, irrespective of their current work status and location, whether they would prefer to work for private business or for the civil service. The results in figure 5-2 show considerable variations across nations. The proportion opting to work for the government is particularly strong in many post-Communist countries as well as in the two developing societies under comparison (Bangladesh and the Philippines). Interestingly the Anglo-American countries have some of the lowest proportions wanting to work for government, and the Scandinavian countries have (perhaps surprisingly) low numbers, while the western European nations are in the middle of the distribution. In a simple cross-tabulation, responses to this item

Figure 5-2. *Preference for Working in the Public Sector*[a]

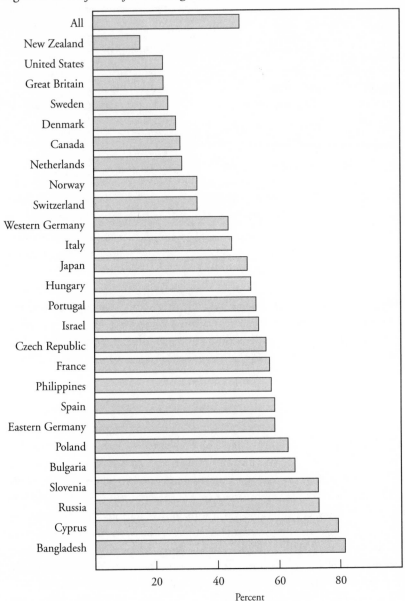

Percent

Source: ISSP, 1997.

a. Question: Respondents were asked whether they would prefer working in a private business or the civil service.

are fairly closely correlated with the actual experience of working in these sectors; the majority (55 percent) of those working for the government say that they would choose to work in the public sector, and the same proportion who are employed in the private sector say that they would prefer to work in business.

The striking variation in the popularity of public sector employment across nations is open to a number of possible explanations. Governments in Anglo-American nations could have a more difficult time attracting workers because of recent public sector reforms. The new public management under Ronald Reagan and Margaret Thatcher may have demoralized workers, reduced their status, and cut down on the perks and sinecures associated with government employment, perhaps boosting organizational performance at the expense of making it harder to recruit new staff. Evidence presented below suggests that people working in the public sector in Anglo-American countries do experience less job security and poorer career prospects than colleagues in equivalent jobs in other regions. Nevertheless similar new public management reforms have been introduced in many countries, not just those in Anglo-American societies, so this seems unlikely to provide a complete explanation of such marked discrepancies as the contrasts evident between New Zealand, the United States, and Britain on the one hand, and France, Spain, and Bangladesh on the other. The contrasts between eastern and western Germany provide an important indication of the root cause.

An alternative and more plausible explanation suggests that cross-national variations may be associated with long-standing structural patterns in the labor force in developing, post-Communist, and postindustrial economies, including the size of the employment pool in the service sector. Careers in the civil service may well be popular in agrarian and industrial economies that have fewer well-paid white-collar jobs for middle-class managers and professionals. The structure of the labor force combined with cultural differences in orientation toward markets and the state may help to explain the residual contrasts between western and post-Communist Europe (and eastern and western Germany). Public sector employment is likely to be more attractive in countries in central and eastern Europe with a culture that tends to be more sympathetic toward government than in countries with long experience of market economies and private enterprise.

The advantage of measuring preference for working in the private or public sector for the initial analysis of motivational values (rather than the actual experience of working in one or the other sector) is that this item speaks to prospective career paths. It therefore covers the recruitment pool—those who are not currently employed in the paid labor force as well as those who would like to work in each sector, irrespective of current employer. To analyze how motivational values relate to the perceived pros and cons of government work, the model in table 5-2 looks at how well values can predict preference for working in the public or private sector. People were asked to evaluate the importance of seven items in considering a job, including high income, job security, and good prospects for career advancement. The analysis allows us to examine the motivational values held by people wanting to work for government. The model breaks down the results by world regions to see whether perceptions of public service careers vary in different areas.

The results in table 5-2 show that, as expected, important differences in motivational values distinguish those who prefer working in the public and private sectors. The primary reason associated with a preference for public service is usefulness to society, a pattern that is strong and significant across all regions except Asia (including Japan, the Philippines, and Bangladesh). In Scandinavia, western Europe, and post-Communist Europe, all nations with strong welfare states and many professionals employed in public sectors, working for the government is also associated with helping other people. The other major advantage of public employment is perceived to be a material incentive; over half the people considered job security a strong priority, and those who value it highly are most likely to prefer public sector work. By contrast people who prefer working for business give greater priority to autonomy and the ability to work independently. This pattern is strong and significant across all world regions, suggesting that the images of government work as rule-bound and circumscribed and private business as allowing more entrepreneurial independence are deeply embedded in public perceptions across many cultures.

The other values queried present a more mixed pattern. Although the private sector might be expected to be associated with more generous salaries, in fact neither public nor private sector work is consistently associated in the public mind with levels of salary, intrinsic interest, or opportunities for advancement. There are indications that those opting to work in the private sector are attracted by the interest or stimulus of those careers as well as by perceived opportunities for advancement, but these patterns are not statistically significant across all regions. The reasons for regional differences in the motivational values associated with the private or public

Table 5-2. *Values Associated with Preference for Working in the Public Sector, Five Regions*[a]

Values	Anglo-America	Scandinavia	Western Europe	Central and Eastern Europe	Asia
Social controls[b]					
Age	.01*	.01***	.01	.03***	−.01**
Gender	.15*	.94***	.39***	.42***	.10
Subjective class	−.04	−.07*	−.03	−.08***	.01
Education	.03	.09**	−.07***	−.09***	−.13***
Motivational values[c]					
Useful to society	.33***	.35***	.23***	.14**	−.01
Job security	.25***	.36***	.33***	.24***	.37***
High income	.13*	−.04	.25***	.07	−.30***
Help others	.06	.24***	.14***	.10**	−.04
Interesting job	−.02	−.15	−.23***	.06	−.10
Advancement opportunities	−.02	−.10	.03	−.11***	−.07
Work independently	−.25***	−.35***	−.29***	−.27***	−.12*
Summary statistics					
Constant	−3.8	−4.2			
Percent correct	78	72	50	67	70
Nagelkerke R^2	.04	.17	.11	.13	.08
Number of respondents	3,368	2,571	8,342	6,201	2,295

Source: ISSP, 1997.

*** p < .001; ** p < .01; * p < .05.

a. Table reports unstandardized beta coefficients and their significance from logistic binary regression models.

b. Age: years; subjective class: 6-point scale; gender: (1) male, (2) female; educational qualifications: 7-point scale.

c. Question: How important do you personally think each of the following items is in a job? (5-point scale from "very important" to "not important at all"). Dependent variable: I would choose to work in a private business (0) or the civil service (1).

sector have to remain speculative at this stage, but they could be explained by a number of factors, including political cultures governing the role and status of the civil service, "objective" working conditions for government employees, such as levels of pay and pensions, employment opportunities in other sectors of the labor market, and the broader role of the state in some societies.

Employment Experience

One way to explore this question further is to look at whether employees in the public and private sectors feel that they reap different benefits and rewards from their work. Accordingly respondents currently active in the labor force were divided by employment sector. The survey asked workers how much they agreed or disagreed with a series of statements about their jobs, replicating the same items already used for analysis. Table 5-3 shows the analysis broken down by region, again controlling for the standard social background factors.

The results suggest a broad congruence between values and experience. Working for government is strongly related to a sense of public service to others and of contributing toward society. Civil service work is also regarded as highly secure in every region except the Anglo-American democracies. (It is unclear how much reforms to this sector during the late 1980s and early 1990s, including privatization and downsizing of the state, contributed toward greater job insecurity in these countries.) On the question of financial rewards, public sector employees in the Anglo-American nations report that they enjoy high salaries, but high salaries are negatively related to public sector employment elsewhere. By contrast people working in the private sector are far more likely to report that their job allows them independence and autonomy, a pattern found across every region of the world. The responses concerning an interesting job and one with opportunities for career advancement proved mixed. We can conclude that the qualities that people most want from work and the qualities that people experience in their jobs both show marked differences by sector, broadly reflecting the mission and ethos of working for government or private business.

Job Satisfaction

What are the qualities that help generate satisfaction with work? If job satisfaction is understood as a function of both value priorities and rewards experienced, we need to compare the difference between the two. Figure 5-3 shows the main contrasts by sector. The largest gaps between the public and private sectors are in job security, income, interest, and advancement prospects. In all these areas experience falls well behind how much these are valued. But the gaps are similar for people working in gov-

Table 5-3. *Values Associated with Working in the Public Sector,*
Five Regions[a]

Values	Anglo-America	Scandinavia	Western Europe	Central and Eastern Europe	Asia
Social controls[b]					
Age	.01	.02**	.01***	.02***	.02*
Gender	.68**	.98***	.32***	.50***	−.08
Subjective class	.06*	−.08*	.03	−.03	.15*
Education	.14**	.29**	.26***	.24***	.39***
Employment experiences[c]					
Useful to society	.50**	.77***	.36***	.46***	.62***
Job security	−.01	.17**	.53***	.07*	.91***
High income	.20**	−.33***	−.03	−.22***	−.45***
Help others	.25***	.34***	.09*	.10*	−.21
Interesting job	.05	−.10	−.02	−.10*	−.24*
Advancement opportunities	−.25**	.05	−.07*	.07	−.24*
Work independently	−.19**	−.42**	−.50***	−.46***	−.40***
Summary Statistics					
Constant	−5.4	−5.9	−5.3	−2.4	−4.8
Percent correct	71	74	79	65	80
Nagelkerke R^2	.20	.34	.19	.17	.38
Number of cases	1,412	2,101	5,629	3,370	992

Source: ISSP, 1997.
*** $p < .001$; ** $p < .01$; * $p < .05$.
a. See table 5-2, note a.
b. See table 5-2, note b.
c. Question: How much do you agree or disagree that these statements apply to your job? (5-point scale from "strongly agree" to "strongly disagree"). Dependent variable: Respondent works (1) for the government, a publicly owned firm, a cooperative, or a nonprofit organization; (0) respondent works for the private sector or is self-employed.

ernment or business. In other priorities, expectations match experience more closely, but public workers are especially satisfied that their work contributes toward society or helps other people. These differences remain significant in multivariate models with controls (not reported here). What this suggests is that all employees desire better financial rewards and conditions of work, yet there is no reason to believe, based on these results, that public sector workers are less satisfied with their positions.

Figure 5-3. *Motivational Values and Employment Experiences, by Sector*[a]

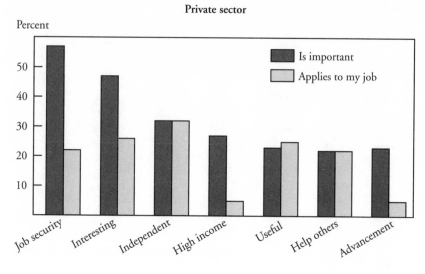

Private sector

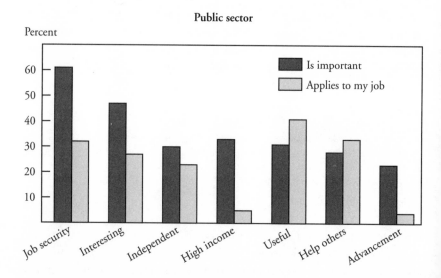

Public sector

Source: ISSP, 1997.

a. Motivational values question: How important do you personally think each of the following items is in a job? (5-point scale, from "very important" to "not important at all"). Employment experiences question: How much do you agree or disagree that these statements apply to your job? (5-point scale, from "strongly agree" to "strongly disagree")

This conclusion was confirmed when people were asked directly, "How satisfied are you in your job?" and responded based on a seven-point scale ranging from "completely satisfied" to "completely dissatisfied." The mean result for public sector workers is 5.22, compared with 5.24 for private workers, an insignificant difference. Greater contrasts occur by occupational rank, ranging from the lowest satisfaction among blue-collar manual workers in both sectors (mean 5.06) to the greatest satisfaction among senior officials and managers in both sectors (5.50).

Conclusions

Although it might be expected that employees would differ by sector in the rewards they seek and get from their jobs, studies have not always supported these assumptions. As Wright observes in his literature review, "The research on sector differences in employee motives should be viewed with some caution. Although some evidence has suggested that a relationship exists between employee motives and sector employment, these findings have not been entirely consistent and the causal direction remains uncertain."[18] Indeed few significant differences between sectors can be detected using the ISSP survey. There is little difference between sectors in people's answers to questions about the importance of work in their lives, how hard they work, the most appropriate criteria for promotion, how easy it would be to get another job, if past work experience or skills are useful in their present job, and relations between management and employees and among colleagues. A comparison across all these dimensions suggests more congruence than divergence between public and private sector employees. The contrasts by occupational rank within each sector are far greater than the contrasts between sectors.[19]

Nevertheless, in some important areas public and private sector workers disagree, areas that relate less to work conditions than to the broad mission of the organizations. Private sector workers experience greater freedom and autonomy in their jobs. Public sector organizations operate with more constraints because of the need to ensure democratic accountability, transparent standards of public policy, and equity in dealing with public service clients. Public sector managers have less freedom than their business equivalents but have a stronger sense of fulfilling a useful societal role and greater job security. The civil service has a distinctive mission, and its employees seem to reflect and value this ethos. Finally, public sector employees are as satisfied with their jobs as those in private employment. The perception that the public sector in the United States has growing problems in recruiting employees is not confirmed by the evidence presented in this study.

We cannot demonstrate that a well-satisfied work force is sufficient to achieve effective and efficient government performance. Even if public sector workers are happy with their lot, feeling relatively well paid and secure, government departments may still fail to recruit the entrepreneurial go-getters and innovative managers needed to achieve key goals. Perhaps the government attracts too many risk-averse people who care too much about job security and too little about innovation and challenges. Nevertheless the evidence presented here suggesting that public sector employees find their work fulfilling and rewarding should prove encouraging for civil service managers, for governments, and indeed for the broader public who depend upon their services.

Notes

1. Christopher Hood, *The Art of the State* (Oxford: Clarendon Press, 1998); David Osborne and Ted Gaebler, *Reinventing Government* (Addison-Wesley, 1992).

2. See John D. Donahue and Joseph S. Nye Jr., eds., *Governance Amid Bigger, Better Markets* (Brookings, 2001); D. Farnham and S. Horton, "Continuity and Change in the Public Services," in D. Farnham and S. Horton, eds., *Managing People in the Public Services* (Macmillan, 1996), pp. 3–42; E. Ferlie and others, *The New Public Management in Action* (Oxford University Press, 1996); Elaine Kamarck, chapter 8 of this volume; Joseph S. Nye Jr. and John D. Donahue, eds., *Governance in a Globalizing World* (Brookings, 2000); B. Guy Peters and Jon Pierre, eds., *Politicians, Bureaucrats and Administrative Reform* (London: Routledge, 2001).

3. See Merilee Grindle, chapter 6 of this volume; Ali Farazmand, ed., *Handbook of Comparative and Development Public Administration* (New York: Marcel Dekker, 1991); Ali Farazmand, ed., *Administrative Reform in Developing Nations* (Praeger, 2002); Donald F. Kettl, *The Global Public Management Revolution: A Report on the Transformation of Governance* (Brookings, 2000).

4. Robert D. Behn, "The Big Questions of Public Management," *Public Administration Review*, vol. 55, no. 4 (1995), pp. 313–24.

5. Donald F. Kettl, "Building Lasting Reform: Enduring Questions, Missing Answers," in Donald F. Kettl and J. J. DiJulio, eds., *Inside the Reinvention Machine* (Brookings, 1995).

6. Norman J. Baldwin, "Public Versus Private Employees: Debunking Stereotypes," *Review of Public Personnel Administration*, vol. 11, no. 2 (1991), pp. 1–27; John Newstrom, William E. Reif, and Robert M. Monckza, "Motivating the Public Employee: Fact vs. Fiction," *Public Personnel Management*, vol. 5 (1976), pp. 67–72.

7. Paul C. Light, "To Restore and Renew: Now Is the Time to Rebuild the Federal Public Service" (www.govexec.com/features/1101/1101plight.htm [October 9, 2002]).

8. Bradley E. Wright, "Public Sector Work Motivation: A Review of the Current Literature and a Revised Conceptual Model," *Journal of Public Administration Research and Theory,* vol. 11, no. 4 (2001), pp. 559–86.

9. For a recent literature review, see ibid.

10. Victor S. DeSantis and Samantha L. Durst, "Comparing Job Satisfaction among Public and Private Sector Employees," *American Review of Public Administration,* vol. 26, no. 3 (1996), pp. 327–43; Mark A. Emmert and Walied A. Taher, "Public Sector Professionals: The Effects of Public Sector Jobs on Motivation, Job Satisfaction, and Work Involvement," *American Review of Public Administration,* vol. 22, no. 1 (1992), pp. 37–48; Anne H. Hopkins, *Work and Job Satisfaction in the Public Sector* (Totowa, N.J.: Rowman & Allanheld, 1983); James L. Perry and Lois R. Wise, "The Motivational Basis of Public Service," *Public Administration Review,* vol. 50, no. 3 (1990), pp. 367–73.

11. Gerald T. Gabris and Gloria Simo, "Public Sector Motivation as an Independent Variable Affecting Career Decisions," *Public Personnel Management,* vol. 24, no. 1 (1995), pp. 33–51; K. A. Karl and C. L. Sutton, "Job Values in Today's Workforce: A Comparison of Public and Private Sector Employees," *Public Personnel Management,* vol. 27, no. 4 (1998), pp. 515–27.

12. See Karl and Sutton, "Job Values."

13. P. E. Crewson, "A Comparative Analysis of Public and Private Sector Entrant Quality," *American Journal of Political Science,* vol. 39, no. 3 (1995), pp. 628–39; P. E. Crewson and I. F. Guyot, "Sartor Resartus: A Comparative Analysis of Public and Private Sector Entrant Quality Reanalyzed," *American Journal of Political Science,* vol. 41, no. 3 (1997), pp. 1057–65.

14. G. A. Boyne, "Public and Private Management: What's the Difference?" *Journal of Management Studies,* vol. 39, no. 1 (2002), pp. 97–122.

15. B. Guy Peters and Christopher Hood, "Erosion and Variety in Pay for High Public Office," *Governance: An International Journal of Policy and Administration,* vol. 8, no. 2 (1995), pp. 171–94; Salvatore Schiavo-Camp, "Government Employment and Pay: The Global and Regional Evidence," *Public Administration and Development,* vol. 18 (1998), pp. 457–78.

16. Hopkins, *Work and Job Satisfaction.*

17. For information on this survey from the International Social Survey Programme, see www.issp.org/surveys.htm.

18. See Wright, "Public Sector Work Motivation," p. 566.

19. Further detailed evidence on all these points can be presented, broken down by sector, nation, and occupational rank. Many other attitudes toward work orientation included in the ISSP survey are not discussed here.

6

MERILEE S. GRINDLE

The Good, the Bad, and the Unavoidable: Improving the Public Service in Poor Countries

VISIT THE MINISTRY of education in just about any poor country.[1] As you make your way down the narrow, ill-lit hallways, you glance into work spaces formed by flimsy and scarred partitions. Bursting with dusty file cabinets, these spaces overflow with equally dusty papers. Although you see many employees, you notice that desks are almost bereft of telephones, computers, in-boxes, paper clips, and other artifacts of the modern office. At the end of a twisting avenue of worn linoleum, you find the minister's office. Three secretaries gossip amiably with a number of messengers, a personal assistant, and a chauffeur, all awaiting the minister's pleasure. Several teachers sit patiently in expectation of a minute with the one person who can resolve their problems—missing back pay, a promotion that was never approved, permission for a transfer to an urban school. You sit down to wait your turn. Although it is 3:30, the minister is still at lunch.

Visit a government rural health clinic in just about any poor country. You may find it closed, the practical nurse or doctor-practitioner absent on some unknown business, not seen in days or even weeks. If the clinic is open, you

I am grateful to Rebeca Sánchez de Tagle of the Fletcher School of Law and Diplomacy, Tufts University, for research assistance for this chapter. I also wish to thank L. David Brown, Calestous Juma, and Iqbal Quadir for comments on an earlier version.

find many there ahead of you—mothers with babies and small children, men and women burdened with ill health. Fly-specked posters on the wall warn about mosquitoes and unboiled water. The district practical nurse, a middle-aged woman with little enthusiasm for the day's work ahead of her, shows you around, pointing out the empty medicine cupboard, the absence of basic supplies, the place where the examining table was before the last district health officer took it away to sell to a doctor in private practice. She blames the patients for the maladies they suffer—they are ignorant, she says, and superstitious; there is nothing to be done for them.

These images are caricatures, of course, but ones not far from the truth in some countries. Bureaucracies in many poor countries suffer from low capacity, often do not deliver effective services, and are frequently staffed with poorly trained, poorly remunerated, and poorly motivated public servants. Yet there is another reality in most of these same countries—a reality of well-trained and committed public servants, well-functioning organizations, and efficient service.

Visit the Central Bank or Ministry of Finance in just about any poor country. You are met at the door by a receptionist who walks you through a tight security system. Behind a counter, energetic clerks respond to the questions and needs of those who stand in short lines before them. You are whisked to the fourth-floor offices of the governor or the minister in a shiny and silent elevator. As you make your way down carpeted hallways, you are stunned by the modernist paintings on the walls; they represent the work of the country's most revered artists. You glance into well-lit offices, where employees focus intently on computers alive with colored graphs that echo the modernism of the artwork. Telephones ring urgently; they are answered immediately. The secretary in the chief executive's quiet, mahogany-paneled waiting room offers you coffee. The chief is able to see you in just five minutes, she says, if you would be so kind as to wait; he is terribly sorry to inconvenience you.

Visit an agricultural extension station in a remote location in one of these countries. The office is worn and small but bustling with energy. You begin to understand the routine—extension agents set out early in the morning to visit even more remote locations and return late at night to finish paperwork. The women who grow food crops are as actively sought by these agents as the men who grow export crops. Back in the office agronomists huddle over a table to design a training session for near-subsistence farmers concerned about pest control for their crops and better grazing for their goats. The station head is proud to show you the experimental fields where improved varieties of the locally grown subsistence crops are being tested. You are invited to join a team that is visiting a nearby village to investigate how an indigenous intercropping system works. The team members joke among themselves, but their commitment to their work and to the needs of the villagers is palpable.

Contrasting conditions of sloth and efficiency, indifference and responsiveness, stasis and reform characterize public sectors in many poor countries. Talented people can be drawn to public service in such countries, and significant reforms can be introduced to set the bases for improved performance. Despite many good experiences, however, governments in most poor countries continue to perform poorly. Improving this bad situation is essential. Like their U.S. counterparts discussed elsewhere in this volume, public sector reformers in developing countries need to consider changes that directly address performance incentives and management practices. But even with such changes, the unavoidable reality of inefficient, ineffective, and unresponsive government is likely to persist for some time to come. Just as in the historical evolution of the United States and other now-developed countries, good public sector performance ultimately depends on the development of political societies that expect and demand efficiency, effectiveness, and responsiveness from their governments.

The Good: Executive Talent and Efforts to Restructure Government

For the average citizen in many poor countries, encounters with government are fraught with risk—of lost time, lost opportunities, lost causes, lost money, and lost self-esteem.[2] And the poorer the country, the less well the public sector tends to perform. Yet these generalizations do not tell the whole story. During the 1980s and 1990s many talented and committed individuals were recruited into government service. During this same period governments adopted numerous public sector reforms. This suggests that the problem of poor public sector performance is not a paucity of executive talent or of reformist initiatives.

Attracting the Best and the Brightest

Throughout the past two decades governments in poor countries attracted numerous skilled executives and managers to important public positions.

Among the most noted examples of this were the reform champions who entered government to lead major initiatives to alter existing economic development policies.[3] Under the guidance of these professionals, governments made radical changes away from inward-oriented and statist development strategies toward export- and market-friendly ones.[4] Economic reformers helped generate new rules of the game about the relationship of the state to the economy, encouraged the creation of institutions to support markets, and promoted the privatization of a host of state-owned enterprises. Many of these "technopols" took over executive and managerial positions in government during times of major national crises.[5] Some of these same people were responsible for introducing a generation of well-trained young people to government service and encouraging them to commit their energies to grappling with some of the most difficult problems of development and change.[6]

In the 1990s economic reformers were joined by energetic and skilled "policy entrepreneurs" in the social sectors. In some countries these reformers exercised considerable power from their positions as leaders of ministries of health, education, or social welfare.[7] Though less well known than the economic reformers, they were responsible not only for major changes in social service delivery systems but also for increasing government budget commitments to these services. Often their reformist initiatives were complicated by the vociferous opposition of service-provider unions and bureaucrats in their own ministries.[8] Despite such obstacles, social sector reformers promoted the professionalization of services, decentralization of responsibilities, improved monitoring and evaluation, community involvement, and other important changes.

Similarly officials in some countries made Herculean efforts to alter long-existing structures in the public sector by cutting public payrolls, restructuring pension systems, decentralizing the administration of services, and improving conditions of work.[9] By providing organizational vision, engendering commitment to their missions, assigning employees meaningful work, and restructuring task management, some organizational managers were able to transform the workplace and the quality of service, even in the midst of poor pay and deficient infrastructure.[10] In organizations such as the agricultural extension unit profiled above, inspired managers resuscitated ailing organizations and increased incentives for providing effective service. Some organizations, such as Ghana's Volta River Authority, gained extensive international recognition for the quality of their management.

Many talented individuals, it seems, were drawn to the public service during those extraordinary times, when the difficulties of national development seemed to open opportunities for making significant policy and institutional changes. In addition, of course, some countries boast long and stable traditions of attracting talented individuals to public service. Certainly the Indian Administrative Service has long enjoyed extensive prestige within India and internationally, despite low salaries and an almost Gandhian ethos of self-sacrifice. While the prestige of the service declined in the late twentieth century, and the structures within which it works can be rigid and unresponsive, there is no question that the IAS continued to attract many of the most promising people in the country, even in the context of a rapidly expanding private sector.[11] Just as impressively, highly trained elite cadres characterize the public service in Hong Kong, Malaysia, and Thailand.

It is difficult to explain why talented people would be drawn to the public sector based on the usual rewards assumed to influence career choices. Public sector executives were paid salaries well below what they might have earned in the private sector. Those who entered government during times of crisis did so with no assurance of job security or tenure. Their reputations were at risk because they faced extraordinarily difficult situations and heavy demands that they resolve major problems quickly. These officials certainly were not counting on short and relaxed hours in the office, given the challenges they were taking on, nor the promise of early retirement and secure pensions. Rather, many were responding to opportunities in which their talents were particularly needed. Career senior executives in India and elsewhere were often pursuing traditions of prestige and service. In addition, opportunities to be part of domestic and international policy networks, to appear in the limelight, and to put particular theories into action were further inducements to take up positions in government.

Searching for Structures That Work

There is more good experience to relate about the public service in poor countries in the past two decades. During this period reformers in government, development professionals, academics, and development assistance organizations focused great attention on improving government performance.[12] In addition major infusions of funds were committed to capacity building in public sectors. Technical cooperation directed at poor countries from international development agencies was significant throughout the

Table 6-1. *Number of Countries Undertaking Public Sector Reforms,*
1980–99

Reform	Number of countries[a]
Privatization	63
Decentralization	39
Downsizing	31
Civil service reform	24
Financial and budgetary reform	22
Regulatory reform	20

Source: Elaine Kamarck, "Globalization and Public Administration Reform," in Joseph S. Nye Jr. and John D. Donahue, eds., *Governance in a Globalizing World* (Brookings, 2000), p. 244.
a. N = 99. Eighteen countries undertook two or more reforms.

1990s, reaching $20 billion in 1995 and totaling over $170 billion by the end of the decade.[13]

Civil service reform was high on the list of actions undertaken to decrease the costs and improve the performance of public sectors. Among the ninety-nine low- and middle-income countries included in a survey carried out by Elaine Kamarck, twenty-four had announced civil service reforms by late 1999 (see table 6-1). Initiatives included establishing clear categories of personnel, linking them to pay scales and career systems, developing job descriptions, and introducing measures to link performance to pay and mobility reward structures. In addition some countries sought to devolve personnel decisionmaking—including standards for hiring, performance, promotion, and firing decisions—away from central civil service commissions or human resource units to operational organizations within the public sector.[14]

Major downsizing efforts were carried out in Bolivia, Cameroon, Chile, Ghana, Sri Lanka, Uganda, Venezuela, and many other countries.[15] Eliminating ghost workers was important in Brazil, Costa Rica, Ghana, South Africa, South Korea, Tanzania, and Uganda, among other countries. Ghana and Laos instituted early retirement and other retrenchment efforts in the 1980s, while Brazil introduced measures to make it easier to hire and fire public servants. In the wake of such reforms, a number of countries were able to increase public sector pay and decompress salaries.[16]

Other public sector reforms helped governments manage development more effectively. In Botswana, for example, improvements in public expenditure management were recognized as an important element of the country's ability to invest its resource boom effectively. Financial management and budgetary reforms also figured as important initiatives in Bolivia, Chile, Hungary, Malawi, Mexico, Mozambique, Peru, South Africa, and South Korea, among other countries.[17]

Few initiatives were more noticed or more politically contentious than privatization. Sixty-three countries had adopted this approach by late 1999 to deal with large public sector deficits, reduce the public sector wage bill, and improve the performance of state enterprises and service delivery agencies. According to a World Bank study, countries in Africa, Latin America, and eastern and central Asia divested 2,735 enterprises between 1980 and 1993.[18] Pressures to privatize government functions also encouraged the development of important innovations, such as performance contracts, contracting out of essential public services, and a variety of joint public sector–private sector ventures. Moreover, in the wake of privatization many governments began to develop regulatory mechanisms to ensure that national goals and standards were respected by the new private owners.

Just as assiduously many countries restructured the relationship between central, provincial, and local governments. As indicated in table 6-1, decentralization was second only to privatization in the number of countries reported to have introduced this reform. Among those whose initiatives were particularly far reaching were Bolivia, Poland, and South Africa.[19] Some of these initiatives were taken at regional or local levels, even when national governments did not pursue similar initiatives.[20] Fiscal decentralization gave new dynamism to budgetary management and local input into resource allocation in some countries. Administrative deconcentration of services such as education and public health was chosen by some to increase government responsiveness and accountability, and other countries took the more radical step of devolution to local levels of government or even to the community level with the same goals in mind. Further, political decentralization introduced the direct election of provincial and local officials in a number of countries, significantly altering political dynamics and the electoral calculations of politicians and parties.[21]

Overall, then, efforts to alter the structures within which public servants work, the conditions under which they work, and the capacities they bring to their work were significant in the late twentieth century. The sources of these changes varied from country to country and reform to reform, of course.[22] Countries differed in terms of the alacrity with which they took up such reforms and the extent to which they actually implemented them after committing themselves rhetorically to change. Similarly countries differed in the extent to which they maintained their commitment to public sector reform over time. Of thirty-one countries reporting efforts to downsize the public service, for example, eleven actually employed more public workers at the end of the 1990s than they had in the 1980s.[23] Many countries introduced broad reform programs but implemented them haltingly.[24] Nevertheless general patterns were clear. Liberalization and privatization encouraged governments to shed many functions, civil service reform and capacity building attempted to alter employment structures, pay, and performance standards, and decentralization altered the roles and power of different levels of government.

The Bad: Poor Performance and Perverse Incentives

"People now place their hope in God, since the government is no longer involved in such matters."[25]

"Teachers do not go to school except when it is time to receive salaries."[26]

"We would rather treat ourselves than go to the hospital, where an angry nurse might inject us with the wrong drug."[27]

"The state steals from us all the time, so deceiving the state is not a sin."[28]

However many talented executives and managers have entered the public sector and however extensive the restructuring of government, the truth remains that, overall, poorly performing public sectors persist into the twenty-first century in a large number of poor countries.[29] Citizens continue to report that their governments are ill prepared to respond to their needs, are corrupt, and lack the capacity to ensure basic levels of human and public security. Investors continue to complain that governments are rife with controls and regulations and that public institutions either do not provide the services they should or act as obstacles to the efficient management of business. Indeed a survey of expert opinion in twenty countries in 2000–01 revealed that, even while government performance was thought to have improved over a five-year period, opinions remained critical of overall conditions (see table 6-2).[30] Expert respondents found their countries seriously deficient on measures such as accountability, transparency, and equity in the provision of public services (see table 6-3). After twenty years of public sector reformism, examples of effective leadership,

Table 6-2. *Perceptions of Government Performance on Six Principles of Governance, 2000–01*[a]

Governance principles	Five years ago	At the current time	Change (percent)
Participation	2.82	3.12	10.06
Fairness	2.71	2.86	5.50
Decency	2.82	3.10	9.90
Accountability	2.52	2.70	7.10
Transparency	2.66	2.87	7.80
Efficiency	2.77	2.93	5.70

Source: Julius Court and Goran Hyden, "Towards a World Governance Assessment: Preliminary Findings from the Pilot Phase," working paper (Tokyo: United Nations University, 2001), p. 22.

a. Respondents in twenty countries rated government performance on a scale of 1 (very low) to 5 (very high), "at the current time" and "five years ago."

inspired management, and efficient service delivery often remain restricted to "islands of excellence."

According to World Bank governance data, only seven countries in Latin America, Africa, Asia, the Middle East, and eastern Europe ranked in the upper 25 percent of countries in the world in terms of government effectiveness at the turn of the millennium. Thirty-three had governments that were judged to be relatively effective (in the second quartile). About eighty countries, however, most of them in Africa, eastern and central Europe, and central Asia, fell into the bottom two quartiles of countries in the world in terms of governance. Similarly, the record of government's ability to be responsive to citizen demand and accountable for its actions was also poor. In 2000–01 only Costa Rica, the Czech Republic, Estonia, Hungary, and South Korea ranked in the upper 25 percent of governments in assessments of the extent to which they gave their citizens voice and had effective mechanisms for accountability. Most African countries and a significant number of eastern and central European and central and Southeast Asian governments fell into the lowest two quartiles.

Civil servants at times have reason to be as unresponsive and unmotivated as these data suggest. Many are poorly remunerated, and some experienced declining pay over the course of the 1980s and 1990s. In Latin America, for example, average public sector incomes were shown to be low in Bolivia, Ecuador, Honduras, Nicaragua, and Venezuela, and in Costa Rica, Honduras, and Venezuela public employees were on average rela-

Table 6-3. *Perceptions of Government Performance, by Country, 2000–01*[a]

Country	Scope for expert policy advocate	Meritocracy in recruitment	Accountability of of civil servants	Transparency in civil service	Equal access to public services	Country average
Argentina	2.92	1.74	2.21	1.95	2.76	2.32
Barbados	3.73	3.32	3.23	3.71	4.36	3.67
Chile	3.00	2.50	2.84	2.94	3.30	2.92
China	2.53	2.69	2.38	2.06	2.36	2.41
India	4.03	4.08	2.29	2.97	2.86	3.37
Indonesia	2.57	2.17	1.97	2.03	2.46	2.22
Jordan	3.03	2.50	2.95	3.03	3.48	3.00
Kyrgyz Republic	2.88	2.03	2.08	2.03	2.08	2.22
Mongolia	3.38	2.68	2.40	2.80	2.70	2.79
Nepal	2.97	2.89	1.97	2.20	2.35	2.48
Nigeria	3.08	2.49	2.97	3.00	2.46	2.80
Pakistan	3.86	2.92	2.41	2.31	1.95	2.49
Papua New Guinea	3.17	2.26	2.44	2.42	2.23	2.50
Peru	3.00	2.16	2.50	2.17	2.65	2.49
Philippines	2.57	2.37	2.14	2.37	2.01	2.30
Russia	3.67	2.39	2.16	2.11	2.58	2.58
Samoa	3.08	2.49	2.97	3.00	2.46	2.80
South Korea	3.29	2.68	2.61	2.44	2.66	2.74
Thailand	3.60	3.00	3.10	3.10	3.17	3.19
Togo	2.79	1.98	1.95	2.02	2.29	2.21
Average	3.21	2.63	2.55	2.57	2.76	2.74

Source: Court and Hyden, "Towards a World Governance Assessment."

a. Respondents in twenty countries rated government on five performance measures on a scale of 1 (very low) to 5 (very high).

tively less well off at the end of the 1990s than they were in the 1980s.[31] These conditions give added insight into the rueful adage that is a favorite among beleaguered bureaucrats almost everywhere: "They pretend to pay us and we pretend to work."

Moreover, conditions of employment often do not encourage public employees to be efficient, effective, or responsive in their activities. In most countries in Latin America the security of public sector jobs is notoriously fragile for all except unionized workers; insecurity as well as low pay undermine professionalism. In countries with professional civil services, such as those in south Asia and much of the rest of Asia, employment is relatively secure, but the rules regarding advancement and the bureaucratization of even minor aspects of jobs often stifle ambition and energy; this same set of structures insulates most officials from public demands for responsiveness. In many African countries political appointments and promotions have gradually undermined structured civil service systems and the commitment of public officials to traditions of service.

Of course this does not mean that public sector employment is not attractive to many people. In contexts in which employment opportunities are almost always extremely limited, a job with government is often sought after, even at low pay.[32] In some countries it offers a modicum of security, benefits such as housing, transportation, and pensions, hours that allow for second jobs, prestige, and, for some, opportunities for rent-seeking.[33] In countries that remain primarily rural, a government job often means a beachhead in the formal urban economy that can open up opportunities to send children to better schools, have access to health care, and invest in small business. Indeed it is for such reasons that public sector employment is frequently used by political parties as a reward for political service or in the service of ethnic, family, or local ties.

As suggested in the vignettes at the beginning of this chapter, poor administrative infrastructure characterizes the governments of many countries in the early 2000s. Crumbling buildings without adequate plumbing and electrical service and offices lacking computers, telephones, and even light bulbs are not unusual in some countries. Dismal environments also meet citizens who come to public buildings to receive services, make inquiries, or pay bills. These are only the most visible signs of organizations without effective record-keeping systems, information, or monitoring capacity.

It should not be surprising, then, that governments and their workers are often accused of high levels of corruption. World Bank governance data indicates that, while nine poor countries ranked near the top of all countries in the world in terms of their ability to limit corruption in 2000–01, the assessment for most countries is much less positive (see table 6-4). According to Transparency International's corruption perception index of ninety-one countries in 2001, Azerbaijan, Bolivia, Cameroon, Kenya, Indonesia, Uganda, Nigeria, and Bangladesh all had scores of 2 or less on a 10-point scale.[34]

Clearly many of the reforms instituted in the late twentieth century were less effective than their creators imagined, and many middle- and lower-level public officials continue to face a series of perverse incentives. Often employment and pay are unrelated to performance. Job responsibilities can

Table 6-4. *Ability to Control Corruption, 2000–01*[a]

Lowest 25 percent	Second quartile	Third quartile	Top 25 percent
Afghanistan	Albania	Bahrain	Botswana
Angola	Algeria	Belarus	Chile
Armenia	Argentina	Brazil	Costa Rica
Azerbaijan	Bangladesh	Bulgaria	Estonia
Burkina Faso	Bolivia	Cambodia	Hungary
Burundi	Bosnia-Herzegovina	Croatia	Namibia
Cameroon	China	Cuba	Taiwan
Dem. Rep. Congo	Colombia	Czech Republic	Tunisia
Ecuador	Congo	Dominican Republic	Uruguay
Haiti	Cote d'Ivoire	Egypt	
Indonesia	El Salvador	Gambia	
Iraq	Ethiopia	Guinea	
Kazakhstan	Gabon	Guinea-Bissau	
Kyrgyz Republic	Georgia	Jamaica	
Libya	Ghana	Jordan	
Madagascar	Guatemala	Kuwait	
Mauritania	Guyana	Latvia	
Moldova	Honduras	Lithuania	
Myanmar	India	Malawi	
Nicaragua	Iran	Malaysia	
Niger	Laos	Mongolia	
Nigeria	Lebanon	Morocco	
North Korea	Liberia	Mozambique	
Pakistan	Macedonia	Oman	
Papua New Guinea	Mali	Peru	
Paraguay	Mexico	Poland	
Russia	Nepal	Rwanda	
Somalia	Panama	Slovak Republic	
Sudan	Philippines	South Africa	
Syria	Romania	South Korea	
Tajikistan	Saudi Arabia	Sri Lanka	
Tanzania	Senegal	Taiwan	
Turkmenistan	Sierra Leone	United Arab Emirates	
Uganda	Thailand		
Ukraine	Togo		
Yugoslavia	Turkey		
Zambia	Uzbekistan		
Zimbabwe	Venezuela		
	Vietnam		
	Yemen		

Source: World Bank, 2000–01 governance database (www.worldbank.org/wbi/governance).

a. Ratings of low- and middle-income countries with population over 1 million in Latin America, Africa, Asia, the Middle East, and eastern and central Europe, with gross national income per capita up to US$9,265.

be ambiguous or even nonexistent. Moreover, the introduction of job descriptions, performance reviews, and finely calibrated pay scales often mean little in contexts in which political affiliation, ethnic or regional identities, or simply seniority continue to be the basis upon which hiring, promotion, and firing decisions are based. Some of the reforms actually increase problems of public sector management. Downsizing, for example, routinely encourages the more active and ambitious to abandon the public sector for other opportunities; they are the most likely to be able to make use of severance packages to begin small businesses, invest in land, or find other opportunities.[35] Those left behind are often the least likely to be efficient and responsive public servants.

First- and Second-Generation Public Sector Reforms

The first generation of public sector reforms focused on downsizing and putting in place measures for improved pay and conditions of work, career structures, rules and regulations to instill effective routines and regularized responses to public problems, and ongoing efforts to improve capacity among public servants. As we have seen, their impact was generally less than anticipated. The reasons for disappointing results are numerous and certainly include political and bureaucratic environments that were unwelcoming of such changes. From another perspective, however, first-generation reforms tackle only one side of a performance problem.

To generate responses to poor performance, public sector reformers in the past two decades asked an important set of questions: Why do public servants behave badly? Why do public organizations carry out their functions poorly? Why is there corruption and lack of efficiency? In asking such questions they arrived at reasonable answers: because public sector personnel are poorly paid, because incentives are perverse, because clientelism rather than merit prevails, and because structures, rules, and public pressure for accountability are inadequate. Given such responses it is not surprising that the resulting reforms focused on bringing order to disordered structures, controlling the activities of public sector workers, keeping them from doing harm, and ensuring that organizations do what is expected of them. These are important considerations in efforts to improve the public sector, particularly in contexts in which most citizens are poor and vulnerable to the misbehavior of the people and organizations that represent the state.

But these first-generation reforms largely ignored a second important set of questions: Why do public servants perform well? Why are they committed and energetic in pursuing the public interest, even when poorly remunerated? Why are public organizations efficient, effective, and responsive? Why do public servants resist opportunities for corruption?[36] By asking such questions, public sector reformers are directed to a different set of factors than emerge when asking why public officials act badly: because they are committed to the missions and norms of their organizations, because organizations have mystiques that motivate their workers, because public servants have meaningful jobs and believe they are involved in finding solutions to important problems, because they gain approval for what they do well, because they have opportunities to work in teams with others who share their commitments.[37]

Asking questions about why people sometimes perform well is as important as asking why they often perform poorly. Indeed there are lessons to be derived from the capacity to draw good people into the public sector and from the evidence of organizations that perform well. Interest in responding to important public problems, a sense of commitment and mission, valuing the work done and the people who undertake it, interest in innovative solutions to long-existing problems, norms of professional expertise, aspirations to acquire prestige and recognition—these are among the lessons that such experiences suggest.[38] A second generation of public sector reformism in developing countries would do well to begin with a distinct set of questions and then to recommend that performance be improved through such reforms as building managerial capacities and developing positive organizational cultures.

Structures and systems—the focus of the first generation of public sector reforms—are important, of course, and little progress in improving performance can be sustained without some minimal level of structure, some basic rules about proper behavior and procedures, and some routinized ways of dealing with recurrent problems and tasks. Indeed, while there are examples of islands of excellence in the midst of public sectors that do not have even the rudiments of good structures and systems, their long-term sustainability cannot be assumed unless basic conditions are met. Certainly the spread of good organizational performance is limited by the absence of structures, rules, routines, and systems. And yet an overemphasis on these factors can also result in public sector organizations that are too cumbersome to be able to resolve problems easily and that dampen the commitment and energy of public servants.

Even wisely developed structures and systems can carry the public sector so far in terms of good performance, however. Equally important are meaningful jobs, commitment to missions, positive responses to jobs well done, teamwork, participation in finding solutions to important problems, loyalty, respect, and managers who recognize and reward excellence. These second-generation reforms are difficult, require considerable investment in developing management skills, and can only be introduced unit by unit and organization by organization. Nevertheless they may be the kinds of changes required to make additional steps toward more efficient, effective, and responsive governments.

Second-generation reforms are implicit in many of the public sector reforms currently being discussed and attempted in the United States and other industrialized countries. As several chapters in this volume indicate, the experience of private sector and not-for-profit organizations, and the scholarly literature that explores this experience, are now being mined for insights into links between structures and missions, the motivational basis of performance, the relationship of organizational mission to authority structures, the development of team-based approaches to work, and many other aspects of organizational performance. Indeed much of the emphasis of current approaches to public sector reform is on moving away from the strict rules and hierarchies of civil service structures toward more flexible and accountable organizations, more concern with relating tasks to skills, and more interest in developing managerial and leadership skills.

The Unavoidable: A Long Haul

Public sectors in poor countries are not devoid of talented executives. In fact there are numerous examples of well-trained and motivated individuals devoting portions of their careers to high-level positions in government, despite low pay, high risks, and sometimes spartan surroundings. Neither are effective managers unknown in the public sector. Most poor countries can point to creative officials who work with few resources to invigorate and lead organizations that are mission focused and innovative and who engage their employees in meaningful jobs from which they derive personal satisfaction and public recognition. Moreover, organizations that deliver good services and are responsive to citizen needs also exist. These organizations often pursue their difficult goals under equally difficult conditions yet set high standards for problem solving and service delivery.

As we have seen, the problem in many countries is not the absence of bright spots in the public sector but rather a series of factors that limit such experiences to islands of excellence. The evidence presented suggests that public sector reforms in the 1980s and 1990s did not make large dents in the overall record of poor performance. Asking different questions may do much to inform a second generation of public sector reforms. These reforms would focus less on the need to control public servants and limit the harm they and their organizations might do and more on ways to motivate people and organizations to do good work and attack important tasks. A second generation of public sector reformism could address some of the limitations of focusing primarily on structures and rules.

Such reforms are likely to be most successful where levels of human development are high. Low levels of human development, a characteristic of most poor countries, significantly limit the overall quality of public sector workers and the range of skills they bring to their jobs. Indeed countries that rank low on the United Nations Development Program's human development index also tend to rank low on the quality of their governments.[39] While this constraint is often much less binding at elite levels, where exceptional executive and managerial talent can be found, at middle and lower levels of government—where much of the routine work gets done and much of the direct interaction with the public is carried out—this is a serious impediment to more general progress in improved public performance.

For this and other reasons, transforming poorly performing public organizations into efficient, effective, and responsive ones is a tough job. It means finding ways to make structures, human resources, and cultures congruent with the responsibilities of each organization or organizational unit. It means widespread training of managers in skills that move employees toward good job performance. It means understanding how formal rules and informal norms shape the activities of organizations and individuals. And these changes will elicit resistance, because they mean the loss of career protection from rigid civil service and seniority systems and more demanding expectations about performance. They unsettle long-existing political relationships between organizations, public service unions, and political parties.[40] Clientelism, having "a friend in city hall," opportunities for rent-seeking, and impunity for privileged individuals and groups are difficult to sustain in the face of such changes.

Because they are politically as well as organizationally difficult, second-generation reforms need interested publics to support them. An important incentive for organizations and officials alike is the capacity of citizens and groups to demand fair treatment, to have information about their rights vis-à-vis government, and to be able to hold officials and governments accountable for their actions. Thus, while better public sector performance is important, so too is demand for it. Even when it is possible to move on to second-generation public sector reforms, organizations that demonstrate the capacity to improve are likely to remain islands of excellence unless civil societies are also strengthened.[41]

The past twenty years has seen extraordinary growth of civil society organizations and clear signs that they are increasing their capacity to interact effectively with government, to organize political pressure to gain attention for their demands, to abandon clientelistic relations in favor of negotiation with government, and to bring to light instances of public malfeasance, ineffective services, and lack of responsiveness.[42] Frequently aided by organizations representing international civil society as well as the media, these groups have at times been able to join in debates about policy and to raise important criticisms. Increasingly civil society groups have organized to denounce corruption and demand basic honesty from government. Ultimately this kind of counterpoint to government is the essential incentive that governments need to make them more accountable for their actions.

Of course countries vary in the strength and vitality of their civil societies, and governments differ in the extent to which they encourage, control, or repress citizens and the groups that represent them. Nevertheless over the longer term the quality of government in poor countries may well be a function of the quality of their civil societies. Reformers concerned about good government, then, need to look beyond government for remedies.

Notes

1. Throughout this chapter I use the term *poor countries* to refer to low- and middle-income countries as they are categorized by the World Bank in *World Development Report* (Oxford University Press, 2002), p. 241, based on data for 2000. Low-income countries are those with gross national income per capita of $755 or less, lower-middle-income countries are those with per capita incomes between $756 and $2,995, while upper-middle-income countries have per capita incomes between $2,996 and $9,265. I have excluded countries with populations of less than 1 million.

2. For examples, see Deepa Narayan, *Voices of the Poor: Can Anyone Hear Us?* (Oxford University Press for the World Bank, 2000).

3. Turgut Özal in Turkey, Domingo Cavallo in Argentina, Kwesi Botchwey in Ghana, Pedro Aspe in Mexico, Sheriff Sisay in Gambia, Leszek Balcerowicz in Poland, Mart Laar in Estonia, Manmohan Singh in India, and Gonzalo Sánchez de Lozada in Bolivia are among a group of reformers widely esteemed for the technical skill and political savvy they

brought to their positions. On policy champions more generally, see Albert O. Hirschman, "Policymaking and Policy Analysis in Latin America: A Return Journey," in Albert O. Hirschman, ed., *Essays in Trespassing: Economics to Politics and Beyond* (Cambridge University Press, 1981); Arnold C. Harberger, "Economic Policy and Economic Growth," in Arnold C. Harberger, ed., *World Economic Growth* (San Francisco: Institute for Contemporary Studies, 1984); T. N. Srinivasan, "Neoclassical Political Economy: The State and Economic Development," *Asian Development Review*, vol. 2, no. 2 (1985), pp. 38–58; Alefandra González-Rosetti, "The Political Dimension of Health Reform: The Case of Mexico and Colombia," Ph.D. diss., University of London, 2001; Joe Wallis, "Understanding the Role of Leadership in Economic Policy Reform," *World Development*, vol. 27, no. 1 (1999); John Williamson, ed., *The Political Economy of Policy Reform* (Washington: Institute for International Economics, 1994).

4. The economic challenges of the 1980s and 1990s heightened the interest of many political leaders in recruiting well-trained economists and planners to help deal with alarming levels of inflation, fiscal deficits, and international debt. These experts were often granted extraordinary scope for reform and at times were shielded from partisan politics by the same leaders. In some countries, international financial institutions and bilateral assistance agencies recognized the importance of their skills in government as well as the need to have counterparts in discussions of stabilization packages, structural adjustment lending, and sectoral reform programs. Such agencies at times provided funds for topping off the salaries of executives and important organizational managers, particularly in African countries, where public sector salaries were very low.

5. Jorge Domínguez, *Technopols: Freeing Politics and Markets in the 1990s* (Pennsylvania State University Press, 1997), uses the term to refer to officials with expertise in particular fields who also exercise political skills in their roles as reformers. See also Williamson, *Political Economy;* Jeffrey M. Puryear, *Thinking Politics: Intellectuals and Democracy in Chile, 1973–1988* (Johns Hopkins University Press, 1994); and Miguel Angel Centeno, *Democracy within Reason: Technocratic Revolution in Mexico* (Pennsylvania State University Press, 1994).

6. In Bolivia, for example, governments in the 1980s and 1990s drew private sector entrepreneurs and technocrats into government to head up major organizations or spearhead important reforms; equally, well-educated young people became actively engaged in the country's social adjustment experience and learned firsthand how the majority of the country's population lived. Some stayed on in government with renewed commitment to address problems of poverty and exclusion in the country. In Uganda under President Yoweri Museveni, well-trained people were drawn into government service to develop and promote a range of policy and institutional reforms. Many in South Africa were eager to join the post-apartheid government in order to begin to bring growth and equity to its majority population. In Argentina in the early 1990s under the wing of Economy Minister Domingo Cavallo, many well-trained young people participated in far-reaching reforms. In the Philippines under President Fidel Ramos, cabinet officials were widely known for their intelligence and commitment to reform. Mexico, Chile, Vietnam, and Malaysia also became noted for the extensive infusion of young technocrats in the public service.

7. For example, Paulo Renato in Brazil, Humberto Belli in Nicaragua, Amalia Anaya in Bolivia, Juan Carlos Lodoño in Colombia, and Cecilia Gallardo de Cano in El Salvador spearheaded major changes in health and education policies in those countries.

8. See Merilee Grindle, *Despite the Odds: The Contentious Politics of Education Reform* (forthcoming).

9. For example, Luiz Carlos Bresser Pereira was the reformer behind major changes in the public service in Brazil; in the Philippines Laura Pascua promoted important innovations in public expenditure management. In Tanzania Francis Nyalali committed his career to building independent judicial institutions. Joy Phumaphi provided able leadership in the Ministry of Health in Botswana.

10. For example, see Merilee Grindle, "Divergent Cultures? When Public Organizations Perform Well in Developing Countries," *World Development,* vol. 25, no. 4 (1997); Luiz Carlos Bresser Pereira, "From Bureaucratic to Managerial Public Administration in Brazil," in Luiz Carlos Bresser Pereira and Peter Spink, eds., *Reforming the State: Managerial Public Administration in Latin America* (Boulder, Colo.: Lynne Rienner, 1999); and David K. Leonard, *African Successes: Four Public Managers of Kenyan Rural Development* (University of California Press, 1991).

11. Currently some 300,000 individuals take the initial IAS examination each year, from which about 7,000 are selected for a more detailed examination, from which 1,400 are selected for interviews, from which some 60 individuals are selected for a two-year training course prior to a first posting in the country's districts (www.civilservices.gov.in/ibsnaa/ info_registration/index.jsp [10/8/02]).

12. See Merilee Grindle, ed., *Getting Good Government: Capacity Building in the Public Sectors of Developing Countries* (Harvard University Press, 1997); David L. Lindauer and Barbara Nunberg, *Rehabilitating Government: Pay and Employment Reform in Africa* (Washington: World Bank, 1994); World Bank, *Bureaucrats in Business: The Economics and Politics of Government Ownership* (Oxford University Press, 1995); and Ali Farazmand, ed., *Administrative Reform in Developing Nations* (Praeger, 2002). Also see Barbara Nunberg, "Breaking Administrative Deadlock in Poland," "Hungary's Head Start on Reform," and "Transforming the Prototype," all in Barbara Nunberg, ed., *The State after Communism: Administrative Transitions in Central and Eastern Europe* (Washington: World Bank, 1999).

13. World Bank, *Global Development Finance: Analysis and Summary Tables* (Washington, 2001), p. 87.

14. Elaine Kamarck, "Globalization and Public Administration Reform," in Joseph S. Nye Jr. and John D. Donahue, eds., *Governance in a Globalizing World* (Brookings, 2000), p. 244. For a case study, see Habib Zafarullah, "Administrative Reform in Bangladesh: An Unfinished Agenda," in Farazmand, *Administrative Reform.*

15. See, for example, Lindauer and Nunberg, *Rehabilitating Government,* p. 129; and Kamarck, "Globalization." I am grateful to Elaine Kamarck for sharing the database from which many country examples are taken.

16. For examples, see Lindauer and Nunberg, *Rehabilitating Government.*

17. Examples from Kamarck, "Globalization." The data are for countries with populations of more than 3.4 million.

18. World Bank, *Bureaucrats in Business,* p. 27.

19. On Bolivia, see Merilee Grindle, *Audacious Reforms: Institutional Invention and Democracy in Latin America* (Johns Hopkins University Press, 2000). On Poland, see Nunberg, "Breaking Administrative Deadlock."

20. This was the experience of El Salvador, Malawi, Morocco, Pakistan, Paraguay, and Slovakia, for example. See Kamarck, "Globalization," pp. 236–51.

21. See Grindle, *Audacious Reforms*.

22. In some cases changes were the result of deep economic crises. At times they were imposed on reluctant countries through the conditionalities of international financial institutions. In some cases reformist politicians and their technical teams wished to deepen the institutional bases for market economies or representative democracies. In some cases the changes were initiated to shift burdens of service delivery or to increase accountability.

23. Data from Kamarck, "Globalization."

24. See, for example, the cases of Poland and Hungary in Nunberg, "Breaking Administrative Deadlock," and "Hungary's Head Start."

25. Narayan, *Voices of the Poor,* p. 100, quoting a citizen of Armenia, 1995.

26. Ibid., p. 93, quoting a citizen of Nigeria, 1997.

27. Ibid., p. 97, quoting a citizen of Tanzania, 1997.

28. Ibid., p. 92, quoting a citizen of Ukraine, 1996.

29. See Carol Graham and Moisés Naím, "The Political Economy of Institutional Reform in Latin America," in Nancy Birdsall, Carol Graham, and Richard Sabot, eds., *Beyond Trade-offs: Market Reform and Equitable Growth in Latin America* (Washington: Inter-American Development Bank and Brookings, 1998), for a framework of public sector institutional weaknesses. See Farazmand, *Administrative Reform,* for case studies.

30. Julius Court and Goran Hyden, "Towards a World Governance Assessment: Preliminary Findings from the Pilot Phase," working paper (Tokyo: United Nations University, 2001), p. 22. A cross-section of between twenty and fifty-five "well-informed people" from government, business, nongovernmental organizations, academia, and international organizations was surveyed in each country.

31. Economic Commission on Latin America, *Social Panorama of Latin America, 1999–2000 Statistical Appendix* (Santiago, Chile: United Nations Publications, 2000), p. 243, calculated using multiples of country poverty lines at various points in the 1980s and 1990s. Equally important, salary compression often meant that employees with major managerial or leadership responsibilities were remunerated only slightly more than workers with the most routine and menial responsibilities. For a vivid example of the impact of wage compression on the public service in Uganda, see David Chew, "Internal Adjustments to Falling Civil Service Salaries," *World Development,* vol. 18, no. 7 (1990). In Russia in the early 1990s a minister earned 5.8 times the salary of a low-level specialist in government (see Nunberg, "Transforming the Prototype"). See also Lindauer and Nunberg, *Rehabilitating Government.*

32. Data presented by Pippa Norris in chapter 5 of this volume indicates a strong preference for public sector employment in nine transitional and developing countries included in a 1997 survey.

33. See Chew, "Internal Adjustments."

34. Transparency International, *Global Corruption Report* (Berlin, 2001).

35. See Lindauer and Nunberg, *Rehabilitating Government.*

36. See John DiIulio Jr., "Principled Agents: The Cultural Bases of Behavior in a Federal Government Bureaucracy," *Journal of Public Administration Research and Theory,* vol. 4, no. 3 (1994).

37. Ibid.; Judith Tendler, *Good Government in the Tropics* (Johns Hopkins University Press, 1997); Grindle, "Divergent Cultures?"

38. See, for example, Tendler, *Good Government.*

39. Court and Hyden, "Towards a World Governance Assessment," p. 30.

40. Grindle, *Despite the Odds.*

41. Robert Putnam, *Making Democracy Work: Civic Traditions in Modern Italy* (Princeton University Press, 1993).

42. See, for example, Jonathan Fox and L. David Brown, *The Struggle for Accountability: NGOs, Social Movements, and the World Bank* (MIT Press, 1998).

II

DESIDERATA
What Should the Future Look Like?

LINDA J. BILMES
JEFFREY R. NEAL

7

The People Factor:
Human Resources Reform
in Government

SIX OUT OF TEN college students say the government does important, meaningful work. Nearly half think that what happens in government affects their daily lives. But most juniors and seniors will not even consider working for the federal government. They view it as an unappealing employer that does not care about its employees and does not let them rise to their full potential.[1]

This disconnect between the perception that government does valuable work and the perception that it is a lousy employer is threatening to bring down the U.S. government machine from within. Despite great attention to government structure since the events of September 11, 2001, the real problem lies elsewhere. The bigger and more intractable issue is that the government is poor at managing people. Successive layers of rules and regulations have rendered an already troubled system almost dysfunctional. This, and not individual incompetence, explains why INS contractors granted visas to dead hijackers, why supervisors at FBI headquarters ignored warning memos from the field about suspicious behavior at flight schools, and why spokespeople at the Centers for Disease Control offered conflicting advice on anthrax.

The federal human resources system has itself become a major obstacle to effective government. It penalizes its best workers and at the same time discourages talented people outside government from joining. A major overhaul is needed; the government must catch up with the rest of the economy and learn how to manage and motivate its work force.

This chapter looks at the government personnel system from the perspective of how to change it into a leading-edge "people" organization. The most successful private sector companies recruit employees carefully, nurture them, and invest in them. They practice "intrapreneurship."[2] They are flexible. They are clever at rewarding people for their accomplishments and creating a caring atmosphere at work. Click on the employee home page of a successful company and you see an enticing array of options: training, travel, promotion opportunities, company achievements, jolly social activities. The typical government employee website lists pages of arcane regulations and instructions for submitting to drug tests.

This chapter shows that the civil service suffers from an acute lack of precisely these people characteristics that are critical to the success of the best companies. We discuss the results of a new survey of over 1,000 college students revealing that young people—much like people already in the work force—want to work in an organization that offers such benefits. Students prefer the private sector not primarily because of the money but because of the people factor. Strikingly, if government were to adopt people factor reforms, our survey reveals that this would double the number of students who would consider a career in the civil service.[3] It would also make government stronger, more attractive, and better able to deal with the challenges of this century.

First Problem: Obsolescence

The current problems of the civil service reflect a long history of good intentions gone awry. Federal employment in the nineteenth century was based on patronage. Job seekers became such a nuisance that President James Garfield complained they were like "vultures lying in wait for a wounded bison."[4] Garfield was prophetic: On July 2, 1881, a mentally unstable job seeker named Charles Guiteau shot him. The Garfield assassination ultimately led to reform: The Pendleton Act was passed in 1883, and it remains in effect today. The act requires open competition and hiring based on merit rather than favoritism. But the rules and regulations subsequently introduced to ensure merit hiring have become so elaborate that few people outside government can navigate the system on their own.

Numerous reforms, including the Classification Act of 1949, the establishment of the federal wage system in 1972, the Civil Service Reform Act of 1978, and the Federal Employees Pay Comparability Act of 1990, have attempted to correct flaws in the system. All of them failed because they did not address the key underlying problem—that the structure of the federal civil service is still based on a management model that was prevalent before today's knowledge economy came into being.

Like the giant industrial enterprises of the 1940s, the civil service is set up on the premise that individuals join at entry-level positions, work their way up the ladder for twenty-five or thirty years, and retire with comfortable pensions. The system is rigidly hierarchical. It was not designed to foster creativity or innovation and, indeed, it discourages them. This approach long ago became obsolete in the private sector, which has evolved into a dynamic, knowledge-based service economy, where the most valuable asset is the human mind. The government has failed to make this leap. Even college students are aware of how ossified management in the government is. In our survey, over 50 percent of students thought the private sector has changed over the past twenty-five years—compared to only 18 percent who said that government has changed.[5]

Second Problem: Structural Deficiencies

The second major problem is that the regulations, policies, and practices that have evolved over the years to implement merit principles have strangled the system by making it slow, unresponsive, and arguably unfair. Although the system prides itself on upholding the principles espoused in the Pendleton Act, the reality is quite different. In a recent study of new hires, the Merit System Protection Board found that over one-third of people newly hired in the government found out about the job vacancy from someone they knew.[6] This is consistent with the opinions of college students. Asked the question "Do you think the federal government hiring process is a fair and open process or is it often based mainly on who you know?" a shocking majority—58 percent—said it was based mainly on who you know.[7]

Deficiencies in the government personnel system extend to every significant topic in human resources management. These include problems with hiring, firing, promotion, organizational structure, lack of lateral opportunities, insufficient training, poor compensation, limited awards and

recognition, few fringe benefits, lack of career development, legalistic dispute resolution, inflexibility, poor performance measurement and evaluation, use of contractors for mission-critical activities, irrelevance of the
strategic planning process, antiquated information technology, and
unhealthy, unsanitary office facilities—to name but a few. It is not the
purpose of this chapter to provide an exhaustive review of the whole personnel system, but two examples—the hiring and classification systems—
illustrate how a system designed with good intentions has become truly
oppressive.

The Hiring System

The federal government employs 1.8 million civilians directly. Over the
next decade it will need to hire hundreds of thousands of new workers.[8]
But applying for a federal job can be a daunting proposition, particularly
for recent college graduates or workers interested in moving from the private sector. The system bears little resemblance to anything in the outside
world.

It is tricky to find out about federal job vacancies in the first place. There
are numerous parallel application processes, based on veteran status, grade
point average in college, disability status, and eligibility for dozens of special hiring programs (such as for former Peace Corps volunteers). The separate merit promotion program is aimed primarily at current or former
federal employees, although applicants eligible for other hiring programs
are sometimes also eligible.

Half the jobs are not open to applicants outside the government.[9] On
close inspection this is because many positions are essentially rigged, in
that the hiring manager has a candidate in mind before starting the recruitment process. The job description may demand knowledge of specific laws,
rules, and regulations (as opposed to the ability to learn them) and direct
experience of internal projects. When the Department of Commerce
wanted to hire a chief information officer, we discovered that the existing
job description was riddled with requirements that nobody outside government, or even outside the Washington metropolitan area, could possibly meet. We rewrote the description and permitted applicants to submit
standard resumes. Even so, the successful applicant (a former CIO at a
major corporation) still had to work for weeks with a government human
resources official to write lengthy and irrelevant essays in the proper format

in order to be approved for the position. The whole process took nine months.

Even for entry-level positions, the application process is cumbersome. In most agencies standard resumes are not accepted. Government has its own tortuous requirements—a system most comparable to writing a graduate school application. Job announcements are bureaucratic, filled with jargon and acronyms. A typical federal job vacancy announcement for a job paying $46,000 to $59,000 is four to six pages of single-spaced type filled with arcane and unexplained references such as "eligibility under 5CFR 330.60(b)." The "how to apply" section alone is well over a thousand words.[10] Incredibly most agencies still accept only paper applications—the Merit System Protection Board found that only 7 percent of applications are accepted online.[11] By design, applicants are typically not given essential information needed to prepare an application. The "crediting plan" used by most agencies to evaluate the applicant's experience is considered confidential, so applicants do not have access to critical information about what is important in the application process. The assumption is that telling applicants what the human resources office is looking for encourages them to falsify their applications. Thus the premise upon which the hiring process is built is that applicants are not to be trusted. One result is that federal job seekers routinely submit applications of forty or fifty pages that describe everything the reviewers might possibly be looking for.

Not surprisingly the process discourages students from applying. In our survey, two-thirds said that "it is difficult to locate and apply for a job with the federal government." Asked for the maximum time they could afford to wait for a government job before taking another offer, 20 percent said two weeks or less, 48 percent said four weeks, and 21 percent could wait up to two months. In fact it takes the government an average of eighty-two days to make a hiring decision. By the time the government's offer letter gets sent out, only 4 percent of our students would still be available.[12]

The Job Classification System

The Classification Act of 1949 mandated equal pay for equal work. In order to implement this, the act introduced the principle of classifying job series. Few would argue with the principle of equal pay, but the execution of this principle is pure lunacy. The federal wage system includes 250 job series in thirty-six job families. It has fifteen nonsupervisory pay grades, fifteen leader grades, and numerous other grades. Job series include WG-3727-Buffing and Polishing, WG-7641-Beautician, WG-5034-Dairy Farming, WG-6903-Coal Handling, WG-6941-Bulk Money Handling, and WG-3716-Leadburning. The federal wage system looks simple in comparison with the general schedule, which includes an additional 422 individual job classifications in twenty-three job groups. Given that there are five or more grade levels in most job classifications, the result is more than 2,000 ways to classify a government job.

The classification system is pernicious for workers and managers alike. It traps government workers in specific jobs and leads to careers that typically follow a narrow path. It is not uncommon to find federal employees who have spent an entire career in one job series. Managers are constrained in their ability to hire people with new skills because when a vacancy occurs it is only for a specific job. The narrow career path combined with a lack of promotion opportunities once workers reach the journeyman level of their occupation leads to frustrated, resentful employees and an extremely rigid organization.

The federal pay system is linked to the classification system. Compensation for general schedule positions is based on grade and the ten pay levels (steps) within each grade. There is little flexibility; it is not easy to link pay to performance. And because the pay system is fixed, managers frequently use the classification system to solve pay problems. That is, they inflate the duties in a job description to make them appear more substantial in order to pay people more. This technique is also used when managers want to avoid hiring a particular individual—for example, in order to get around the law that gives preference to veterans.

By contrast, leading-edge companies in the private sector have moved in the diametrically opposite direction—creating flat organizations with multiskilled employees. The software developer SAP has only four job classifications in the entire company: board member, manager, worker, and support worker. Every SAP employee must learn at least two jobs (for example, sales and marketing or software development and technical support) so the work force will be versatile.[13] Students are well aware of the government's shortcomings in this area. When asked to compare the federal government with the private sector, 43 percent said that "a flat organization with few layers of management" applies to industry; only 12 percent said it applies to the federal government. Thirty-nine percent said that industry gives "diverse assignments so you can develop different skills"; only 16 percent said government does the same.[14]

Third Problem: Short-Termism

A peculiar inversion within the federal government is that those who run it (the political appointees) have a shorter time-horizon than the rest of the work force. In this respect government truly is a different animal from both private and nonprofit organizations, where senior managers often come up through the ranks and typically stay with the organization for years. The average tenure of a Senate-confirmed political appointee is fewer than twenty months[15]—less than half the average tenure of a senior executive in the private sector.[16]

The implications of this fact are far-reaching. It means that long-range planning—a key strategic tool in the private sector—is virtually absent in the government. Corporations, museums, and universities expend a good deal of brainpower putting together five-year plans, long-term investment strategies, and so forth, for everything from research and development to raising capital. Planning exercises help set goals and priorities both for the organization and for individuals. Career planning, training needs, recruitment, physical office design, performance measurement, and other aspects of human resources are pegged to long-term goals.

Since the enactment of the Government Performance and Results Act (GPRA), federal government departments have been required to develop five-year strategic plans and performance metrics. But the process is hollow: Who is held accountable for a five-year goal if all the managers have since left? Indeed, despite an enormous amount of time spent on them, the plans have little impact on day-to-day management. Many departments hire outside consultants to write their five-year strategic plans.[17]

Most other democracies do not suffer from this affliction. Civil servants in other governments typically gain experience working in several ministries and several disciplines in order to progress up the career ladder. Ministries usually have powerful permanent secretary positions and only a handful of political appointees. As Harvard president Lawrence Summers commented, "As a civil servant in the British treasury you can be one of the top four people; in the U.S. Treasury you can't be in the top forty."[18]

Apart from a handful of U.S. agencies, such as the Internal Revenue Service, short-term political appointees occupy the senior management positions in government. At the Department of Commerce, we had some brilliant senior executives who had been doing the same job for many years. Because they could not progress any further up the ladder, they turned their talents, Darth Vader–like, to the "dark side," expending much effort in internal turf battles, jockeying for bigger budgets and more staff. They knew ways to invest money in their department that would save millions for the taxpayer over a fifteen-year period, but the system did not reward them for putting such ideas into practice.

This glass ceiling is a deterrent to talented young people. The students in our survey rated the "opportunity to go as high in the organization as your abilities take you" as the single most important quality in a potential employer. Fifty-one percent rated this attribute a 10 on a scale of 1 to 10. Another 24 percent rated it a 9. Zero percent said it was "not important." When asked whether this attribute applies more to government or to private industry, 46 percent said it applies more to industry; 10 percent said it applies more to government. In a separate question 62 percent of the students said career advancement in government is "limited."[19]

Why Is the HR Crisis Coming to a Head?

The government's human resources travails might continue indefinitely were it not for a looming demographic crisis. The crisis is the result of a huge bulge of near-retirees at the top of the civil service and an inability to attract talented young people to join at the bottom.

The Retirement Crunch

The retirement crunch stems from the fact that 71 percent of the senior executive service (SES), 50 percent of the GS 13–15 level workers (from which the SES are usually drawn), and 35 percent of the rest of the civil service will be eligible to retire within the next four years.[20] Regardless of the precise speed with which they depart, this means that virtually the entire generation of public-service-minded individuals who joined the government in the 1960s and 1970s, and who occupy pivotal positions, will shortly be leaving. There is an acute shortage of internal candidates to replace them. A near freeze on hiring in the 1990s combined with the departure of many talented young people for more glamorous jobs during that decade's boom years means there is a deficit of young workers in general and particularly in some of the most needed disciplines. For example, at the Department of Energy, which manages national energy policy and oversees the disposal of nuclear waste, 44 percent of employees are over the age of fifty, while only 23 percent are under age forty.[21] According to leading demographer Nicholas Eberstadt, "The demographics of the federal government resembles East Germany in the early 1960s—what you have is a curious-looking curve with a high percentage of older people and a scarcity of young people from the next generation."[22]

Problems in the Job Market

Two-thirds of college students in our survey said they are not considering a government job.[23] Other recent studies have shown that growing numbers of graduate students in public policy are forsaking government employment for the private and nonprofit sectors.[24] Our survey asked college juniors and seniors to rate the importance of thirty-three specific employment attributes, such as "strong pension plan," "casual and fun work environment," "rewards and encourages ethical conduct," and "ability to try new things and think outside the box." It then asked them to compare how well government and private industry perform on each attribute. We also tested their reaction to specific reforms to the government personnel system.

The results contain both good and bad news for government. The good news is that college students are not negative about government per se. Of the overall sample 21 percent said they were "very favorable" and 54 percent "somewhat favorable" toward government employees. Students rated federal employees more favorably than they did investment bankers, lawyers, management consultants, journalists, and state and local employees. They rated federal workers less favorably than doctors, teachers, public safety workers, military personnel, and workers at nonprofit firms. Private companies, such as Wal-Mart, General Electric, Proctor & Gamble, Microsoft, and IBM, scored about the same or slightly better than the federal government. Students also said that government offers better job security, a stronger pension plan, a discrimination-free environment, and a better place to contribute to society than the private sector.

On the other hand the federal government has a long way to go in its efforts to compete with America's companies for the best and brightest. Even in the post-Enron environment, college students view the private sector as a far better employer on almost all the things that really matter to them.

Money is not what matters most. Only one in three students said that "competitive salary" is extremely important in choosing an employer, while less than a quarter say that an uncompetitive salary is preventing them from working for the federal government. The main reasons why students eschew government service are the perceived lack of softer, people benefits. The five most important criteria they cite for choosing a job are:

—the opportunity to go as high in the organization as your abilities take you

—an organization that really cares about its employees

—an environment that is diverse and free from discrimination

—balance between work responsibilities and personal and family life

—challenging and interesting work.[25]

As figure 7-1 shows, students rate the private sector higher than government in almost all criteria that are most important to them. They also believe government jobs are too difficult to apply for, too politicized, and too bureaucratic. They pick up negative attitudes toward government service from the media. For example, of the two-thirds not considering a government career, over 50 percent agree that "media and politicians project such a negative image of the federal government that I am less likely to work there."

Enlightened Employment: Lessons from the Private Sector

What students want is remarkably similar to what working people want in any job: reasonably good pay, interesting work, and an employer that cares about them and gives them recognition for their ideas.

There are many excellent models for human resource management in the private sector, where substantial resources have been devoted to people issues in the past thirty years. A growing body of research shows a strong positive link between enlightened employment practices and financial performance.

In an earlier piece of research we carefully analyzed eighty-four U.S. and German companies in ten industrial sectors over a period of eight years. We ranked them using a "people scorecard"—a yardstick for measuring investment in human resources and intrapreneurship across industries (see table 7-1). We found that the high-scoring companies were consistently more successful (measured in terms of total stockholder returns) than their peer group. Those that scored highest on the people scorecard had an annual average total stockholder return (TSR) of 27 percent, compared with 8 percent for the lowest-scoring companies. In each industry sector the highest-scoring company had a TSR well above the industry average and in two-thirds of the cases had the best TSR in its sector. Companies with the worst financial performance always scored worst or second worst on the people scorecard.[26]

Companies that put the people factor into practice have two distinct characteristics. The first is exceptional attention to traditional human resources issues, including recruitment, performance evaluation and feedback, training, and career development. The second is intrapreneurship— the degree of freedom, autonomy in decisionmaking, and scope for individual initiative, reinforced by the reward system. The combination of both is critical for success. For example, companies that excelled at both HR and intrapreneurship delivered stock market performance three times better than their competitors, whereas those that focused on HR alone showed only average performance.

In addition to our own work, a growing body of literature supports the linkage between financial performance and investment in people. In a landmark 1996 study of bank tellers, John Delery and Harold Doty were able to predict 11 percent of stock price variations based purely on the human resource strategies used in hiring and training tellers.[27] In 1999 Watson Wyatt, a human resources consulting firm, conducted a large study of 405 companies and found a strong correlation between "human capital strategies" and TSR. According to Wyatt the primary drivers of TSR growth are "recruiting excellence," "clear rewards and accountability," and "collegial, flexible workplace."[28] Research published by Jeffrey Pfeffer of the Stanford Business School, Mark Huselid of Rutgers University, Dave Ulrich of the University of Michigan Business School, and Brian Becker of the State University of New York at Buffalo have all added weight to the view that investment in human resources is critical to companies' financial success.[29]

Not surprisingly, people who work for enlightened employers are happier and more loyal to them. In our original research we conducted a survey of 2,000 employees working in different kinds of companies in Germany and the United States.[30] We tested twenty-six specific benefits related to the people scorecard. We found that, above all, people want to receive credit for their ideas, to be recognized financially for their contribution to the firm, to receive training and constructive feedback on their performance, and to work in a team-based, nonhierarchical, caring atmosphere. These aspirations are similar to those Paul Light identified in surveys of government workers.[31] Our research found that nearly 60 percent of employees who worked for companies that provided these benefits were

Figure 7-1. *Relative Importance of Employer's Attributes to Job-Seeking Students*

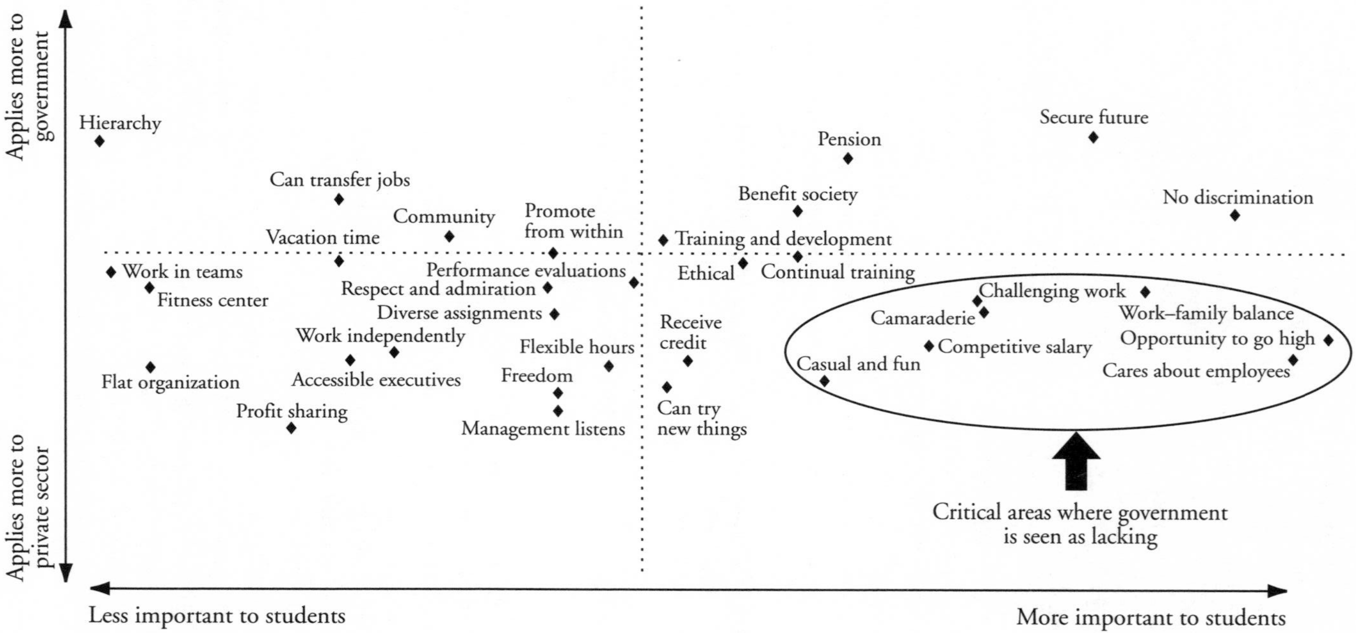

Applies more to government

Applies more to private sector

Less important to students

More important to students

Hierarchy

Can transfer jobs

Vacation time

Community

Work in teams

Fitness center

Performance evaluations

Respect and admiration

Promote from within

Diverse assignments

Work independently

Flexible hours

Accessible executives

Freedom

Flat organization

Management listens

Profit sharing

Secure future

No discrimination

Pension

Benefit society

Training and development

Continual training

Ethical

Receive credit

Can try new things

Challenging work

Work–family balance

Camaraderie

Opportunity to go high

Competitive salary

Cares about employees

Casual and fun

Critical areas where government is seen as lacking

Table 7-1. *"People Factor" Criteria Used to Rate Companies*

Human resources criteria	Intrapreneurship criteria
Staff training and education	*Flexibility*
Expenditures per day per employee	Structure of work content
Career-long training opportunities	Hours and scheduling
Employee-driven curricula	
	Organizational structure
Loyalty of employer	Fewer levels of hierarchy
Layoffs compared to industry	Prevalence of teams
Strength of outplacement efforts	Decentralization of decisionmaking
Worker-friendly work reductions	
	Versatility of employees
Corporate recognition of employees	Lateral transfers within company
Breadth, frequency, and consistency	Cross-functional exposure and training
Quality of policies	*Entrepreneurial opportunities*
Recruiting incentives	Recognition of innovation and contribution;
Benefits	awards, bonuses
Detail of performance evaluations and	Profit-sharing opportunities at business, team
feedback	unit, or product level
Promotion from within, career	Linkage of compensation to individual
development	performance
Job satisfaction indicators	
Employee sick days taken	
Employee turnover	

very satisfied with their jobs, and 70 percent were highly loyal to their employers. In both cases this is much higher than the median job satisfaction level of 34 percent and the median loyalty level of 46 percent.

In sum, the state-of-the-art thinking in the private sector is that companies that invest in their employees perform better and have contented and dedicated work forces. Whether companies that invest in their people become more successful or whether successful companies simply invest more in their people, the result is that a number of highly successful companies have developed best practice in human resources management—practices that have largely passed government by.

Is the People Factor Model Applicable to Government?

The people factor is not a management tool like total quality management or time-based competition, nor is it universally well practiced. But at its best it is a management philosophy in which the focus is on making every worker feel valued and recognizing his or her contribution to the success of the enterprise. In order to do this companies tailor their personnel systems to the individual worker and the specific type of job, in terms of how they recruit, train, evaluate, compensate, reward, and promote. Even the most cursory examination shows that the current civil service is virtually the opposite of this model (see table 7-2).

The question we should ask is whether government would improve—become more appealing to young people, a better place to work, and better serve the United States—if it were reconfigured along these lines. Certainly, from the student perspective, government would become a much more attractive employer if it made such changes.[32] In our survey students were asked, "If you were offered a full-time job that was identical in job description, compensation package, and location at the U.S. federal government and at a private company, which offer would you accept?" In this horse race 50 percent said they would work for the government and 50 percent said private industry. The number of students that would choose government increased significantly, however, when changes were put in place.

Some of these changes are a matter of the government becoming like any normal twenty-first-century employer. For example, if one could apply for a public sector job "using your standard resume instead of filling out government forms," 64 percent of students said they would work for government versus 36 percent for private industry. Similarly 28 percent said they were more likely to work for government if the current benefit system was replaced with one that offered cafeteria-style benefits. This concept, available for years throughout industry, means that people with different needs can select from a menu of benefits. (For example a single mother with three children might choose a different medical or life insurance plan than a gay couple.) With this change, 61 percent said they would choose government employment.

Two fundamental structural reforms were overwhelmingly popular among all students, even those who had been negative toward government initially. The first reform was "making it easier to go back and forth be-

Table 7-2. *Attributes of a "People-Factor" Company Compared with Civil Service*

Attribute	People-Factor Company	Civil Service
Flexibility	Flexible	Inflexible
HR benefits	Generous	Below industry standards
Training and skills development	Frequent	Little, sporadic
Pay	Linked to performance, benchmarked to competitors	Fixed to classification system, unrelated to private sector equivalent
Recognition	Additional, for achievement	Few avenues of credit
Innovation	Risk-taking rewarded	Risk-taking discouraged
Organization	Flat structure	Hierarchical structure
Performance evaluation	Detailed	Perfunctory
Accommodation of individual	Accommodates needs, variety	One size fits all
Culture	Caring about employees makes good business sense	Focus on mission, not employees
Character of work force	Versatile	Narrow job classifications, stovepiped work force
Career development	Aligned with long-term planning	Little, if any

tween government and the private sector." Over 50 percent said this would make them more likely to take a government job, and a remarkable 73 percent said they would take the identical government job. Among students who were already considering government, 89 percent said that, if this reform were enacted, they would choose government. Among those not considering government work, 63 percent said this reform would change their minds and tempt them to take government jobs.

The next most popular reform was "replacing some of the political appointees with career civil servants who rise from the ranks so that more senior jobs go to career civil servants." One in three students said this would make them much more likely to take a government job. Of those already considering government, 73 percent said they would work for government if this change were enacted; among those not considering government, 51 percent said this reform would make them work for government.

Each of the changes that would make government more flexible, more accessible, less hierarchical, higher in prestige, and richer in skills training and benefits made students more likely to work for government. If all the proposed reforms were adopted, nearly three out of four students said they would work for the government rather than for the private sector if offered an identical position. The least popular reform we tested was "appointing a chief human capital officer for every department."[33] This proposal, which Congress is likely to enact, actually made students slightly less inclined to work for the government.

The shortcomings of the federal personnel system are so overwhelming that it cries out for root and branch reform. But, as President Bill Clinton once remarked about the Middle East, "If this was easy to fix, it would have been fixed by now." Numerous efforts by successive administrations to improve the workings of government have not been able to overcome the opposition of entrenched interest groups. Despite a looming terrorist threat and widespread public support for the creation of the Department of Homeland Security, the Bush administration was not able to introduce more than mild changes to civil service rules. Labor organizations fought changes to the end, and business interests convinced the Senate to add sweetheart deals to the bill.

The Clinton administration's efforts fared little better. Vice President Al Gore's "reinventing government" initiative sought out business leaders and asked for their help in adapting good ideas for the public sector. But actual changes were piecemeal and limited in scope. Over the years numerous government agencies have appealed to Congress to exempt them from particular rules that interfere with their ability to accomplish their mission. But apart from tinkerings here and there, change has remained elusive.

These experiences—and in particular the recent example of the Department of Homeland Security—offer valuable lessons for the proponents of reform. Civil service reform needs to avoid being a tool for partisan gain. This is not the time to gut the federal labor relations statute, nor is civil service reform an appropriate vehicle to stop or increase outsourcing. Truly effective reform will require something equivalent to the Base Realignment and Closure Commissions that were designed to minimize political interference in the process. The objective should be to take the civil service back to its foundation and rebuild it to serve the knowledge economy based on the original merit principles. The present combination of a demographic crisis in the public sector and increased public recognition of government's important role in national life could provide the ideal opportunity to achieve this.

Rebuilding the Civil Service: Agenda for Reform

A civil service designed around people concepts would not look anything like the existing one. As an image, it is perhaps most helpful to think not of a business but of a university, with a minimum of hierarchy and major differences in how each department recruits its faculty and students, conducts its work, and achieves its purpose. The federal government needs to shed its monolithic approach. Each agency should tailor its recruiting to the job markets in which it competes. Those seeking to hire scientists must be able to provide particular incentives to attract and retain them, as should those seeking to hire accountants, lawyers, fish experts, security experts, economists, claims specialists, and everyone else. We must recognize that a single hiring system, a single compensation system, and a single recognition and reward system will not suffice.

We are not suggesting a laissez-faire approach to federal government. The civil service should be based upon a governing set of core principles. It must still be based upon merit rather than favoritism and a political spoils system. Equal opportunity must continue. Military service should still be rewarded. The civil service is a public trust and must be treated as such. Nevertheless, a merit-based system need not be a monolith. In fact we believe that structured flexibility in the civil service will lead to more emphasis on merit, as agencies build programs to recruit, develop, and retain the work force needed for their missions.

Structured flexibility means that many aspects of the civil service would vary. Pay, benefits, job classification, hiring practices, and other hiring decisions would be selected from a menu of available options. In this "flexistyle" civil service, each agency could select from a central, preapproved list of human resource options, drawn from existing best practice in federal agencies, state and local governments, and public, nonprofit, and private sectors. This menu of options would become a platform to enable each agency to design a personnel system for its own needs, without reinventing the wheel or seeking congressional action for every circumstance. Congress would retain its proper oversight authority over the civil service by voting to approve the items on the master menu. (This aspect of our recommendation is critical; proposals that involve Congress ceding its oversight authority to the executive branch are unrealistic, as the dispute over the Department of Homeland Security showed.)

Therefore, instead of the current system (where individual agencies beg Congress to exempt them from certain civil service rules), the flexistyle civil service would provide proven alternatives that agencies could use to customize programs appropriate to their circumstances. There would be numerous options for every aspect of personnel practice, such as compensation, benefits, and career type.

This implies a reform agenda that focuses on the following best people practices:

—Eliminate the classification system.

—Replace the general schedule with a flatter system. For example, many companies use a four- or five-layer system, with managers, specialists, doers, and support staff. The overwhelming majority of government employees would be in the doer category.

—Allow each agency to select policies for recruiting, hiring, promoting, performance measurement, and compensation from a menu of approved options.

—Guarantee a minimum of two weeks annual training for each employee, the bare minimum for people companies. Every employee would carry with them a nonrescindable training account, equivalent to two weeks of annual salary.

—Offer flexibility in working hours, structure of assignments, sabbaticals, telecommuting, team arrangements, and benefits. The objective would be to achieve parity with best practice in the private sector.

—Modernize the hiring process. The next generation of public servants is technologically savvy. All federal government agencies should post vacancies on the Internet and on job websites and should accept ordinary resumes. Simple web-based hiring systems or off-the-shelf software products could be used.[34] The average hiring time should be cut from the current eighty-two days to no more than twenty-eight days for entry positions. Recruiters from government agencies should be able to make provisional offers on the spot.

—Reduce the number of political appointees by eliminating the majority of line management slots below the level of assistant secretary. This means that deputy assistant secretary and similar slots should go to career employees. Senior political appointees who have not previously served in government should be given orientation training before taking up their positions.

—Appoint a one-year commission to draw up the human resources menu. The president would have veto power over such a list, and Congress would approve it, thereby retaining its proper oversight role.

There is no doubting the difficulty of enacting such radical reforms, which would amount to the biggest structural changes in the machinery of government for over a hundred years. The history of government reform is not encouraging, and the opposition of special interest groups is assured. Nonetheless the scale of the crisis facing government today and the new focus of public attention present a real opportunity for change. We need to seize it now.

Notes

1. A survey of 1,011 college students, designed by the authors, was conducted over the Internet by Penn, Schoen & Berland Associates during April and May of 2002 (hereafter referred to as student survey). The sample comprised college juniors (48 percent), seniors (46 percent), and recent graduates (within the previous month) (6 percent).

2. Gifford Pinchot coined the term *intrapreneurship* in the Netherlands in 1978. His company, Pinchot & Co., began leading seminars on the topic in 1984. It refers to the creation of entrepreneurship within a large organization, either individuals who act like entrepreneurs or entrepreneurial opportunities throughout an organization.

3. Student survey.

4. U.S. Information Agency, "Backgrounder on the Pendleton Act 1883," Basic Readings in U.S. Democracy (http://usinfo.state.gov/usa/infousa/facts/democrac/28.htm [February 11, 2003]).

5. Student survey.

6. Merit System Protection Board (MSPB), "Competing for Federal Jobs: Job Experiences of New Hires," report to the president and the Congress (2000). The MSPB surveyed 2,000 randomly selected new employees who were hired competitively during the period June 1996 through December 1997.

7. Student survey.

8. Estimates based on data from the Office of Personnel Management (OPM).

9. A study by the Partnership for Public Service released February 22, 2002, shows that 47 percent of all midlevel federal job vacancies were not open to outside competition. It also found that in 2000 only 13 percent of midcareer hires were candidates who did not already hold government jobs (www.ourpublicservice.org).

10. Department of Interior, Announcement GLBA-02-03, July 1, 2002.

11. MSPB, "Competing for Federal Jobs."

12. Student survey.

13. SAP is the leading software company in Germany and the fifth largest in the world. It is further described in Konrad Wetzker, Peter Strueven, and Linda Bilmes, *Gebt un das Risiko zuruck* (Carl Hanser Verlag, 1998).

14. Student survey.

15. The RAND Corporation estimates the tenure of senior political appointees at eleven to twenty months; see Cheryl Y. Marcum and others, "Department of Defense Political Appointments: Positions and Process" (RAND, 2001). A second estimate by Thomas Mann and Norman Ornstein is that "the average tenure of presidential political appointees has been steadily declining and is now barely fourteen months"; see Thomas Mann and Norman Ornstein, "After the Campaign, What? Governance Questions for the 2000 Election," *Brookings Review*, vol. 18, no. 1 (Winter 2000).

16. According to "Backgrounder on the Pendleton Act 1883," a 2000 study conducted by the Department of Labor, the average length of time a worker remains in a given job is 3.6 years. More senior executives stay longer, while wage-level employees stay for less time.

17. In 1999, according to the Office of Management and Budget, at least nine of the thirteen cabinet-level agencies engaged consultants to help in the preparation of their strategic plans, annual performance plans, or accountability reports.

18. Lawrence Summers, interview by author, April 19, 2002.

19. Student survey.

20. Projections compiled from several sources: Office of Personnel Management, "Fact Book: Federal Civilian Workforce Statistics, 2001"; OPM, "Employment Trends, 2001"; OPM, "Demographic Profile of the Federal Workforce, 2001"; and Comptroller General David Walker, "Human Capital: Meeting the Governmentwide High-Risk Challenge" (GAO-01-357T), testimony before the Senate Subcommittee on Oversight of Government Management Restructuring, and the District of Columbia Committee on Governmental Affairs, February 1, 2001.

21. OPM, "Fact Book."

22. Nicholas Eberstadt, American Enterprise Institute, interview by author, February 25, 2002.

23. Student survey.

24. See Carol Chetkovich, "Winning the Best and Brightest: Increasing the Attraction of Public Service," Human Capital Series (Arlington, Va.: PWC Endowment for the Business of Government, July 2001).

25. Student survey.

26. We surveyed forty-eight companies in Germany from ten sectors and thirty-six companies in the United States in six sectors, choosing publicly traded companies producing similar goods and services. Stockholder return was analyzed over an eight-year period, 1989 through 1997 in the United States and 1987 through 1996 in Germany. To measure relative stock performance we used the highly specific metric of total shareholder return (TSR) and its corollary, the relative total shareholder return (RTSR). TSR measures the actual cash value (share price increases plus dividends) of an investment. To avoid cross-industry comparisons we divided the TSR of each company by an average TSR of its industry peer group, therefore using RTSR. To identify comparable companies we used standard sources, such as the Fortune 5000 list and Datastream.

27. John Delery and Harold Doty, "Modes of Theorizing in Strategic Human Resource Management: Tests of Universalistic, Contingency, and Configurational Performance Predictions," *Academy of Management Journal,* vol. 39 (1996), p. 820.

28. Watson Wyatt, "Human Capital Index: Linking Human Capital and Shareholder Value," North American Survey Report, Washington, September 1999.

29. See Jeffrey Pfeffer, *The Human Equation: Building Profits by Putting People First* (Harvard Business School Press, 1998); and Brian Becker, Mark Huselid, and Dave Ulrich, *The HR Scorecard: Linking People, Strategy, and Performance* (Harvard Business School Press, 2001).

30. Survey commissioned by Boston Consulting Group GmbH, conducted by Penn & Schoen Associates.

31. See Paul Light, "What Federal Employees Want from Reform," Reform Watch Brief 5 (Brookings, March 2002).

32. Student survey.

33. One of several proposals included in the Federal Human Capital Act of 2001.

34. Some government agencies have attempted to use these off-the-shelf packages or develop web-based hiring systems. At the Department of Commerce we developed Commerce Opportunities On-Line (COOL), a web-based hiring system derived from work originally done by the Defense Logistics Agency.

8

ELAINE CIULLA KAMARCK

Public Servants
for Twenty-First-Century
Government

FOR MUCH OF the twentieth century the implementation of government policy has taken place through the creation of hierarchically organized entities known as bureaucracies. But by the end of the twentieth century leaders and ordinary citizens in many democracies, both modern and emerging, harbored a deep dissatisfaction with bureaucratic government.[1] In addition, in the last two decades of the twentieth century, governments around the world began to shrink, reversing a trend and reflecting a feeling that government had gotten too big.[2] Finally, to participants in the exciting initial decade of the Internet revolution, government looked pretty old and obsolete in contrast to the self-organizing energy of the cyberworld.[3]

To some this has looked like the end of government. But, as I have argued elsewhere, it is not the end of government but merely the end of government as we know it.[4] Government in the twenty-first century is not going away (as some hope and others fear); it is merely changing. These changes are in response to the failure of the Communist experiment around the world and to the emergence of a postindustrial economy, both of which in their own ways repudiate centralized hierarchical organizational structures. The evolving models of government are not intrinsically liberal or conservative, effective or not effective—they are simply different and new and thus require some careful thought on the part of those who care about good governance and well-functioning public administration.

Twenty-first-century government will implement policy in three new ways: through reinvented public sector organizations, through networks created and managed by government, and through markets shaped and monitored by government. Each of these forms will require new systems of accountability and new skills for the public servants who manage them. Effective management of these new forms will stem from the perfection of new accountability mechanisms, many of which are still evolving and are poorly understood. Thus, in trying to anticipate what skills the future public servant will need, we must define these new modes of government, understand how the accountability mechanisms might evolve, and then catalog the skills that future public managers will need.

Each new mode of government implementation attempts to correct the problems and dilemmas associated with traditional bureaucracy, such as slowness, poor performance, lack of flexibility, and lack of innovation. But, in spite of these problems, detailed with enthusiasm by American politicians from Reagan to Bush to Clinton to Bush, the traditional government bureaucracy has one big advantage: Accountability mechanisms are clearly spelled out in copious detail. It is not unheard of for even medium-size agencies in the federal government to have hundreds of pages of internal rules and regulations. When I was in the government, I used to refer to these as an agency's "self-inflicted wounds" because they were usually additive to the rules and regulations promulgated as a result of legislation. In some cases they were added on to already highly detailed legislative or judicial mandates (a problem that has been especially severe in the area of environmental policy implementation).

But these rule-based systems, for all their complexity, have one key advantage for the public servant: clarity. Every action—from the purchase of an office chair to the filling out of forms to establish benefits—has its rules. The performance of all actors in the system is judged by their adherence to the rules. In the late 1970s the American government added to every major federal organization an office of inspector general. For the most part these positions have been filled by former law enforcement officers, who reinforce the dedication to rules by monitoring internal infractions, large and small.[5] Very few of the items included in the inspector generals' reports ever get to the stage where they are referred to the Department of Justice for criminal prosecution.

These rule-based systems evolved, in the United States and other countries, as a way to combat governmental corruption. In the American system, at least, this approach was highly successful but, as Robert Behn and others have pointed out, a system meant to deal with the problem of corruption ended up creating a government plagued by poor performance.[6] One book's title says it all: *The Pursuit of Absolute Integrity: How Corruption Control Makes Government Ineffective.*[7] Nevertheless the problems of poor government performance are sufficiently complicated that they can be blamed on a myriad of causes outside the governmental organization in question. In the meantime for most individual public servants the best protection has been to simply follow the rules.

In traditional bureaucracies the rules are created and enforced by central control mechanisms. Among the first scholars to point out the performance problems created by these central control units (usually budget, personnel, and procurement) was Michael Barzelay. In a 1992 book he relates how the government of the state of Minnesota decided that its staff positions and functions were becoming serious impediments to the performance of those on the line.[8] This theme was picked up in David Osborne and Ted Gaebler's best-selling book, *Reinventing Government,* as well as in other studies.[9]

Reinvented Public Sector Organizations

The movement to reinvent public organizations began in Great Britain in 1982, in New Zealand in 1984, in American statehouses in the 1980s, and in the federal government in 1993. In all cases reformers tried to replace the typical accountability mechanisms with accountability for performance. In most of Europe the reform movement was called new public management, but in the United States it became known, after Osborne and Gaebler's book, as reinventing government, the label borne by the Clinton-Gore administration's eight-year reform campaign.

Successful government, according to Osborne, is catalytic—it does not row, it steers. It is community-owned; it empowers employees; it uses competition to produce and improve results; it is mission-driven, results-driven, and customer-driven. This new kind of organization is entrepreneurial, a term so infrequently associated with government that it is almost an oxymoron. Successful government draws from the entrepreneurial spirit to revitalize itself and in so doing takes on concepts and modes of operation previously associated only with the private sector. While the project of reinventing government includes networked and market-based forms, as governments began to implement reforms they generally focused first on public sector organizations.

Reinvented government bureaucracies are still public entities, composed of public sector employees and relying on public sector funding. But reinvented government tends to be shorn of its public sector trappings, especially rigid rules regarding budgets, personnel, and procurement. The underlying assumption behind reinvented government as practiced in the Anglo-American countries, which have had the most serious public sector reform movements, is that, with respect to management, there are few significant differences between the public and the private sectors. A second but equally important assumption behind entrepreneurial government is that the goals of public sector organizations can be clearly articulated and measured.

Thus, as David Osborne says, the "grand bargain" within traditional bureaucracies seeking to remake themselves is one in which the strict, sometimes stultifying rules of the organization are replaced by performance measures. There have been many experiments in implementing this grand bargain across the globe, but for our purposes three merit attention—the New Zealand experiment, the creation of "next steps" or executive agencies, in the British government, and the Government Performance and Results Act (GPRA) in the U.S. government.

New Zealand's government reform efforts have been more comprehensive and revolutionary in scope than those of any other country. A clear division of responsibility has been established between ministers and departmental heads, giving the traditional civil service both more autonomy and more responsibility for results than ever before. Ministers contract with public servants for the accomplishment of certain goals, and the civil service is given free rein in how they accomplish the goals. Everything in the government is competed out, or put out to a bid—even policy advice. The monopoly of government on governance has been broken. While officials in the United States were asking, "What is a core governmental function?" New Zealand found the answer: nothing.

Public managers in New Zealand thus find themselves in a situation closer to that of managers in the private sector than to managers in the traditional public sector. Similarly Great Britain has created executive agencies that hire chief executive officers on contracts, called framework agreements, that specify the performance outcomes desired by ministers, complete with the potential for bonuses far above civil service pay—once again a move in the direction of private sector incentives. These CEOs have more control over their budgets, personnel, and other management systems and can be fired at will (and some have been). Of course public managers in reinvented organizations must still abide by statutory rules and regulations but, where performance measures have been adopted, managers have the incentive to change or work around whatever rules are impeding achievement of those measures. In Great Britain, where by the late 1990s about three-quarters of the government was working under the new arrangements, the results have been impressive. Britain boasts of improvements in the processing of passport applications, savings in the administrative costs of the National Health Service Pensions Agency, decreases in waiting times for the National Health Service, and reductions in per-unit costs at the Patent Office, among others.[10]

In the United States the movement toward an explicit performance-based bureaucracy has not been as rapid as in New Zealand and Great Britain. In 1993 Congress passed the Government Performance and Results Act, legislation that mandated the creation of performance goals for every part of government and that tied the achievement of those goals not to the personal evaluations of civil servants but to the budgetary process. Thus an incentive structure was created that sought to make performance a critical factor in congressional appropriations. In most agencies the general schedule system dominated, in which a bureaucrat's pay was more or less in lockstep with seniority. Some agencies attempted to extrapolate from their GPRA goals to create performance agreements within their management structure, but by and large the shift to a performance accountability structure in the U.S. government has been to make agencies, not individual managers, accountable to the congressional appropriations process. So far there is little evidence that performance measurement is affecting congressional appropriating behavior. Appropriations seem to follow the policy preferences of the administration in power and the pressing need for security in a dangerous world.

Even though the shift in accountability away from process and toward performance is not as explicitly linked to the behavior of managers in the American system as it is in the British system, the existence of performance measures as part of an accountability scheme has had the effect of moving public sector management into a more entrepreneurial mode, even in America. In 1996 President Bill Clinton announced that the next step in Vice President Al Gore's reinventing government initiative would be the creation of Performance-Based Organizations, or PBOs—government agencies that were to be reinvented, on the British model of next steps or executive agencies, to include CEOs appointed on contracts. Progress on this front in the

U.S. government has been much slower than in the British government, primarily because the exceptions required to create PBOs involve congressional authorizations. So far only three PBOs exist—the Patent and Trademark Office, the Student Loan Office in the Department of Education, and the Saint Lawrence Seaway Development Corporation. Nevertheless the PBO concept lives on: When the administration of George W. Bush set out to create a Department of Homeland Security, they tried to incorporate into it the very management flexibilities that were at the core of the PBO concept. While many of the performance measures set by the federal government in the initial stages of reform were low, so that they could easily be achieved, their very existence will affect behavior, simply because they provide baselines from which various actors in the process can evaluate the organization.

The emphasis on performance over process has already manifested itself in the U.S. system in a willingness on the part of civil servants to seek legislative exceptions to the old-fashioned control systems that were impeding agency performance. For instance, in 1996, when it became clear to the Clinton-Gore administration that the Republican-dominated Congress would not pass a civil service reform bill that President Clinton could sign, Vice President Gore's National Performance Review encouraged and aided agencies in their efforts to get out from under the civil service laws that they felt were most detrimental to performance. One by one, agencies went to their appropriators and their authorizers in Congress to fashion personnel systems better suited to their mission. As a result by 2000 more than 50 percent of the civil service work force was not covered by the civil service law but by "excepted" personnel systems.[11]

In some cases the move to reinvention was initiated by Congress in response to serious agency performance deficits. In the summer of 1995 Congress, alerted to the technological deficiencies of the air traffic control system by a series of potentially dangerous lapses and eager to avoid responsibility in the event of a serious accident, passed a bill giving the Federal Aeronautics Administration authority to create its own personnel and procurement systems. The new system began showing results right away, as procurement times for the purchase of new computers dropped from more than eighteen months to just under four months.[12] Similarly in the summer of 1997 Congress held a series of sensational hearings featuring tales of Internal Revenue Service agents harassing little old ladies. This resulted in passage of a major IRS reform bill that reinvented the agency along more flexible personnel and procurement lines.[13] And most recently President

Bush's proposal to create a new Department of Homeland Security includes provisions for the continual adjustment of the civil service system by the new secretary.[14]

In a reinvented government that emphasizes performance-based accountability, public sector managers will be expected to innovate much as do their private sector counterparts, innovation that will often entail a deft political dance to remove agencies from statutory and regulatory restrictions that were put in place to ensure compliance with the law and prevent corruption. Thus public managers in reinvented government agencies will also have to be adroit politicians with close relations to their relevant congressional committees.

Furthermore, managers of these new organizations have been and will continue to be subject to increased scrutiny. Bob Stone, one of the earliest and most famous new public managers and the project director for Vice President Gore's National Performance Review, exercised what he called "creative subversion" and in so doing stayed sometimes just one step ahead of trouble. In a forthcoming book Stone refers to the time he reduced the Department of Defense's incomprehensible tome of rules and regulations regarding the administration of military bases to a short book that could fit into a shirt pocket. For this he was investigated by the department's inspector general, who was sure an infraction had been committed if so many regulations could be reduced to so few.[15]

The public managers of reinvented agencies will face continual suspicion from those government organizations accustomed to control. When the Clinton-Gore administration introduced the concept of PBOs, the Office of Management and Budget attempted to create a "template" into which all PBOs would fit—thus undermining the idea that each new organization would structure itself according to its unique mission. And, in spite of the many exceptions to and flexibilities in the federal government's personnel laws, the perception among civil servants that the Office of Personnel Management will "regulate" the exceptions so as to make them impracticable keeps many public managers from sticking their necks out and using those flexibilities.

And finally, public managers of reinvented government agencies will find that sometimes their political leaders are not interested in performance measures. Serious efforts to improve performance can often have unintended consequences. The first attempt to allow Americans to get their Social Security earnings records from the Internet exploded amidst concerns over privacy. The initiative had to be pulled and retooled before it was acceptable to the public. Career-minded elected officials may not want experimentation and innovation in the public organizations they oversee, because change brings with it risks that are difficult to predict.

Government by Network

In recent years the term *network* as applied to government has come to have at least three meanings. *Networked government* is often used to describe the constellation of public, private, and semipublic organizations that influence policy—a policy network. *Network* has also been used to describe emerging relationships among nation states in an increasingly globalized world. As Anne-Marie Slaughter and others have documented, one response to the need for international governance has been for subunits of national governments to develop relationships in which both law and administrative processes are harmonized, thus allowing for world governance in the absence of world government.[16] And John Peterson and Laurence O'Toole have used the term *network* to apply to the complex, mutually adaptive behavior of subunits of states in the European Union that, while often slow and opaque, solves an important supranational governance problem.[17]

But, when *network* is used in the context of describing new ways of implementing policy, it refers to those instances where the government chooses to create, through its power to contract and to fund, a network of nongovernmental organizations. In government by network the bureaucracy is replaced by a wide variety of institutions, almost all of which have better reputations (and sometimes better performance) than bureaucratic government. In government by network the government stops trying to do anything itself; instead it funds other organizations to do the work the government wants done. An immense variety of organizations are part of government by network. Churches, research labs, nonprofit organizations, and for-profit companies have been called on to perform the work of the government.

While some see this trend as a weakening of the state, there are two major advantages to networked government. The first is that elected officials can cause something to happen without incurring the direct costs—both political and financial—involved in the creation of a new public sector organization. The second is that networks have huge potential to innovate, because the governmental task is being carried out by different organizations in different ways. Government by network has been used where government valued innovation so much that it was willing to give up a certain degree of control.

The most long-standing example of government by network is the famous (and sometimes infamous) military-industrial complex. During the cold war the United States engaged countless corporations, along with their own internal research laboratories, in developing sophisticated weaponry. At the same time the Soviet Union kept its weapons research within the bureaucracy of the Communist state. By 1989 this real-world experiment was over. When the Soviet empire fell, we learned that its technological and military capacity had fallen behind that of the United States. Government by network had won; bureaucratic government had lost.

Government reliance on outside organizations to do its work has long been practiced in the social service area, where a wide variety of organizations, especially nonprofits, owe their existence largely to government funding. In the landmark 1996 welfare reform bill, which transformed the system into one based on work, the network concept took a leap forward, as churches and for-profit organizations were added to the welfare-to-work network. Giant corporations like Lockheed Martin also won contracts in the new system.

The diversity inherent in networks is likely to make them staples of law enforcement and the fight against terrorism. In order to effectively protect our critical infrastructure (those computer systems that regulate just about everything from emergency responses to the financial system) the government will have to develop a sophisticated network that includes state and local governments and private sector actors. The private sector has so far been reluctant to cooperate in the war against cyber-crime. In a recent survey 94 percent of companies responding reported detecting security breaches of their information systems in the previous twelve months, but only 34 percent reported the intrusions to law enforcement.[18] But government cannot fight this new kind of crime without creating networks that include private sector security operations in a community of trust with public sector law enforcement.

Government by network is especially important in those policy areas that defy one solution or one set of routines. That is why government has created networks in areas such as research and development and social services. When it is difficult to foresee outcomes other than in the broadest, most general terms, government seeks the diversity and flexibility inherent in the network form.

Government by network comes with its own set of managerial challenges, however, challenges that arise, as they do in reinvented government, from accountability mechanisms or the lack thereof. In the broad sweep of history, the military-industrial complex may be remembered for winning the cold war. In the meantime, it is much maligned for recurring instances of corruption, waste, fraud, and abuse. So far the extensive contracting that has been part of the welfare reform system seems to be working; there are many stories of women emerging from dependency into employment, and some early statistics back up that success. But it is just a matter of time before one of the new (or old) organizations becomes involved in a scandal that reflects upon the entire network. The soft underbelly of government by network is the nearly 100 percent probability that, over time, some actor in the network will steal money or will simply prove ineffective. Because government by network has often been a sort of default mode of implementation, very little attention has been paid to what makes for its success.

In a previous volume in this series, Steven Kelman argued that "the third element of strategic contracting management, the administration of contracts once they have been signed, has been the neglected stepchild of these efforts." He notes that opponents to contracting out government work, especially government employee unions, are quick to point out that no one is minding the store, and that academics who warn of the creation of a "hollow state" are also sounding alarms.[19] Kelman argues for making contract management a key rather than a peripheral area of management expertise inside an agency and for recognizing "contract administration as in the first instance a management function."[20]

Kelman's call for upgrading contract management is critical for those agencies like the Department of Defense, which contract out a large part of their work. But in the purest form of government by network there is no agency to manage contracts. Many grants to state and local governments are awarded on a formula basis; the federal government audits for financial compliance, but no one ever asks whether the money is achieving the intended purposes. In the field of welfare-to-work, a small division of Health and Human Services (the Office of Families and Children) and fifty state governments administer a network of funds, most of which are federal, some of which are state and local, and some of which are private.

Hence the major problem with government by network goes far beyond management of contracts: It is the lack of an accountability mechanism. Management in many networks is still defined in the rule-based terms of the traditional bureaucracy: Audit contracts periodically, and make sure that no one is spending money improperly. While academics and think tanks occasionally get inspired to find out how a network is doing, the government that is funding the bulk of the network often seems to have little interest in the question.

One of the chief advantages of government by network is that it allows for innovation, in ways even reinvented government cannot. Like managers in reinvented government, network managers must be able to set performance goals for the overall endeavor but must also be able to understand and analyze the contributions of all parts of the network. That means understanding the consequences of various strategies and why they work, a different skill set than the one described in the classic public administration literature. Robert Agranoff and Michael McGuire sum up the challenge as follows: "The classical, mostly intraorganizational-inspired management perspective that has guided public administration for more than a century is simply inapplicable for multiorganizational, multigovernmental, and multisectoral forms of governing."[21]

The leader of a government network must have an almost academic ability to find out what is working and why. Like the leaders of reinvented government, who have to muster the political support to overturn obsolete bureaucratic obstacles to effective action, the leader of a network has to muster the political support to eliminate ineffective organizations and to resist the pressure to pull new ones in. Too often relationships in publicly funded networks suffer from the protection of special interests and powerful politicians, and woe to the conscientious bureaucrat who upsets the arrangement. In addition network leaders need to constantly define the purposes and goals of the network as a whole.

The ability to evaluate performance and to constantly adjust the players so that results are achieved is critical to the preservation of any network. In its absence the inevitable bad behavior will have one of two results. In some cases the network experiment will simply end, a likely scenario when remnants of an existing bureaucracy are looking for reasons to destroy the network. In other cases management will exercise so much control over each organization that the network functions no better than an old-fashioned bureaucracy. The work becomes routinized, and the chief attraction of the network—its ability to innovate—is lost.

Government by Market

The third emerging model—government by market—requires few public employees and little public money. In this model the state uses its power to create markets that fulfill public purposes, which often means taking account of what economists call externalities. Some scholars, such as B. Guy Peters, use the term *market government* to describe "the basic belief in the virtues of an idealized pattern of exchange and incentives."[22] (When Peters and other public administration scholars talk about market-driven government, they are usually talking about what I have previously referred to as reinvented government or networked government.)

Government by market is a specific form of policy implementation involving public power but little or no public organization. For instance, in 1971 the state of Oregon passed the nation's first "bottle bill" in response to growing concern about the beer and soft drink bottles littering the landscape and posing problems for overflowing landfills. Instead of creating a Bureau of Clean Highways and hiring state workers to pick up bottles, government did something unusual—it created a market. By passing laws that require deposits on bottles and soda cans, the state created an economic incentive to keep people from throwing bottles out of car windows. For the hard-core litterbugs who persist in throwing bottles away, the law created an economic incentive for other people to pick them up.

Similarly, in the 1991 Clean Air Act, Congress decided to put a price on sulfur dioxide emissions (the major cause of acid rain) from industrial plants. The government determined how much sulfur dioxide the environment could handle and then developed a trading system that allows clean plants to sell permits and dirty plants to buy permits. Most analysts feel this system has worked well. Sulfur dioxide emissions have dropped. The cost was high enough to encourage plants to get new equipment for cleaner air but low enough that companies could determine their own timetable and their own technology.[23]

In retrospect government by market applied to some environmental problems has been a success, but only recently has it become politically acceptable. Rob Stavins, one of the early advocates of this approach, recalls how just a decade ago environmentalists chafed at the idea of "buying and selling pollution."[24] That reaction, he reports, has changed dramatically in recent years. The most ardent environmentalists admit to the attractiveness of market government and often seek to apply it even where it will not work.

The United States is about to embark upon another grand experiment in government by market—school vouchers. In what has been called the most important Supreme Court decision on education since *Brown* v. *Board of Education,* in the summer of 2002 the Cleveland voucher plan for elementary school education was ruled constitutional. Voucher advocates have long argued that the best way to improve education is to assign public money to each student and then give them (or their parents) the choice of where to go to school. This approach would presumably encourage competition, innovation, and general improvements in education—the very things the public school system, a more or less traditional bureaucracy, has had a hard time doing.

The government by market idea has been cropping up in many disparate policy areas, but we rarely think of it as an intentional policy choice, and therefore we know little about what makes these markets work. A well-functioning market in the private sector is a marvel to behold. In our lifetimes the competitive marketplace has given us color TVs, microwaves, and VCRs, and every year they have gotten better and cheaper. But what does a well-functioning market look like in the public sector, and what skills should the designers and managers of public sector markets have? Let us start with four considerations: price, range, rule of law, and information.

The first challenge for the creator and manager of a government market is to get the price right. If the price on beer bottles in Oregon had been too low (say, a fraction of a cent) there might not have been enough incentive for people to collect them. If the price had been too high, it might have seriously harmed the beverage industry, thus creating a different set of problems. As state and local officials have to decide whether to move to a voucher system for education, a great deal will depend upon the price set for each voucher. So far cities like Cleveland have set the price of vouchers so low that the market has comprised religious (especially Roman Catholic) schools, where the church subsidizes the cost of the education. What will happen if the price of a voucher is the actual per-pupil expenditure in a public school system—which in some places could be as high as $8,000? Will that stimulate the creation of new and better schools?

In some instances government will have to continually adjust prices in order to achieve the social good desired. In the environmental area a declining price can mean that undesirable products, such as sulfur dioxide emissions, are decreasing and the social good is being achieved. But in other forms of government by market, such as pure vouchers, it is conceivable that the initial price might be set appropriately but over time could fail to bring about the desired consequences in terms of quality and innovation in education.

The second consideration is the range of the market. Elected officials often get cold feet in the establishment of a new market; they want to have their cake and eat it, too. That was part of the story in the deregulation of the California energy market. The government deregulated the wholesale market without deregulating the retail market. False expectations (that energy prices would continue to go down) and political pressures to reassure voters that the changes would not cost them more money (along with some evidence of market manipulation) ended up contributing to a crisis. Thus the second challenge for the public official interested in government by market is the political pressure to retain the certainty that goes with traditional government.

The third challenge facing those who would create and manage markets for the public good is to make sure that the rule of law is effective enough to prevent cheating. This problem is clearest in emerging democracies and countries with long histories of corruption. All markets, public and private, need rules to operate and an effective enforcement mechanism. Although market government applied to environmental problems has proven a success in the United States, talk about using market mechanisms to implement the Kyoto accords falls on skeptical ears in other countries.

Finally, well-functioning markets depend on adequate information. As American consumers we are accustomed to having at our fingertips reliable sources of information about everything from cars to bread-making machines. But will consumers of education in newly voucherized school districts have reliable information about schools? The failure of traditional educational bureaucracies (until recently) to standardize and measure performance means that parents are not accustomed to evaluating the potential benefits of one school versus another. They do not really know what to "buy" when it comes to education. Lurking behind the failure on state ballots of so many voucher plans is the suspicion that parents will make bad choices. Comparing the quality of one second-grade education to another is simply not the same as comparing the quality of one car to another. A similar problem emerges in health care: Evaluating it is filled with methodological pitfalls. Good markets require good information, and in two critical areas of our public life—education and health care—the measurement of performance is difficult.

This means that the creator and manager of a state-established market must be constantly monitoring the quality of information available about it. This is difficult enough in the private sector. In 1999 Arthur Levitt, head of the Securities and Exchange Commission, implemented new order-handling rules, which require that customer limit orders in all markets be publicly exposed and two-tiered pricing eliminated. He cited this as an example of the mission of the SEC—to create "quality markets."[25] The spate of corporate scandals in the spring and summer of 2002 testify to the continuing need for the government to be alert to the quality of the information provided to the private market.

The government leader who wishes to create and manage a quality market for the public good has to be just as vigilant against cheating and just as concerned about the quality of the information as are those regulatory agencies that monitor private markets. The trick will be, as it is in government by network, to regulate without bleeding those networks or markets of the creativity and capacity for innovation that are their strongest features. Problems aside, government by market is a powerful alternative to traditional bureaucracy precisely because is allows unlimited adaptations in the service of the public good. It is therefore perfectly suited to the United States, where citizens place a high value on individual choice.

Conclusion

Each of these emerging forms of postbureaucratic government has its strengths and weaknesses. Each is prone to creativity and innovation and to cheating and stealing from the public purse. The secret to success is in the quality of the leadership and management brought to these organizations. As table 8-1 illustrates, leaders of these new methods require new and different skills. And yet they all require courage, integrity, and a belief in the public mission—qualities that have made for good public leaders no matter what the century.

Table 8-1. *Four Governing Systems*

System	Accountability mechanism	Management tasks	Management pitfalls
Traditional government	Rules and regulations	Implement rules and regulations	Accountability crowds out performance
Reinvented government	Performance goals for the organization	Reduce traditional control mechanisms that interfere with performance Innovate within the law Use flexibilities in the law Change the law when necessary	Increased scrutiny Tendency of elected leaders to ignore performance in favor of traditional accountability measures
Government by network	Performance goals for the network and for each actor	Define successful network performance Analyze elements of success and failure Weed out bad performers and reward good performers	Political difficulty of replacing poor performers Temptation to over-regulate organizations and drive out creativity
Government by market	Performance goals for the the market	Set and adjust prices as necessary Provide quality information Prevent cheating and gaming the system	Temptation to over-regulate the market and drive out creativity Over time pricing becomes obsolete and fails to achieve the public good

Notes

1. See Joseph S. Nye, Philip D. Zelikowe, and David C. King, eds., *Why People Don't Trust Government* (Harvard University Press, 1997), for a description of dissatisfaction with government in the United States. For a similar review of attitudes toward governance in the rest of the world, see Pippa Norris, ed., *Critical Citizens: Global Support for Democratic Government* (Oxford University Press, 1999).

2. See Salvatore Schiavo-Campo, "Government Employment and Pay: The Global and Regional Evidence," *Public Administration and Development,* vol. 18 (1998), pp. 457–78.

3. See George Gilder, *Microcosm: The Quantum Revolution in Economics and Technology* (Simon and Schuster, 1989); and Nicholas Negroponte, *Being Digital* (Basic Books, 1996).

4. Elaine Ciulla Kamarck, "The End of Government as We Know It," in John D. Donahue and Joseph S. Nye Jr., eds., *Market-Based Governance: Supply Side, Demand Side, Upside, and Downside* (Brookings, 2002), pp. 227–63.

5. Paul Light, *Monitoring Government: Inspectors General and the Search for Accountability* (Brookings, 1993).

6. See Robert Behn, *Rethinking Democratic Accountability* (Brookings, 2001).

7. Frank Anechiarico and James. P Jacobs, *The Pursuit of Absolute Integrity: How Corruption Control Makes Government Ineffective* (University of Chicago Press, 1996).

8. Michael Barzelay with Babk J. Armajani, *Breaking through Bureaucracy: A New Vision of Managing in Government* (University of California Press, 1992).

9. David Osborne and Ted Gaebler, *Reinventing Government: How the Entrepreneurial Spirit Is Transforming the Public Sector* (Plume, 1992).

10. Christopher Mihm, acting associate director, Federal Management and Workforce Issues, General Accounting Office, quoted in *Performance-Based Organizations: Lessons from the British Next Steps Initiative,* GAO/T-GGD-97-151, July 8, 1997.

11. See James R. Thompson, "The Civil Service under Clinton," *Review of Public Personnel Administration,* vol. 21, no. 2 (Summer 2001), pp. 508–21.

12. See "Vice President Al Gore and the National Performance Review," *The Best Kept Secrets in Washington: A Report to President Bill Clinton* (Government Printing Office, 1996).

13. The Internal Revenue Service Restructuring and Reform Act of 1998 (Public Law 105-206) contains a section called "Improvement in Personnel Flexibilities" (section 1201), which includes civil service reforms such as pay banding, streamlined demonstration authority, and category ranking.

14. The Homeland Security Act of 2002 contains two sections that have been especially controversial. Section 9701 gives the secretary of the department authority to create a "flexible and contemporary" human resource management system. Section 763 gives management authority to transfer appropriations between accounts with only sixty days notice to the relevant congressional committees, a provision that Senator Robert Byrd (D-West Va.) finds especially troublesome.

15. See Robert Stone, *Confessions of a Civil Servant: Lessons in Changing America's Government and Military* (forthcoming).

16. See Anne-Marie Slaughter, "The Real New World Order," *Foreign Affairs,* vol. 5, no. 76 (September/October 1997), pp. 159–71.

17. John Peterson and Laurence J. O'Toole Jr., "Federal Governance in the United States and the European Union: A Policy Network Perspective," in Kalypso Nicolaidis and Robert Howse, eds., *The Federal Vision: Legitimacy and Levels of Governance in the United States and the European Union* (Oxford University Press, 2001), pp. 300–35.

18. Cyber Security Institute, "Cyber Crime Bleeds U.S. Corporations, Survey Shows: Financial Losses from Attacks Climb for Third Year in a Row," press release, San Francisco, April 7, 2002.

19. See Steven Kelman, "Strategic Contracting Management," in Donahue and Nye, *Market-Based Governance,* p. 90.

20. Ibid., p. 93.

21. Robert Agranoff and Michael McGuire, "Big Questions in Public Network Management Research," *Journal of Public Administration Research and Theory,* vol. 11, no. 3 (July 2001), p. 296.

22. B. Guy Peters, *The Future of Governing: Four Emerging Models* (University Press of Kansas, 1996), p. 22.

23. See Robert N. Stavins, "What Can We Learn from the Grand Policy Experiment? Lessons from SO2 Allowance Trading," *Journal of Economic Perspectives,* vol. 12, no. 3 (Summer 1998), pp. 69–88.

24. Personal communication from Rob Stavins, June 23, 2001.

25. Arthur Levitt, "The Changing Markets," speech at Columbia Law School, September 23, 1999.

9

STEPHEN GOLDSMITH

Local Problem Solving: Empowerment as a Path to Job Satisfaction

ASHINGTON'S CURRENT DEBATE about human capital appropriately emphasizes the shortage of skilled, dedicated public sector workers. Discussions focus primarily on issues such as salary, recruitment, and occasionally other workplace conditions. Noticeably absent from conversations are popular and scholarly commentaries addressing systemic human capital problems. The examination of poor public sector labor-management relations, outdated bureaucratic organizations, and jobs detached from tangible results is critical to understanding employee job satisfaction.

Many individuals enter public sector positions so they can feel that they are making a difference and so they can see the results of their efforts. Certainly not enough talented individuals that obtain public service jobs feel satisfied. Paul Light notes that only 38 percent of nondefense federal employees feel challenged in their jobs and believe that they accomplish something at work.[1] And the Partnership for Public Service, a nonpartisan orga-

Municipal consultant Michael Huber conducted interviews excerpted in this chapter. Mark E. Schneider contributed to a paper with this writer to be published by the *Journal of Labor and Employment Law,* University of Pennsylvania, on some of these same themes.

nization whose mission is to restore public confidence in the federal civil service, found that few federal employees believe that their organizations provide tools essential for high-quality job performance.[2]

This chapter looks at the lessons that might be learned from one city's efforts to create a new set of conditions for employee fulfillment. Drawing on the experience of Indianapolis from 1992 to 2000, what follows is an account of how systematic and structural changes in organization, procedure, and relationships alter the attitudes of managers and line workers.

By the mid-1980s American cities and their employees were under siege. Tax revenues collapsed as citizens and businesses migrated to the suburbs, leaving behind urban decay and surging crime. Federal assistance to urban areas failed to resolve many of the problems it was designed to eliminate. As the issues affecting cities became increasingly more frustrating, local public employees themselves became more discouraged. Reforms initiated decades earlier (for example, hierarchical, rule-driven procedures with centralized staff services and highly structured collective bargaining contracts) seemed to impede solutions and further frustrate workers. These reforms in large part succeeded in reducing corruption but at the high cost of creating a narrow, often dispirited public sector work force.

Transforming the nature of public work through changes in labor-management policies can apply in some degree at any level of government, but the municipal level provides the best opportunity for meaningful reform. In Indianapolis, city hall and union leaders agreed on the vision: a competitive city with safe streets, vibrant neighborhoods, and a thriving economy. A strong mayoral form of government allowed leadership substantial executive flexibility, even though many of the most important reforms required legislative action. Local government employees are close to the "customer," and Indianapolis officials worked to connect employees and customers more directly. City leaders are in direct contact with a high percentage of their employees, so communication is simplified, and the possible negative influence of a disgruntled manager or union steward can be offset. In Indianapolis there was also a rigorous effort on the part of leaders to remove bureaucratic obstacles to change. Though sometimes disguised as safeguards for professional standards, bureaucratic hierarchies—dominated as they are by internal monopolies, narrow job definitions, and restrictive collective bargaining agreements—tend to reduce the efficacy and satisfaction of work.

Approaching a Shared Vision

Indianapolis began its efforts in a hostile environment, where the mayor was advocating privatization and the union was threatening lawsuits, pickets, and workplace disruption. The city, like others in the early 1990s, faced more demands for public services than existing resources would allow, and raising taxes was expected to exacerbate the outward flow of people and capital to the suburbs. Maintaining the status quo simply was not an option. The friction surrounding major changes in public employment policy often make the political costs of change exceed the benefits, thus deterring action. But Indianapolis leaders eventually agreed to expend political capital to transform the workplace.

The message from city hall was clear and emphatic: Taxes had to be increased to pay for services. Citizens and workers knew that enhanced productivity was a necessity, if not by public work force changes then through privatization. The message began to alter the political calculation. The top union official in the state, Steve Fantauzzo, had already seen fellow union workers lose their jobs in New York state hospitals. He understood the ultimate risk to the city and its employees if population and wealth continued to flee to the suburbs. This union acknowledgement that sometimes conditions require change provided a small opening that deserved a major investment in time and resources if it could eventually transform the way the city operated.

Productivity had to be improved; better results had to be gained from each tax dollar. Threats to privatize and shrill union reactions eventually progressed to a cease-fire and weekly meetings between the mayor's office and each union. Better and more financial information was made available, so union leaders could understand in which areas public employees were competitive. These efforts led to two major initiatives, both of which required leadership from the union and from city hall: The city would move to a competition model, allowing and assisting the unions to bid for tendered work, and major initiatives would be undertaken to improve practices so that public employees could fairly compete.

The Indianapolis effort to enhance productivity and change the working environment was led from the mayor's office. The obstacles to reforming workplace rules and approaches sometimes came from the city council, sometimes from managers, and other times from regulated industries or unions. A clear core leadership was needed to bypass the obstacles and translate the vision into concrete steps. A small office that reported directly to the mayor was created called Enterprise Development. This entity had full authority to crosscut bureaucracy, manage performance, and provide legitimacy to alter the then-adversarial labor-management environment. Skip Stitt, head of the office, helped arrange direct access to the mayor for labor and its leaders. These efforts led to monthly meetings with labor representatives, e-mail access to the mayor and deputy mayors, open financial books, site visits by the mayor, and appreciation letters and events for employees.

Management, however, continued to produce unnecessary obstacles, and even the department directors who were appointed became captive to the information flow from the managers reporting to them. Therefore Charles Snyder, a chief operations officer who understood the vision and believed in labor partnerships, was employed to manage the two departments with the greatest number of union workers. But change required more than new offices or people; it required leadership on the part of the union, invested resources, and trust based on fairness.

Union-Management Teamwork

Union local presidents eventually also advocated change, albeit with somewhat different priorities in mind. The stick of privatization did indeed secure the attention of union leaders, but the most substantial advances occurred after tension had been reduced. Tensions eased when the city created a safety net, assuring displaced workers that they would be placed in other open city jobs. Employees were promised that innovative ideas and shaved costs would not cause job loss; reforms and competition would eliminate jobs only as positions became vacant through attrition, retirement, or aggressive outplacement efforts.

As one city worker explained, "We wouldn't have accomplished nearly as much if we hadn't had the safety net. If you went to a new position, at the most you'd get a one grade cut in pay." The cooperative approach facilitated by the safety net was summed up by manager Charles Snyder: "What we did was try to get out of work that we were not good at and get into work that we were good at. The safety net provided more employees a chance to do what we were good at. It wasn't that we had more employees than we needed, what we had was too many employees in one area."

AFSCME (American Federation of State, County, and Municipal Employees) local president Steve Quick agreed: "Getting out of business we were not good at and into business we were good at was really a joint venture between employees, union, and management. What we did was meet in a room for about a week and put everything that we did up on a board. And we said, Do we really want to pick up trash on the side of the road? We eliminated a lot of stuff that we were basically reacting to and started doing things that the employees liked doing, and it built morale."

These structural changes created a less arrogant management and a more willing labor pool. Said Snyder, "The key is involvement. We involved employees in decisions such as what equipment to purchase, how to staff the crews, and what routes we ran. For example, we overlapped and wasted time picking up trash and plowing snow. We asked the guys what they thought about it, and they said, Here's how we should be picking up trash and plowing snow, and here are the routes we should be running."

Added Quick, "From my position, employees liked the changes, because they had an opportunity to have a voice in the process. Before, they didn't have a voice at all. So when those changes were made and the employees were in power to make the day-to-day decisions—especially on how the work was to be done—it lifted morale and energized employees. They knew their ideas were actually being produced."

Partnership Investments

The rhetoric of partnership sets the stage for worker satisfaction and productivity, but of course more is required, especially the tangible investment of resources. In Indianapolis these investments took two major forms, other than pay: training and equipment. Quality training enhanced the skills, confidence, and pride of employees. One city employee observed, "We had a variety of drivers across departments who would only serve their department. We decided to make them all the same [classification]. We asked city hall for an additional $300,000 to train those drivers and bring them to the right level. That, to me, was probably the best thing, bar none. You want to motivate people and have more people be more encouraged in their job? Give them training that will give them better work and more money for their family. When I'm an old man, I'll remember that."

Manager Jody Tilford agreed: "The work force was more flexible; they weren't doing the same job over and over again. They were offered training in any area they wanted, so if they had a desire to go into computers or backhoes, they could. Then management implemented a certification program, so if people wanted to better themselves and their credentials, they had the opportunity to get the training. And as a reward they would get an hourly rate increase. That really benefited the work force as a whole."

Increases in productivity and job satisfaction require that workers have essential resources, and this goal is best accomplished when they participate in choosing their equipment. Indianapolis trained its workers, managers, and union leaders in activity-based costing (ABC) to support a common language for reform. To the surprise of many, the union used ABC to recommend better equipment: "We said to the city, If we're going to be competitive with our work, we have to know the numbers," said Jerry Richmond, a water department employee and United Water Union local vice president. "That's where we found out that purchasing costs us an arm and a leg. If a broom costs three dollars but we're paying Indianapolis six dollars because of the way the purchasing process is run, we can't be competitive. So that educated us tremendously. Management sent everybody through ABC, and that really opened our eyes. We saw that instead of having ten guys on a job, we only needed four. We got to thinking then that we could make more money."

Equipment decisions enhanced productivity. "Before we started having the employees in power, you'd have about ten or twelve people out there sealing cracks on the road," said AFSCME president Quick. "Once the employees were empowered to determine a better way, it dropped down to six guys doing the same job. They needed better equipment, and they knew what they needed but never could get it, because previously they had no voice in the process. When employees had an opportunity to talk about different types of equipment, they requested a do-all, a truck equipped with a conveyor belt. It's much more productive for many tasks. That was an idea that came from the employees."[3]

Teamwork, leadership, and communication built a sense of respect and trust.[4] As union vice president Jerry Richmond stated, "Workers felt more comfortable. Instead of having one boss for every three or four workers, you had one boss for every twelve or fifteen. I think it was more of a trust thing versus a fear thing. You didn't have a boss behind every door."

Louis Davis, local president of the Public Housing Union, added, "Any time you give employees some buy-in, some authority to make decisions about their work and job, they take more personal ownership of their jobs. In housing we eliminated levels of supervision. The union leaders then stepped forward and made some members team leaders and working fore-men. So we started really exercising a lot of discretion in taking more con-trol over the jobs and the tasks that we were doing on a day-to-day basis. I think productivity increased dramatically as a result."

The Indianapolis experience required substantial investment to provide the tools necessary for public employees to exercise more discretion more productively. These resources included technology (e-government) invest-ments, better training, and improved equipment. For example, in the build-ing permit office employees previously toiled in highly specialized tasks that were organized in sequential, linear steps and required much paper passing, chasing, and botched handoffs. Rules built into new information technol-ogy (IT) systems guided newly trained employees to better decisions. For example, permit applications for locations not appropriately zoned simply could not be completed. New technology coupled with advanced training meant city workers exercised discretion and solved more problems with fewer errors, resulting in more interesting and satisfying jobs.

Nonfinancial Problem Solving

Some of the approaches undertaken in Indianapolis could easily be applied to other levels of government. For instance it became apparent that, despite years of participating in highly structured reform efforts, such as total qual-ity management, managers were not acting on employee requests or sug-gestions. So senior city staff, using information gathered directly from workers and from the small meetings with union leaders, began evaluating managers on how well they were capturing and quickly implementing employee suggestions. Solving nonfinancial issues quickly and effectively became an important part of enhancing job satisfaction. Union vice presi-dent Jerry Richmond commented, "The biggest key is you've got to com-municate, no matter what level you're on. Gestures like providing water for employees and little things that they need—we provide whisk brooms for our drivers so they can clean out their trucks. You wouldn't think that those things make any difference, but they're a huge morale boost. When you do things like that to help workers enjoy their everyday jobs, you get it back tenfold in productivity."

Employees expected fair and equitable treatment in return for their pro-fessionalism. "We used to have a problem with managers' accountability. If one of the workers wrecked a vehicle, he was suspended or disciplined. If management wrecked a vehicle, they got another vehicle and no discipline at all. We created this partnership in which everybody was treated the same. Accountability for one was accountability for all. And that made a difference," said union president Quick.

Issues of race required immediate resolution. As Quick noted, "We used to have an all-white male management structure. When [the new administration] came through, they started promoting women and blacks and other ethnic groups into decisionmaking positions. Those actions sent a clear message that was different from the past."

Appreciating the importance of and moving to solve these nonfinancial problems was both critical and relatively easy once managers were held accountable for implementing reforms recommended by employees.

Closeness as Motivator

Job satisfaction requires pride, and pride requires reinforcement from both overseers and customers. Employees needed to see top city officials personally articulating the vision and the reason for change, but they also needed to see the effect of their work on citizens. Highly restricted tasks, with no opportunity for reinforcement or complaints from citizens created a work force where narrow rules mattered more than results. The city's experience involved extensive personal communication with as many workers and labor leaders as possible, both from officials above and constituents below. The effort to communicate directly with workers produced an important and visible reaction. As one union president said, "The mayor visited every garage and asked us questions. He wanted to know what the city could do to make our jobs better. That was a positive thing. It was something to get a letter thanking us for a job we did. You would think, Man, he took time out to do something like that? That did a lot for the morale. We hadn't seen anything like that before." Another commented, "You eliminate three or four levels between the mayor and the workers, that's all you need."

A third union president had this to say: "The mayor introduced monthly meetings with labor leaders. We got a lot of good out of those. We were pretty confrontational originally with the level of change that the mayor introduced to the city. [We were all] quite protective of our turf. But the meetings diffused some of that resentment. That way you get straight off the presses what's going on and what the honest truth is, without sugarcoating it."

Yet another union president commented, "At that time the union participated in every level with the mayor's office, even improving the budget. We knew exactly what our budget was and how we had to capture costs. That really helped motivate us. The main thing is stepping down off that platform and looking eye-to-eye with your hourly employees. I think when you do that, they'll work harder for you."

Technology provided employees with real-time customer complaint information. It also allowed employees to subvert the bureaucracy and directly access any city official. "The mayor gave his e-mail address to all city employees," noted union president Quick. "Before, if I had a problem with my supervisor or manager, I could never get the message to the top boss. That provided another check and balance for management. They knew that if things weren't working right or in line with the mayor's vision, managers would be e-mailed. We're talking labor, workers—everybody had the mayor's e-mail address."

One of the major areas of job satisfaction for public employees is the opportunity to serve the community. To create a satisfied public work force that solves community problems, workers need contact with that community. This important reform is easiest to accomplish at the local level.

Initially in Indianapolis few of the approximately 5,000 city employees "owned" a problem or neighborhood or served customers. Rather, they completed work order assignments or engaged in professional but narrow technical activities. They were motivated neither by the opportunity to solve problems nor by the fulfillment that comes by correcting a neighborhood eyesore and receiving thanks from real people. Of all city employees, only firefighters regularly used the vocabulary of public service in describing their work. The firefighters' palpable pride in serving the public differed significantly from other public employees.

These observations led to changes in the language and character of government employment. A systematic effort began to connect as many employees as possible to customers. Work crews met with neighborhood leaders, development officials received geographical assignments, and city representatives attended all community meetings. Beat officers—not just community relations officers—met with and were accessible to constituent groups. The following comments from a union leader characterize the response to these initiatives: "Everybody took more pride. In the past our work force would throw litter out the window, knowing someone else would have to pick it up. When the changes started happening, we had a cleaner city. It was great to be here during that time and see how city employees went from the bottom of the barrel to where citizens really took pride in what we did."

The effect of the initiative on both managers and employees is reflected in these comments from union president Quick and manager Snyder. Quick: "The employees knew that it was their work, and they were proud of it, because their ideas and vision were taking place." Snyder: "For example for a special event, where in the past you couldn't get anybody to work, now everybody in the city worked, because they were proud of what they could accomplish. People wanted to get out and clean the streets and make Indianapolis look good."

To increase contact with citizens in neighborhoods, the city work force, from planning officials to work crews, was reorganized around geographic regions. Some teams were virtual, as employees from various departments joined together, mostly through intranet systems, to solve a problem that a neighborhood association listed as a priority. Quick notes that "for the first time we partnered with the neighborhoods." This approach contrasted to employees' earlier experiences of operating from a work order that resulted from a request to the call center. The evolution brought city employees in closer contact with neighbors. "You'd see people picking up trash in neighborhoods that used to be a mess. They saw us cutting weeds and picking up trash, and they knew we were really committed to making the city look better," said one employee.

Indianapolis implemented additional measures to solidify the employee-customer connection. For example, service requests and complaint tracking systems were enhanced and made transparent. More city managers and workers reviewed complaints and service requests, and citizens who complained were later surveyed to see if their problem was solved. Their responses allowed departments to be compared to one other by a third-party survey company that assessed service quality by geography and type of service. Both customer service and employee morale were improved by managers explicitly advancing the model of public servants serving the public good.

Bureaucracy-Busting as a Path to Satisfaction

Indianapolis had been a well-run city historically. It had adopted all the reforms suggested for progressive municipalities: professional human resource offices, centralized staff services like IT and purchasing, job classifications, grievance systems, and well-negotiated collective bargaining agreements. These efforts, coupled with the natural specialization that comes from professionalism, created a substantial bureaucracy; workers were circumscribed and disconnected from ownership of problems or neighborhoods.[5] The goal became how to maintain fiscal accountability while broadening discretion and increasing the percentage of the work force involved in direct service delivery.

Indianapolis clearly illustrated what David Osborne and Ted Gaebler call "good people working in bad systems."[6] Bureaucracy often hid behind other labels, protecting a class of professionals and midmanagers who were both frustrated by their jobs and resistant to change. This bureaucracy crowded out job satisfaction. The behavior of public managers often has a negative effect on employees, according to labor economist Richard Freeman.[7] As Edward Deci notes, "Supervision experienced as controlling undermines intrinsic motivation."[8] Controlling, adversarial relationships are also dissatisfying to managers. Mark Emmert and Walied Taher found that if public employees "enter professional fields to enjoy greater autonomy, task significance, and identity . . . the results suggest they are disappointed with their experience in the public sector."[9] By changing the system—that is, by deregulating the labor environment—it is possible to motivate these employees and increase productivity.

Increasing Authority to Solve Problems

In Indianapolis the issues dominating labor-management relations in the 1980s seemed designed to create tension and advocacy around needless matters. Lawsuits and bargaining often centered on whether job classifications were appropriate. Trying to make sure that similarly classified jobs in differing areas did exactly the same work aggravated relations and diminished accomplishment. Eventually, though, the union began to advocate for something quite different: fewer job classes that granted employees broader discretion and more complex jobs with higher degrees of autonomy. Employees and their union officials no longer preferred narrow job bands within which pay was measured by the difficulty of a repetitive task and the number of times the task was completed.

Senior managers were asked to read Rosabeth Moss Kanter's *Change Masters* and to establish "flexible vehicles . . . for encouraging entrepreneurs from the entire work force to perform better and be more professionally satisfied."[10] The goal was similar to that described by Greg Oldham and Anne Cummings: "When jobs are complex and challenging, individuals are likely to be excited about their work activities. . . . In addition, complex jobs may actually demand creative outcomes by encouraging employees to focus simultaneously on multiple dimensions of their work, whereas highly simple or routine jobs may inhibit such a focus."[11]

The city human relations department, traditionally the enemy of reform, was recast as an internal management consultant and was asked to assist managers and union officials in an effort to create fewer and broader job classifications. The fleet operation department dropped from thirty-three job classifications to eleven. The public housing force slimmed from twelve to three. The results inspired the work force, as indicated by the following union employee comments.

Art: "They took truck drivers and changed their description to Maintenance Operation Tech (MOT). Therefore they were not just truck drivers, they did everything."

Lenny: "Our guys in traffic that paint can't paint in the winter. We got those guys to install signs. We used them to also plow snow."

Public Housing Union President Louis Davis commented, "Now, instead of plumbers, carpenters, electricians, and many more, you have Maintenance Tech 1, 2, 3, and 4. Level 4 technicians are the most skilled. We found that people were limited by titles. Carpenters tended to focus on only carpentry, and so on. We requested that management implement a program to cross-train. As a result of cross-training, we have people that are more skilled, more competent, and more versatile."

A Department of Public Works employee concurred: "If I used to be a concrete finisher, I didn't used to jackhammer that concrete out. Now I do the whole job—I help tear it out, make the repair, and pour the concrete. That helped in every aspect of the city [because it was harder] to manage the work force and be efficient if you had thirty job descriptions as opposed to ten. [With thirty descriptions], you had thirty specialists. No one would step outside their job descriptions. You can now perform a lot of different functions."

Not only did this broadband initiative enhance productivity, but it also had a personal impact on employees. Said one union employee, "We are more versatile. It's really up to you to go as far as you want to go. You have different experience and knowledge now about different [areas]. I think it makes life as a whole more stable. I don't just have to depend on one thing. I have other skills under my belt now."

Similarly reform in the area of procurement forced authority down in the organization, communicating to employees that officials trusted them to solve problems. Fleet maintenance manager Jody Tilford commented, "Giving employees more decisions in purchasing was one of the biggest changes that helped. City government used to have so much red tape to go through. They streamlined and pushed down many decisions previously made by the city to employees; that made a big impact." Employee satisfaction soared, as did customer approval. The city added new decentralized purchasing, tracking, and auditing systems to complement the broader authority.

Structural Congruence: Competing to Improve Performance

External pressure combined with internal reform to create a workplace that concentrated on productivity. Years of aggressive internal auditing and heavy-handed discipline had created a risk-averse work force. Employees had little incentive to innovate, because mindless commitment to the status quo produced no adverse effect. Compliance with rules and processes —not outcome—was the measure of achievement. Performance measurements and competition together produced the hoped-for change in employee attitude.

"Contractors were lined up at city hall, waiting for our jobs, waiting to do the same things we do," said one city employee. "It forced the rank-and-file members to get on the ball and think about working more efficiently. It made better workers and managers out of all of us."

"Competitive bidding let us take new ownership of our work," noted another. "Suddenly we had to be much more conscious of materials, waste, and overhead. It made us mean and lean. We recognized that other groups wanted our core work. For that reason we stepped up to the plate and got much more competitive. The whole process benefited us immensely."

Equally important was the delayering that accompanied—and was accelerated by—competition. Structural changes in management empowered and exhilarated the remaining managers and workers. A discussion between senior manager Snyder and union president Quick reflects this change:

Snyder: "When we went to work to create a new partnership between management and the union, we found that the toughest area to work with was middle management. Once we reduced middle management, the partnership took off."

Quick: "Many in middle management thought that the city was going to privatize everything and that they would stick around as inspectors. When we reduced middle management, it sent a message to everybody that they had to work together as a team to come up with quality ideas."

This delayering liberated employees. Union teams designated a crew leader in place of the manager. As Louis Davis, president of the public housing local, noted, "It used to be that we wouldn't budge until a supervisor exercised authority. Now, by giving us discretion and authority to make everyday decisions that impacted the residents' lives, I think our residents found much better service. The employees took more responsibility for their actions and made good decisions. Previously they had to call a supervisor and wait on the supervisor to come and review the potential problem and guide them."

Competition combined with internal reforms changed the dynamic, emphasizing better communication. But communication needs flow up as well as down. Delayering, e-mail, and personal visits all facilitated this process and helped transform managers from information gatekeepers to facilitators of employee-generated ideas. As one manager finally noticed, "Some of our best suggestions on how to save money came from janitors and warehouse people that never had the opportunity to submit ideas." The ability to remove controlling layers of supervision created a team atmosphere, which produced higher job satisfaction and productivity.

Budgeting and Shared Savings

Bonus payments and gain sharing permitted work teams to benefit from their own good ideas by giving them more input into how the work was completed. These reforms, coupled with revolving and flexible funds, allowed employees to respond to budgeting changes by husbanding resources and working toward better results. For example, as one union leader explained, "We corrected problems and found ways to save money that we hadn't thought of before. Employees started turning out lights when they weren't in the rooms to save on electricity; it's amazing how much money you can save through little things."

Added another worker, "We didn't do preventive stuff in the past. We let things run, and then fixed them when they broke. We realized that doing preventive maintenance makes costs cheaper. Then we share more money through gain sharing. In the past nobody cared if the nut on that machine was loose—you worried about it when the machine broke. Now a guy tightens it as soon as he notices it, because that saves money."

Financial rewards are especially meaningful if they can be structured so that public good and personal gain are congruent. In most government environments, systems actually constrain productivity increases, and officials argue with employees about how to share the pain of limited revenue. However, if government establishes a system in which productivity produces shared value, then the positive effects can be powerful.

One worker put it well: "Performance bonuses worked out great. The first year, people were skeptical. They all thought, We're not going to make anything. Well, when the first checks came out, they saw the light, because city leaders said, Hey look, if these folks save money, I'm going to give it back to them. That had never happened in city government in the twenty-one years that I had been around."

Union leaders convinced city officials to replace the individual incentives plan with team-based awards. Union and management both viewed this as an important tool for encouraging teamwork. The chance to share in savings turned peer pressure from a negative factor to a positive force. One manager commented, "I think the bonuses enabled management and union to work together, because they were working toward the same common goal. The bonuses were an extra incentive for us to work together, which made us more cohesive." Added another manager, "Not only did management receive a bonus, but hourly employees received one also. It was a good incentive; it created a bond between management and hourly employees, because we were in the same boat. We had to bring up our production levels in order to receive performance bonuses, and the hourly employees were held to that same standard."

Union president Quick explained how his local went from 300 grievances a year to none: "Grievances vanished overnight, because now the union managed itself. Attitudes changed dramatically because, again, people had ownership of their jobs. They made the decisions, they did the work, and they suffered the consequences when they did something wrong. But people took a lot more pride in what they did."

If procurement, classification, and supervision reduce work to carefully controlled tasks, and if financial systems are dissociated from performance, individuals with little discretion will have equally little job satisfaction. When these systems support productivity, worker satisfaction and performance can increase dramatically.

Conclusion

If most individuals find their way to government jobs in order to make a difference, then the best way to attract and keep them is to ensure that they can make a difference. A concerted effort led by city and union leaders in Indianapolis produced significant results at the local level. The efforts described above resulted in workers feeling proud of their accomplishments. Better services were produced by teamwork among employees rather than by controlling supervisors.

This kind of environment inspires loyalty, reduces boredom, makes work meaningful, and creates vibrant public service. As one employee explained, "When you give employees opportunities to exercise their ideas, [they will] go above and beyond the call of duty. I got to exercise gifts and ideas that I didn't even know I had. Now I have the authority to go to [managers] and say, I don't think you recognize that we need this or we need that, and they listen. Thank God for the improvements."

Notes

1. Paul Light, *The Troubled State of the Federal Public Service* (Brookings, 2002).

2. Amit Bordia and Tony Cheesebrough, "Insights on the Federal Government's Human Capital Crisis: Reflections of Generation X," paper prepared for the Future of Public Service Executive Session, John F. Kennedy School of Government, Harvard University, June 24, 2002.

3. Many of these tools are inventoried in David Osborne and Peter Plastrik, *The Reinventor's Fieldbook: Tools for Transforming Your Government* (Jossey-Bass, 2000).

4. Donald G. Zauderer, "Workplace Incivility and the Management of Human Capital," *The Public Manager*, vol. 31, no. 1 (Spring 2002), pp. 36–42.

5. Mark A. Emmert and Walied A. Taher, "Public Sector Professionals: The Effects of Public Sector Jobs on Motivation, Job Satisfaction, and Work Involvement," *American Review of Public Administration*, vol. 22, no. 1 (March 1992), pp. 37–48.

6. David Osborne and Ted Gaebler, *Reinventing Government: How the Entrepreneurial Spirit Is Transforming the Public Sector* (Penguin, 1993).

7. Richard Freeman, "Through Public Sector Eyes: Employee Attitudes toward Public Sector Labor Relations in the U.S.," in Dale Belman, Morley Gunderson, and Douglas Hyatt, eds., *Public Sector Employment Relations in a Time of Transition* (Madison, Wis.: Industrial Relations Research Assn., 1996).

8. Edward L. Deci, James P. Connell, and Richard M. Ryan, "Self-Determination in a Work Organization," *Journal of Applied Psychology,* vol. 74, no. 4 (August 1989), pp. 580–90.

9. Emmert and Taher, "Public Sector Professionals," p. 39.

10. Rosabeth Moss Kanter, *The Change Masters: Innovation for Productivity in the American Corporation* (Simon and Schuster, 1983).

11. Greg R. Oldham and Anne Cummings, "Employee Creativity: Personal and Contextual Factors at Work," *Academy of Management Journal,* vol. 39, no. 3 (June 1996), pp. 607–34.

10

KENNETH WINSTON

Moral Competence in the Practice of Democratic Governance

SCHOOLS OF GOVERNMENT shape their curriculum around three types of inquiry: policy analysis and design, strategic management, and a more encompassing focus on the political environment, including electoral activity, advocacy, and public leadership. The mission is not just to educate professionals, serially, in these three areas but to enable them to integrate the three in depth and move across them in the course of their careers. What does the person look like who can do that? Are there generic skills and capacities that this person would possess?

The aim of this chapter is to address these questions in part, as a prerequisite to addressing the question we now add to the above: Must the list of skills and capacities be revised as governance responsibilities migrate away from the central state to other locations? My focus is on one dimension of professional skill, which I shall refer to as moral competence, understood as the set of individual attributes and dispositions (latent moral resources) that make for good governance. These are traits that governing

I am indebted to Mark Moore for discussion of the issues addressed in this chapter. For their generous comments and sage advice on an earlier draft, I am grateful to Mary Jo Bane, Michael Blake, Brent Coffin, Cary Coglianese, Archon Fung, Fred Schauer, Philip Selznick, and participants in the Visions of Governance project. Thanks also to Chambers Boyd Moore for her skillful research and editorial assistance.

institutions should either select for in recruiting or, more likely, cultivate on the job through an appropriate ethos and well-designed structural supports—which then constitute the moral competence of the institutions themselves. To give content to the idea of good governance, my working assumption is that the duties of practitioners and the nature of the polity are inextricably linked. What a practitioner should be depends crucially on what the practitioner is legitimately expected to do, and that depends on the polity. The central question, then, is what constitutes moral competence for a practitioner of democratic governance?

I begin by identifying some important aspects of democratic governance (without offering a full-blown theory). Then I sketch five generic virtues that I regard as constituent components of the moral competence of the good practitioner.

Features of Democratic Governance

Democracy is a moral order of a certain sort, based on a commitment citizens make to one another. Only a people with such a mutual commitment attempts to answer the main question of politics: How should we live together? A democratic polity, I want to suggest, has moral foundations, moral ends, and moral structures.[1]

Moral Foundations

It is a sociological commonplace that the legitimacy of political institutions depends on general societal acceptance, not coercive threats. This acceptance, in turn, is sustained over time only if supported by citizens' appreciation of official efforts to achieve orderly, fair, and decent governance. Political institutions are the work of their everyday participants, a continuous effort to construct and maintain a common framework to meet the exigencies of a shared existence, to resolve recurrent conflicts fairly, and to realize the aspiration of just and workable relations among citizens. Good institutions are ones that enable citizens to lead what they regard as decent lives *with others*. Democratic order, then, is emergent rather than imposed and receives its validation from the people whose lives it organizes. It relies on historical understandings and customary expectations in particular social contexts. As a result, democratic legitimacy is variable, fluid, and often problematic: something constantly to be achieved, not taken for granted.

One implication is that citizens are owed respect and have a standing claim to forbearance, even when their views are ill-founded or confused. We need not believe they are always right to recognize that practices and social norms based on shared experience, reflecting shared sentiments, have a presumptive validity. The presumption is rebuttable, of course, but the official who acts toward citizens from an Archimedean point outside the existing culture is likely to experience moral isolation and self-doubt—a precarious circumstance for even the most foresighted among us. Joseph Ellis's compelling portrait of Thomas Jefferson, who had such difficulty sustaining his early commitment to racial equality against opposing social pressures in his beloved Virginia, is a telling, if troubling, case study.[2]

Since democracy is a collective project, the affinities between official rules and procedures on the one hand and social expectations or norms on the other must be close. Not that each rule or decision has to be regarded as morally compelling: A citizen may well follow a rule out of calculated self-interest or to avoid coercive threats. But such an attitude cannot be at the core of citizens' relation to government; it must lie at the periphery or operate only with regard to certain limited obligations. Instead, egoism must be harnessed and bounded by attachment if we expect to see the trust and cooperation necessary for a life together. Of course, if we are too demanding on individual motives, the polity is bound to fail. So it is vital, as John Rawls observes, to rest the commitment to democracy on a reasonable moral psychology. Citizens have the capacity to follow principles and act for the sake of ideals. When they believe that social practices are fair, they are prepared to do their part, provided they have assurance that others will also do their part. The more they believe that others are doing their part for the right reasons, the more they will develop trust and confidence in others.[3] Instrumentalism to personal ends is a possible attitude to have toward social and political institutions and is characteristic of those who think the principal function of government is to protect private spheres of activity. But instrumentalism by itself impoverishes political life. In contrast democratic citizens value civic goods, including the goods of association and collective self-rule. The state itself is an association whose members are citizens, and it has a practical preeminence in compelling them to think about a common good beyond the goods of special groups.[4]

Moral Ends

I follow Amartya Sen in thinking that, for moral purposes, our conception of democratic citizens has a double aspect. We view citizens in terms of well-being and in terms of agency. The first has to do with how well off citizens are: whether they enjoy favorable life circumstances, security, prosperity, and so on. Regarding citizens as agents means respecting their ability to set goals, develop commitments, pursue values—and succeed in realizing them.[5] In the context of a democratic polity, valuing agency is at the core of self-government. Strictly, what is fundamental is not so much the realization of what (let alone everything) one values, but recognition of the moral space within which one can exercise deliberate choice, typically in conjunction with others. Liberty is not a presocial attribute of individuals that government (or society) inevitably restricts; it is the exercise of self-determination that the polity makes possible. A fundamental aim of public policy, therefore, is to empower citizens and foster the conditions for engaging in meaningful activities together. This goal is one criterion for selecting among policy options.

From the importance of agency flows the principle of citizen participation in decisionmaking—not "maximum feasible participation" but participation that is appropriately structured and relevant to the activity in question. (I say more about specific structures below. The forms of participation that come most readily to mind are elections and political advocacy, but every decision mechanism needs to be viewed along this dimension.) Further, to value agency does not mean we should preclude exacting scrutiny of how it is exercised. People are known to enter voluntarily into relationships—of employment, family, politics—even when they are ill-informed and the relationships are demeaning. We need to retain a critical perspective on such choices. Thus, at least for decisions with public implications, it is a benefit to the polity if institutional mechanisms operate to transform initial preferences into thoughtful judgments, the way litigants in constitutional disputes are required to formulate their complaints in terms of authoritative readings of our collective compact or juries are required to reach unanimous agreement and thereby strive for impartiality. In general, well-designed institutions do not leave citizens just as they are but transform them through participation, making possible the reconciliation of partial and general perspectives, which it is the special task of good practitioners to bring about.[6]

Since the exercise of agency requires enabling social conditions, valuing agency entails a collective commitment to capacity building—that is, providing citizens with basic resources and opportunities for realizing the kind of life they have reason to value, individually and collectively. Background conditions include public policies that diminish the threat of famines, epidemics, and terrorist attacks. For individuals, basic capacity development typically requires education, adequate health care, and employment opportunity. We should also note the importance of opening channels of communication—especially today by exploiting the potential of new information technologies—and easing barriers to mobilizing coalitions and forming associations. Beyond these are formal structures of decisionmaking.

Moral Structures

A crucial ingredient of citizens' capacity to exercise choice together is the availability of mechanisms of collective decisionmaking. To act effectively as a member of a democratic polity requires structures that bring each citizen's actions into meaningful relation with the actions of others. This is the civic dimension of freedom—the capacity to engage with others in self-rule.

Traditional decision mechanisms can be sorted into certain basic types, such as election, contract, adjudication, legislation, mediation, administrative regulation, and choosing by lot. Each comes in many variations. For example, voting can take the form of simple majoritarianism or of proportional representation; it can be single or cumulative, and so on. These alternatives are obviously incompatible. Without some method of counting, a collective decision cannot occur, but each method has its own implications for the polity that adopts it. Each is qualitatively different and makes of the polity something that, morally, it would not otherwise be.

The moral quality is highlighted by observing these structures from both sides of the relationships they establish, that of practitioners and of citizens. From the side of practitioners, we can see that certain duties to citizens flow from the purpose of the decision mechanism itself, quite apart from substantive outcomes. For example, if the point of a legislature is to promulgate general rules and give meaningful direction to citizen conduct, then legislators have a duty to make statutes clear and consistent and capable of execution. A carelessly drafted law fails to respect citizens in their capacity as responsible agents. Similarly a retroactive statute (imposing an obligation today on conduct undertaken yesterday) is inherently problematic and requires special justification for the limited cases in which it might be employed. In general, agencies of governance not only have tasks to perform; they have relationships to sustain. The commitment to these relationships determines, to some extent, the kinds of tasks they are able to take on and how the tasks are accomplished.

From the side of citizens, fundamental to the structures of decision are the methods by which participation occurs. Self-rule, whether individual or collective, must be appropriate as well as effective. In adjudication, for example, litigants present evidence and reasoned arguments in support of their claims. Respect for litigants is optimized when the judge's decision is based, as far as possible, on those arguments, even though this entails a reduced role for the judge as policymaker. In that way the fate of litigants is made to rest on their own efforts and their own understanding of their situation. Similarly the important feature of a market, in this view, is that it brings human choices, and the cost of realizing them, into a common calculation. Thus efficiency is not the driving consideration; it is participation, as an equal, in the allocation of social resources. (Closer is the idea that the market is a sensitive mechanism for coordinating a myriad of activities, without requiring agreement on values.) In sum, each structure recognizes a mode of participation, and hence of self-rule, that fits its purpose and mode of functioning.

Institutional forms are not fungible or infinitely malleable. Distinct principles and values regulate different spheres of activity, and appropriately so—for example, marriage and divorce, commercial relations, religious associations. Thus each form, we could say, has a comparative advantage in addressing certain issues and not others. Democratic governance entails due regard for the integrity of institutional forms and respect for the distinctiveness of each sphere. Thus extending an institutional form (such as the market) beyond certain bounds may mean subjecting some spheres of activity to an inappropriate set of values. At the same time institutional forms should be viewed dynamically—not as static and determinate structures of rules or procedures but as purposive mechanisms designed to foster self-government. To accomplish specific aims, participants must follow set forms. But since forms may become dysfunctional in relation to aims, the commitment to form is always open to reassessment. This brings out the moral as well as purposive aspect of decision mechanisms and is especially important to keep in mind as we search for new forms of social architecture in a world of migrating responsibilities. Because people reflect on what they are doing, they construct mental models of possible structures, which then guide the emergence of specific practices and provide patterns for evaluating their success. Such reflection requires evaluative judgments about the interplay of means and ends. The models are focal points of human striving; they embody moral aspirations and define moral relationships. At the same time the ideals we are interested in are not just fantasies of the imagination; they must take concrete form and prove themselves workable in practice. The contextual factors that enhance, or impair, the effectiveness of particular structures determine whether or not an existing social problem can be managed democratically—and how.

Moral Competence of the Practitioner of Democratic Governance

In broad terms *social capital* refers to the fund of human resources (traits of character, moral conventions, social networks) that a society has available to accomplish its collective goals and sustain itself over time. I am concerned with just those resources (dispositions, orientations, training) that constitute moral competence for practitioners of democratic governance. The features of a democratic polity sketched above have powerful implications for what these resources are and how they challenge the profession's current understanding of its work. In particular I focus on five generic attributes that I regard as defining features of the good practitioner—and variable attributes of actual persons. They are not character traits in the ordinary sense but qualities of officials, acting in their official capacities, as required by the duties of office. (Thus we would not expect individuals necessarily to exhibit these traits in other aspects of their lives.) The five are fidelity to the public good, the duty of civility, respect for citizens as responsible agents, proficiency in social architecture, and prudence.[7]

Fidelity to the Public Good

Because the democratic polity is based on a mutual commitment to living together, the good practitioner is crucially preoccupied with determining the content and scope of the public good. This may seem platitudinous, but the challenge is formidable.

The aspect I want to stress is the inescapable dual responsibility of officials in democratic polities. Almost every official gets into office via a process that incurs legitimate obligations to specific individuals or limited constituencies. At the same time officials have a duty to enlarge their vision beyond these connections to encompass considerations of the public good. A key requirement of the good practitioner, then, is the ability to reconcile partial with general perspectives. Members of Congress, for example, are elected from particular districts and have duties to their electoral constituents. But they are also lawmakers for the whole country and thus have responsibilities to every citizen—their constitutional constituents, we could call them. Similarly, top-level administrators owe allegiance to their appointing officer and the officer's political agenda, but they are also bound to the statutorily created mandate of their office, which may or may not coincide with the boss's wishes. Policy analysts face this dual responsibility derivatively when they take on public officials as clients. Only judges appointed for life—and the occasional special prosecutor—escape the need to grapple with it.

The task of reconciling partial and general perspectives is a standing test of the integrity of the good practitioner, and its execution often demands considerable imagination and creative leadership. It may require, for example, open disagreement with (and attempts at educating) one's constituents or reexamining prior personal commitments in light of a new understanding of one's responsibilities. The challenge is compounded for practitioners who attempt to adopt a global perspective. An illustrative case is that of Senator Patrick Leahy who, beginning in 1990, made repeated attempts (all unsuccessful) to enact legislation restricting the export of pesticides whose sale is forbidden in the United States. He offered two principal reasons for this measure. First, he feared the pesticides' return to the United States in the form of poisonous residues on imported food. Second, he was concerned for the health of farm workers, most of them in developing countries, who use these toxic chemicals under conditions that too often produce illness, sterility, and death.

The first reason is not controversial. Surely members of Congress have a legitimate regard for the health and safety of their constituents, both electoral and constitutional; if there are questions about Leahy's efforts, they have to do with the best means for achieving these ends. The second reason is less clear-cut. Why are farm workers in developing countries Leahy's business? Can a legislator have responsibility for a constituency—let us call them Leahy's moral constituents—to whom he or she is not directly accountable? If the category of moral constituent is not empty, how should one weigh duties to constituents to whom one is directly answerable (including the U.S. chemical industry) against duties to constituents where no accountability mechanism exists? How does one configure the public good in these cases? I sympathize with Leahy's felt sense of responsibility to workers harmed by U.S. products in developing countries, but these questions, I believe, are not easily answered.[8]

The Duty of Civility

It is often said that if one heeds one's conscience and does what one sincerely believes to be right, one needn't fear the consequences. The moral life, however, is more complicated than that. If by *conscience* we refer to the personal moral convictions by which one guides one's life, it matters little—except to the person whose conscience it is—what those convictions are and whether they are shared by anyone else. But in the public realm we no longer have the luxury of idiosyncratic moral conviction. Principles that are important, even foundational, to oneself do not necessarily have a claim on anybody else. Thus sincerity of conviction is not an acceptable basis of public action. Since public decisions affect others, often profoundly, including those who have conflicting convictions, good practitioners are obligated to reach out beyond what is personal to what can be shared and agreed to by others. Personal beliefs of course generate felt imperatives and may legitimately function as starting points of public discussion. But reaching common ground is indispensable for collective endeavors. Accordingly one of the moral capacities necessary for responsible public decisionmaking is the ability to regard one's own opinion as only one among others and not decisive simply because one holds it, even passionately. (It is in this light that I take one of Nietzsche's observations: "A very popular error: having the courage of one's convictions. Rather it is a matter of having the courage for an attack on one's convictions.")

The good practitioner, we could say, has a duty to act in accordance with a *public conscience.* The conscientious democratic official is one whose grounds of decision are beliefs and principles that citizens generally are committed to—or could be, after deliberation and reflection. The hypothetical is crucial. Assent by others need not be immediate; that would compel consideration of every prejudice, no matter how vicious, and every opinion, no matter how ill-considered. On the other hand we must have a sense that assent is available, that the principles invoked are current at some level, even if only emergent and inchoate. Consider the example of Abraham Lincoln on slavery. If the goal of emancipating the slaves had been based on a personal (or idiosyncratic) conviction that slavery was wrong, there would have been no moral ground for calling upon the nation to endure the great sacrifices in prosecuting the war against the South. Lincoln appealed, rather, to the ideal of equality expressed in the Declaration of Independence, the nation's defining statement of moral principle. Even though he saw implications in that document that not everyone saw, the logic of his appeal was public, not personal.

Or consider the case of human rights advocacy by nongovernmental organizations. These groups champion essential conditions of human agency and well-being, yet the principles they espouse are not everywhere recognized. Actual acknowledgement of their principles by others cannot be a precondition of their appeal, as Michael Ignatieff emphasizes.[9] But it is also true that NGOs act illegitimately if they have no reasonable basis for supporting their claims on grounds everyone could accept. And that is where questions arise. Do human rights advocates have the correct understanding? Do they have defensible grounds, for example, for giving priority to civil and political rights over social and economic rights, in all societies? There is reasonable disagreement on these matters.

The duty to act only on the basis of principles that citizens could reasonably accept is what Rawls refers to as the duty of civility.[10] This duty requires the good practitioner to strive always to attain a vantage point for assessing and revising particularistic claims and partial viewpoints. It helps the practitioner move in reasoning from the individual to the communal and, where appropriate, from the communal to the universal.

Respect for Citizens as Responsible Agents

Regard for human agency is at the core of the value of self-government. Accordingly good practitioners do not attend to well-being alone. In teaching strategic management, for example, we focus on managers as entrepreneurs for public value. But if public value has to do only with citizens' well-being, not their agency, it omits a critical aspect of what good practitioners have a responsibility to care about. Recognition of this point allows us to distinguish two opposing conceptions of the democratic practitioner and the proper exercise of political power. (The contrast is no doubt a bit overdrawn, but it should help define the terms of debate.) The first sets forth the image of rule by an elite cadre of experts, who are needed because modern democratic society has become so complex that it has outgrown the capacities of even an active, informed citizenry. In this scenario the role of citizens is to choose among competing elites who define policy alternatives. Here political power consists in the capacity to achieve citizen compliance with goals set by practitioners. Let us call this the directive style of governance.

Every government of course uses coercion to secure compliance with some of its rules and decisions; that is unavoidable. Yet, in a democracy, coercive threats are always disfavored; they are a necessary means only if alternative methods have failed or are unworkable. The search for alternatives is therefore a constant imperative. In contrast to the directive style, the opposing conception starts from the premise that democratic self-government is too important to abandon to elites; the modern polity simply poses new challenges to engaging citizens actively in decisionmaking. To require that practitioners be expertly trained and informed is not to cede all control to them. To be sure, they have an active role to play, especially in ensuring that goal-setting is informed and deliberative. But respect for citizens as responsible agents goes further, by giving weight to the goals that citizens have adopted for themselves and enabling them to be realized, within the constraints set by the reconciliation of partial and general perspectives. Thus the orientation is different: While the practitioner's input is critical, the process is interactive. Power then consists in the practitioner's capacity to facilitate citizens' capacity for self-direction. The good practitioner is disposed, wherever feasible, toward a *facilitative* rather than directive style of governance, one that enhances citizens' exercise of effective agency.

In conformity with the first image of the democratic practitioner is command-and-control government, issuing prescriptive rules and backing them with the threat of sanctions. One step removed is official manipulation of incentives to achieve citizen compliance, which still exemplifies the directive style—governance as social engineering. Incentives are designed to provide motivation or encouragement to individuals to act in ways conducive to fixed objectives. The implicit assumption is that manipulation is needed because citizens would not otherwise act as desired. Incentives, however, change people's calculations, not necessarily their minds. They respond to external stimuli, unmediated by appreciation of their warrant, engaging in acts of expedience rather than conviction. Even worse, material incentives to do socially desirable things sometimes crowd out rather than supplement civic motives to do them, with the result that citizens are less inclined to act in socially beneficial ways. For these reasons the manipulation of incentives appears to be an inherently unstable strategy of governance.

For example, in environmental policy, tradable permits and pollution fees take firms' economic motives for granted, attempting to make it in their interest to meet official goals. That is fine, as far as it goes. But regarding these techniques as an improvement over prescriptive rules makes sense precisely because they acknowledge citizen purposes and use local information in decisionmaking. Once this step is taken, it is possible to imagine further moves that give citizens greater opportunities for meaningful engagement. With deliberative environmental regulation, local parties have a significant say in policy implementation and sometimes in goal-setting itself.[11] Instead of attempting to achieve specific outcomes by issuing top-down directives, backed by threats, or by micromanaging citizen activity, practitioners identify broad measures of success (for example, preserving endangered species) and let affected parties work out the details. With problem-centered regulation, practitioners demonstrate their respect for socially valued private activity by adopting its viewpoint, in a cooperative effort to understand the needs of the enterprise and achieve shared goals.[12] With so-called management-based regulation, at least in a generous interpretation of it, citizens are asked to undergo a consciousness-raising planning process, but how—and whether—to meet targeted outcomes is left for them to decide.[13] (This process could also educate practitioners, since private parties might develop solutions to problems too complex for government officials to figure out on their own.)

   This sketch of regulatory options is crude and meant only to be suggestive. The common thread is increased citizen participation, which enhances governance values without losing central oversight. The chief concern for the good practitioner is to reconcile partial and general perspectives, which requires (among other things) serious attention to the principle of subsidiarity. Simply stated, the principle of subsidiarity is this: Do not assign to a higher level of governance what can be done effectively at a lower level. The criteria of allocation are typically economic (maximizing efficiency) and epistemic (aligning tasks with the location of relevant knowledge). For the good practitioner a different criterion is democratic—favoring units of moral commitment, loci of self-determination where mechanisms of citizen engagement can be protected and enhanced. With this concern higher units will attempt, if possible, to exercise less exacting forms of authority over lower units, employing nondirective modes of governance that may take the form of expressions of value, guidelines based on best practice, expert reports, or various "reputational" mechanisms, such as performance scorecards—rather than prescriptive rules and regulatory directives. (These nondirective modes comprise what recent European writers call soft law.)[14]

The point is that, in governance, relationships matter as well as goals. Citizens are objects of concern as whole persons.[15] Therefore the criteria of success in policymaking are incomplete if they fail to take into account how policy options are likely to engage citizens. Not because citizen participation necessarily makes desired outcomes more likely; rather, since citizens are moral agents, the good practitioner aims to release human energies and create structures of opportunity, no less than constraint.

Proficiency in Social Architecture

I have not yet found an apt term for this virtue; perhaps I need to invent one. My aim is to capture an attribute of competence, distinct from technical skill, which involves deliberative judgment about ends and means. Lawyers who value this trait refer to it simply as craft and regard it as essential to law as a professional vocation. Lon Fuller identifies the key features when he speaks of lawyers as architects of social structure, fashioning legal instruments for effective collaboration among citizens and establishing frameworks for the future dealings of affected parties. In elaborating this idea Fuller stresses the continuity between private and public architecture. The orientation and qualities of mind involved in drafting a contract for two parties, for example, represent in miniature what is needed in drafting statutes for the polity, because every legal instrument is a kind of constitution establishing a framework for future interaction. When the client is the public as a whole, the lawyer "could, without any question of propriety, regard himself, in Justice Louis Brandeis's words, as 'attorney for the situation.'"[16]

For this reason legal education, Fuller thinks, should include the teaching of social architecture. Whatever the merits of that view, I believe the virtue of institutional craftsmanship is an attribute of the good practitioner. (Lawyers are not thereby excluded; they may constitute a subset of the class.) As I observe above, institutional forms establish or affirm certain moral relationships, or fail to do so, which is why it is important to get them right. The good practitioner has the skill to identify the appropriate form for a given type of problem, guided by the types of relationships that would obtain among citizens if the form were realized. Institutional design is moral legislation. Any specific decision structure leads us to conduct our lives one way rather than another. It provides access to some citizens and excludes others; it facilitates certain problem definitions, makes certain types of information available and not others. So good practitioners have a responsibility to ensure that the ends of governance are served, as well as are substantive social ends. Governance values are always at risk, subject to displacement, attenuation, and corruption. A major task of the good practitioner is "to preserve inherently precarious values against ruinous competition from the cheap, the easy, the cost-effective, and the urgent."[17]

It is worth emphasizing that the architect of social structure is not just a technician. The responsibility of setting up and monitoring frameworks of interaction and collaboration cannot be carried out without a simultaneous focus on ends and means—not just because both are important, but because ends and means invariably interact and involve each other.[18] This point is especially important in thinking about the implications of moving governance responsibilities to private firms or NGOs. The critique should indeed be familiar. For example, it is commonly assumed that practitioners can use the market as a means for pursuing the ends of governance, without thereby changing the ends of governance. The interaction of means and ends suggests otherwise. Two things may happen: Practitioners may focus on only some ends of governance, especially narrowly managerial ones, and they may fail to grasp how new ends intrude through market mechanisms. A mechanism such as contracting out does not, typically, improve citizen participation, let alone transparency or responsiveness. Demand-side financing (for example, education vouchers) may improve accountability but impair collective self-government. In general, markets are not value-sensitive unless they are made deliberately so. This is the rationale for building "social markets," in which specific political values—such as racial and gender equality, workers' rights, habitat preservation—are incorporated into market calculations.[19] Thus applauding new management forms, as the "new public management" is wont to do, without thinking about their implications for governance, is like creating new life forms without thinking about ethics. No doubt experiments in social architecture will proceed willy-nilly, as the lure of technological innovation pushes ahead of thoughtful deliberation, but good practitioners surely should reflect on their ramifications before leaping to embrace them, asking in particular whether they are opening up or closing down opportunities for democratic governance.

Prudence

In the classical sense prudence is the cardinal political virtue: the exercise of practical wisdom in governance. Since governance is about sustaining valued relationships, ruling requires more than technical expertise. But can we suppose that those who rule in a democratic polity are endowed with superior wisdom? Does their expertise disclose to them a better range of beliefs, which gives them authority to control our conduct and alter our lives? Democrats are cautious about such implications.

In a more specific sense prudence is practical wisdom in deciding how to act in specific cases—not expediency, focusing on the assessment of means to specified ends, not opportunism, taking advantage of institutional dysfunction to achieve predetermined outcomes, but making sound moral judgments in concrete situations. Prudence is thus the capacity and willingness to engage in ethical inquiry when the occasion requires. Beyond the traits described above, this includes skill in managing competing claims and the ability to tolerate moral ambiguity. The commitment to core values is balanced by an appreciation of recurrent perplexities and tensions. In this endeavor the prudent official learns more from cumulative experience than from philosophical reason.

Max Weber addresses this matter when he asks: "In which area of ethics, so to speak, is [politics] at home?"[20] His response is that the animating passions of politics (the pursuit of "ultimate ends") must be tempered by an "ethic of responsibility." This ethic requires an attitude of detachment toward events and people, the ability to contemplate things as they are with inner calm and composure. So, while politics is born from passion and nourished by it, it becomes a mature human activity when disciplined by the exercise of judgment. The ethic of responsibility constrains the commitment to grand principle by a sensitivity to consequences for specific persons. Responsible politicians have a feel for the particularity as well as the complexity of political action. They appreciate the fallibility of human planning and the inevitability of unintended consequences.

Consider Lincoln on slavery: Although he proclaimed his opposition to slavery from early on ("If slavery is not wrong, nothing is wrong.") he refused to align himself with the abolitionists. Up to (and into) the Civil War his effort was to prevent the extension of slavery into new territories, not to abolish it where it already existed. Accordingly, in setting out the position of the Republican Party in 1858, he declared: "If there be a man amongst us who does not think that the institution of slavery is wrong . . . he is misplaced, and ought not to be with us." However: "If there be a man amongst us who is so impatient of it as a wrong as to disregard its actual presence among us and the difficulty of getting rid of it suddenly in a satisfactory way . . . that man is misplaced if he is on our platform." Lincoln realized that unwavering commitment to principle, although indispensable, is not the only determinant of action; he had also to take account of hard facts and constitutional strictures. This was not abandonment of principle but prudence, no less moral than the abolitionists and perhaps more so.[21]

Lincoln's case illustrates prudence on a large scale, but it is worth emphasizing that prudence is required in everyday decisionmaking, in the application of rules to cases—whether the rules be statutes, administrative regulations, or general directives. As Frederick Schauer reminds us, rules reflect the limits of human language and are always imperfect or incomplete in relation to their animating purposes.[22] (They may require more than the purpose warrants, or less.) Consequently faithful rule-following depends on second-order competencies, such as the ability to discern the purpose of a rule and the integrity and self-restraint necessary to pursue it. The prudent official tries to avoid what Fuller refers to as the problem of absentee intellectual management: using today's general language to decide tomorrow's unknown cases. The good practitioner has the ability to discern when rule-departure more effectively meets official responsibilities than rule-following: for example, selective enforcement by police and prosecutors despite a contrary statutory obligation or a jury's nonreviewable decision to "nullify" a law and acquit a defendant as an act of moral protest, in plain violation of judicial instructions. Flexibility, openness to further inquiry (including fact-finding), postponing matters if possible until they are ripe for decision—these are qualities of the prudent official.

The Good Practitioner in a World of Migrating Responsibilities

Let us recall the question motivating this inquiry: Will the moral competence of the practitioner of democratic governance have to change as governance responsibilities migrate away from the central state to other locations? My effort has been to identify which qualities might need to change. But whether they would in fact have to change is a question I would prefer to pose for discussion than attempt to decide.

Today social and economic forces seem to impel us inexorably toward alternative architectures of governance. We live in a time of institution creation, not unlike the postrevolutionary period of the American republic. I take it as a basic assumption, however, that the current order of states is not destined to disappear in the near future. Nor is it outdated; the state is still the most favorable location for democratic governance. Hence the special worry that, if international economic integration is not done with care, it will accentuate domestic inequalities and undermine the mutual commitment among citizens that makes democratic life possible.[23] I would not claim that workable democratic self-government has a natural or optimal size, but I do think that mutual commitment to effective participation in appropriate forms of decisionmaking requires shared sentiments and attachment and perhaps a common vocabulary of understanding with ongoing and inclusive deliberation—all of which place limits on territorial possibilities. At the same time these hard facts should not serve as an excuse for skepticism or resistance to new developments. Rather they define the challenge faced by the good practitioner. As responsibilities migrate to new locations, the special challenge is to stay focused on the moral dimensions of governance.

Notes

1. In elaborating these ideas I am employing the framework I have developed for interpreting the work of Lon Fuller. This essay focuses on the democratic underpinnings of Fuller's jurisprudence. See "Introduction to the Revised Edition," in Kenneth Winston, ed., *The Principles of Social Order: Selected Essays of Lon L. Fuller* (Oxford: Hart Publishing, 2001).

2. Joseph J. Ellis, *American Sphinx: The Character of Thomas Jefferson* (Knopf, 1997).

3. John Rawls, *Political Liberalism* (Columbia University Press, 1993), p. 86; John Rawls, *The Law of Peoples* (Harvard University Press, 1999), pp. 149ff. James Madison wrote: "Is there no virtue among us? If there be not, we are in a wretched situation. No theoretical checks, no form of government, can render us secure. To suppose that any form of government will secure liberty or happiness without any virtue in the people is a chimerical idea." Quoted in the documentary history of the ratification of the Constitution by Lance Banning, *The Sacred Fire of Liberty: James Madison and the Founding of the Federal Republic* (Cornell University Press, 1995), p. 247.

4. For a critique of instrumentalism, see Kenneth Winston, "Why Are Libertarians Afraid of Democracy?" *The Good Society*, vol. 8, no. 2 (1998), pp. 48–52.

5. Amartya Sen, "Well-Being, Agency, and Freedom," *Journal of Philosophy*, vol. 82, no. 4 (1985), pp. 185–87, 203–08.

6. I am not arguing that thoughtful citizens would not sometimes rationally prefer to delegate decisionmaking authority to others. But, in policy analysis, it is too easy to assume that the act of delegation has already occurred and need not be revisited. I believe rather that delegation should be considered not as a one-time transfer of authority but as a condition that needs sustaining through continuing communication. And we need to be more imaginative about involving citizens in decisions, where that is feasible. For reflections on the economy (or diseconomy) of participation in decisionmaking, see Robert Dahl, *After the*

Revolution: Authority in a Good Society (Yale University Press, 1970); and Jane J. Mansbridge, *Beyond Adversary Democracy* (Basic Books, 1980).

7. For a more expansive account of what constitutes virtue for officials in democratic societies, see Mark H. Moore and Malcolm K. Sparrow, *Ethics in Government: The Moral Challenge of Public Leadership* (Prentice-Hall, 1990).

8. The story of Leahy's efforts is told by Esther Scott, "Breaking the 'Circle of Poison': Senator Patrick Leahy and Pesticide Export Controls" (KSG case C14-00-1583.0). The relevant moral arguments are canvassed in the "Teaching Note" for the case (C14-00-1583.2). I should add that Leahy achieved a limited victory when he inserted a provision in an overseas spending measure enacted in January 2002, requiring coca-eradication herbicides used by the United States in Colombia to meet U.S. health and safety standards. See *New York Times*, July 11, 2002, p. A10.

9. Michael Ignatieff, *Human Rights as Politics and Idolatry* (Princeton University Press, 2001), p. 10.

10. Rawls, *Law of Peoples*, p. 56.

11. Charles Sabel, Archon Fung, and Bradley Karkkainen, *Beyond Backyard Environmentalism* (Beacon Press, 2000). See also Archon Fung and Erik Olin Wright, "Deepening Democracy: Innovations in Empowered Participatory Governance," *Politics and Society*, vol. 29, no. 1 (2001), pp. 5–41.

12. Eugene Bardach and Robert Kagan, *Going by the Book: The Problem of Regulatory Unreasonableness* (Temple University Press, 1982).

13. Cary Coglianese and David Lazer, "Management-Based Regulatory Strategies," in John D. Donahue and Joseph S. Nye Jr., eds., *Market-Based Governance: Supply Side, Demand Side, Upside, and Downside* (Brookings, 2002), pp. 201–24.

14. For recent examples of soft law in the European Union, see Adrienne Héritier, "New Modes of Governance in Europe: Policy-Making without Legislating?" in A. Héritier, ed., *Common Goods: Reinventing European and International Governance* (forthcoming). See also W. J. Witteveen and B. M. J. van Klink, "Why Is Soft Law Really Law?" *RegelMaat: Journal for Legislative Studies*, no. 3 (1999), pp. 126–40. Perhaps the EU is fertile territory for soft law because of its peculiar nature as a "postmodern polity," in which the EU is more of a supplement to than a replacement for national governments. (See Joseph S. Nye Jr., *The Paradox of American Power* (Oxford University Press, 2002), p. 32, quoting Andrew Moravcsik.) But a long-standing U.S. example is the work of the American Law Institute in periodically producing nonbinding but exemplary "restatements of law," which are then available for legislatures to enact (or not) as they choose.

15. Philip Selznick, *The Moral Commonwealth: Social Theory and the Promise of Community* (University of California Press, 1992), pp. 289ff. Aaron Wildavsky suggests the same view when he says: "The highest form of analysis is using intellect to aid interaction between people. Policy analysis, then, is about relationships between people." *Speaking Truth to Power: The Art and Craft of Policy Analysis* (Little, Brown, 1979), p. 17.

16. Lon L. Fuller, "What the Law Schools Can Contribute to the Making of Lawyers," in *Education for Professional Responsibility* (Carnegie Press, 1948), p. 34. For the difference between an "architect of social structure" and a "transaction cost engineer," see David Luban, "Rediscovering Fuller's Legal Ethics," in Willem J. Witteveen and Wibren van der Burg, eds., *Rediscovering Fuller: Essays on Implicit Law and Institutional Design* (Amsterdam University Press, 1999), pp. 208–13.

17. Selznick, *Moral Commonwealth*, p. 245. Since practitioners are often not just drafters of the rules but also players in the game, many ethical conflicts arise simply from the simultaneous occupation of multiple roles. (I call this the problem of many hats.) The debate on campaign finance reform provides an obvious example for U.S. legislators, since they are both drafters of the rules and its potential beneficiaries.

18. John Dewey, *Theory of Valuation* (University of Chicago Press, 1939).

19. Dani Rodrik, *Has Globalization Gone Too Far?* (Washington: Institute for International Economics, 1997). Much of the literature on market-based governance focuses on the good of efficiency, forgetting that efficiency is a secondary and parasitic value. Whether efficiency is good depends on what one is being efficient at; efficiency at mass murder, for example, is not good. Historically the design of the U.S. federal government has been praised for its inefficiency. This is perfectly intelligible from a political perspective. The counterargument must also be political.

20. Max Weber, "Politics as a Vocation," in W. G. Runciman, ed., *Weber: Selections* (Cambridge University Press, 1978).

21. Bernard Crick, *In Defense of Politics* (Continuum, 2000), pp. 154ff. Crick's argument is anticipated by Alexander Bickel, *The Least Dangerous Branch: The Supreme Court at the Bar of Politics* (Yale University Press, 1986), pp. 65–72.

22. Frederick Schauer, *Playing by the Rules: A Philosophical Examination of Rule-Based Decision Making in Law and in Life* (Oxford University Press, 1991).

23. Merilee Grindle voices the concern that asymmetrical relations between states can force the less powerful to adopt a studied indifference to their own people's needs and wishes. See "Ready or Not: The Developing World and Globalization," in Joseph S. Nye Jr. and John D. Donahue, eds., *Governance in a Globalizing World* (Brookings, 2000), pp. 178–207.

PART **III**

PRESCRIPTIONS
How Do We Get from Here to There?

11

ROBERT D. BEHN

Creating Leadership Capacity
for the Twenty-First Century:
Not Another Technical Fix

IF ONLY WE COULD fix our administrative systems. Better still, if only we could fix our political systems, which drive our administrative systems. Then government agencies would produce the results that we citizens will require from the public service in the twenty-first century.

Clearly improvement is required. After all, citizens are unhappy with the results that government is producing. Moreover, the people charged with leading these agencies are unhappy with the conditions under which they must work to produce these results. In the twenty-first century, the public service—and thus the agencies that it staffs—will have to elevate its performance. Yet, as we seek to improve public service, we are in danger of ignoring the necessity of improving the capacity of public managers to lead their agencies.

What should we do to improve the performance of our public agencies? What do we need to fix so that the public service is better able to produce the results that citizens value: excellent schools, rewarding jobs, a healthy environment, safe communities, a safe world? One attractive strategy is to concentrate on systemic reforms—fix the problems created by both the political and administrative systems within which the public service must

The author thanks John D. Donahue, Steven Kelman, and Frederick Schauer for their valuable comments and suggestions on a draft of this chapter.

work. Why tinker at the margins? Why not undertake serious, systemic, structural reform?

Unfortunately the historical record of both political and administrative fixes (a.k.a. reforms) suggests that such efforts will, at best, produce only small improvements. What looks like a fundamental change in an administrative system might do nothing more than require skilled civil servants to jump through a few more bureaucratic hoops. Or it might produce some improvements but require much time and effort of many people to create merely marginal benefits. Little wonder that the governmental landscape is littered with discarded reforms: the Planning, Program, Budgeting System; Management by Objectives; Zero-Based Budgeting; Total Quality Management. Each was designed to force fundamental change, to require public agencies to improve performance. Moreover, any effort to obtain authorization and implementation of such systemic reforms is very expensive—expensive in resources, expensive in time, expensive in political capital.[1]

A more promising strategy is to fix the managers—to help them develop the leadership capacity necessary to produce results within the inherently convoluted labyrinth created by our administrative apparati and the multiple contradictions inherent in our political demands. Rather than reformulate the systems of government to conform to some administrative ideal, we ought to help our public managers to function effectively given the restrictions and opportunities created by these systems.

Is this suboptimizing? Perhaps. It is, however, much more realistic. Fixing our political behavior or our administrative apparatus might prove much more productive—if we could, indeed, fix them. Unfortunately this strategy has repeatedly proven inadequate. As citizens we have consciously built into our political and administrative systems important features that implicitly (and often very explicitly) hinder the ability of public managers to produce results. We did this neither whimsically nor perversely. We did it because we wanted these systems to achieve public purposes that we thought more important than merely facilitating the task of public management. We did this because we agreed with the philosopher Karl Popper when he argued that the primary question of political theory is: "How can we organize our political institutions so that bad or incompetent rulers (whom we should try not to get, but whom we so easily might get all the same) cannot do too much damage?"[2]

So, rather than bemoan the crudeness and instability of our political life or the inefficiencies and contortions of our administrative structures, we ought to accept them for what they are—inherent to our human pro-clivities, our political heritage, and our contemporary values. Then we ought to get on with the task of helping public managers function effectively within these constraints.

The Search for a Technical Solution

Government is not particularly efficient. Just ask anyone. Citizens bemoan it. Politicians bemoan it. Public managers bemoan it. The curse word *bureaucracy* is so associated with government that the phrase *government bureaucracy* is considered redundant. What kind of government organization is there other than bureaucracy? What kind of government administration is there other than inefficient? Every citizen can tell a horror story about his, her, or a friend's personal interaction with a public bureaucracy—be that a municipal school, a state drivers' license bureau, or a federal regulatory agency.[3]

Thus we search for administrative reforms or some kind of technical fix that will force public agencies to stop behaving bureaucratically and start improving their performance:

—"If only public agencies would make it easier for good people to learn about and apply for public-service jobs. Then these agencies could be staffed with quality people, not bureaucrats. Thus let's require them to streamline the application procedures and create a formal recruitment process."

—"If only public agencies would measure their performance. Then these agencies could get some clear feedback about how they could improve. Thus let's require them to generate performance measures."

—"If only public agencies would stop reacting to immediate crises and short-term political demands and start focusing on long-term improvement. Then these agencies could produce the outcomes we really want. Thus let's require them to establish a five-year strategic plan."

—"If only public agencies would focus their resources on the activities that really produce results. Then these agencies could deploy their resources most effectively and efficiently. Thus let's require them to use a system of performance budgeting."

—"If only public agencies would pay their employees according to their performance. Then these agencies could motivate all their employees to produce real results (encouraging the high performers to remain in government

and work even harder and smarter, while also prompting the low performers to leave). Thus let's require them to institute pay for performance."

The logic of the technical fix is alluring.

—"If only public agencies would . . . Then these agencies could . . .
Thus let's require them to . . ."

The "if only" diagnosis seems so obvious. The "then" conclusion follows
so smoothly. The "thus" solution appears so rational. If only our public
agencies would function better. Then these agencies could produce the results that we citizens desire. Thus let's require them to function better.

Consequently we are repeatedly reforming our administrative systems.
Yet none of these technical fixes has ever quite lived up to its promise. Nevertheless, this history produces little learning; it fails to deter us from trying again.[4]

Where is the flaw in this impeccable logic?

The Search for a Zero-Abuse, High-Performance Government

At the end of the eighteenth century James Madison and Alexander Hamilton were a team. In 1787 and 1788, sharing the nom de plume of Publius,
Madison wrote twenty-nine and Hamilton fifty of *The Federalist Papers*—
the broadsides that convinced the citizens of New York state, and the new
nation, to replace the diffused authority of the Articles of Confederation
with the more centralized government fashioned by the proposed Constitution. Yet Madison and Hamilton had very different concerns about the
constitutional challenge of establishing the new nation. Madison worried
that the new government would be too strong, that it would have the power
to tyrannize citizens and deny them their human rights. Hamilton worried
that the new government would be too weak, that it would lack the power
to create effective public agencies and foster economic prosperity.[5]

Hamilton did not advocate a government that misused its authority; he
just focused more on performance. Hamilton wanted "energy in the executive." Madison was not indifferent to performance; he just worried more
about the abuse of power. Madison was concerned about "the preservation
of liberty."[6] At the beginning of the twenty-first century our dilemma continues to be that we want our government to be both Madisonian and
Hamiltonian. As citizens we agree with them both.

Still, when it comes to constructing our administrative systems, we are
often forced to choose. More performance? Or less abuse?[7]

Hamilton won our political rhetoric. A staple of American campaign oratory is the promise "to make government more businesslike." We citizens know that our government is often inefficient, and we want our political leaders to fix that. We know that our government is often ineffective, and we want our political leaders to fix that. We know that our government does not perform as well as it might, and we want our political leaders to fix that, too.

Madison, however, won our administrative systems, and not by stealth, either—not by some clever line smuggled into the Constitution. When it comes to the administrative apparatus of government, Madison continues to win, two centuries later. Madison continues to win because we do not like the abuse of power. Madison continues to win because we do not like specific, individual examples of the abuse of power, be that a police officer engaging in racial profiling or a regulatory official arbitrarily denying a permit.[8]

The Search for a Low-Discretion, High-Performance Government

A century after Madison crafted a Constitution to prevent the abuse of government power, the Progressives added another concern: corruption. And again we citizens were receptive. We did not like the corruption of political favoritism and financial kickbacks any more than we liked other abuses of governmental powers.[9] Thus the Progressives won more of our administrative systems. They won because we do not like corruption. And they continue to win because we do not like specific, individual examples of corruption, be that a municipal official soliciting bribes or a state executive hiring a relative.

The Progressives were not opposed to efficiency; they just worried more about corruption of public officials.[10] The dilemma arises because the systems that we deploy to prevent corruption also function (just like the systems that we deploy to thwart the abuse of power) to inhibit performance.[11]

So, whenever a public employee abuses the government's power or engages in some form of corruption, we take it as yet another sign that government is not to be trusted and create yet another rule or regulation—or perhaps another entire administrative system—to prevent this mistake from ever happening again. The objective of this new rule, regulation, or system is inevitably the same: to eliminate the discretion that permitted the original offense. In our zeal to further institutionalize our distrust by controlling official discretion, we tend not to notice that we have added one more administrative constraint to nibble away at the governmental performance that we also cherish. Individually each rule makes perfect sense; collectively they create some unintended but still very real costs.

Unfortunately these costs are often hidden and usually impossible to measure. Not only do the rules frustrate agency performance. The proliferation of rules can also drive out of government those who strive to produce results, and it can deter others from even considering public service.

Thus the history of the administrative structure of American government can be characterized as the slow accretion of rules to prevent the abuse of power and corruption, punctuated by major efforts to rationalize, minimize, or eliminate these rules so as to improve performance. Yet many of the rules remain (and continue to function as a powerful constraint on the performance of public agencies).

Why? Why don't we just get rid of the rules? Because our administrative systems are driven by our political behavior. Because our administrative systems reflect our political values. Because, in the hierarchy of our political values, deterring the abuse of power and preventing corruption are more important than improving performance. In our hierarchy of political values, limiting discretion tops producing results.

And our politicians are not dumb. They behave in ways that we reward. If we demonstrate more concern about the abuse of power and corruption (than about performance), our politicians will notice. And they will respond. Where do you think all those rules and regulations came from? Madison did not sneak them into the Constitution; he simply drafted a Constitution that reflected our early concern about the abuse of power. He simply drafted a Constitution that permitted us—as we saw fresh examples of the abuse of power and new examples of corruption—to add more rules. The plethora of rules reflect our collective concerns. They will not disappear quietly.

Our Political Behavior and the Conundrum of Public Trust

The proliferation of rules to limit discretion reflects our Madisonian distrust of government. Indeed the rules institutionalize our distrust. They reflect not merely our contemporary distrust of government but also our long, deep, historic distrust.[12]

After all, James Madison did not believe in trust. Consequently he created a system designed to ensure that King George III could never again exercise power.[13] The Progressives did not distrust the king (who had not been a serious threat since the British burned Madison's White House in 1814); instead they distrusted democracy—specifically, Jacksonian patronage democracy. They worried about the evils of too much democracy and thus set out to reinvent our administrative systems to ensure that Boss Tweed and Tammany Hall would never again exercise power. The Progressives did not believe in trust either.

Madison and the Progressives did, of course, have reasons for their distrust. Indeed the political leaders and business executives of today seem no more like angels than they did two centuries ago when Madison penned, in *Federalist* No. 51, "If men were angels, no government would be necessary."[14] Unfortunately neither men nor women are angels. Thus we do not trust them. More significantly (for the performance of public agencies at least), our distrust causes us to create numerous mechanisms—both formal (inspectors general) and informal (investigatory journalists)—to act upon this distrust, to constantly deny public officials the discretion that they could use to abuse our trust.[15]

We want to be sure that neither King George nor Boss Tweed can get away with anything again. For, sadly, not only are men and women not angels, they can actually be quite clever at not being angels. Thus, the political descendants of the King and the Boss (and I don't mean Elvis and Springsteen) continuously prove to us that we too should not believe in trust. In response, we create even more aggressive institutions to limit the discretion of those with power—those whom, we know, we should not trust.

All the mechanisms that institutionalize distrust by limiting discretion make the task of improving the performance of government more complicated. These mechanisms for assuaging our distrust may appear to be merely inefficient; they "just" require more paperwork, more approvals, more time. Yet these inefficiencies (about which we, as citizens, do constantly complain) create real waste. Moreover this waste—either in budgetary costs or opportunity costs—lowers a public agency's performance. And sometimes the mechanisms for alleviating our distrust can actually preclude an agency from choosing the most effective means for producing its promised results. And again this climate of distrust can deter conscientious citizens from joining the public service.

The Instability of Political Purpose

Management and leadership require stability. Otherwise what should the executives, who are managing and leading, attempt to accomplish? This year's purpose, last year's purpose, or next year's purpose? If a nation wants the managers of its space agency to land some of its citizens on the moon, the nation cannot turn on this policy one year and turn it off the next.[16] Rather the nation needs to commit itself to this purpose and then be stead- fast. For years!

A democracy, however, cannot guarantee stability in policy. Citizens can change their elected officials and thus change their public policies. Indeed this is why we change legislators and elected executives; citizens vote to replace incumbents with challengers precisely because they want a change in policy. They want government to pursue different results. They seek a different kind of government performance. And even if the incumbents are reelected, they can change their own minds. A basic rule of legislative pro- tocol is that no legislature can bind the next one.

The resulting instability creates a challenge for public managers. For to gain support and effort within their agencies, they are constantly negotiat- ing with subordinates, peers, and superiors: If you produce this, I will get you that.[17] Sometimes they negotiate a formal, legal contract. More often they negotiate an informal agreement, sealing it more with a smile or a nod than with a handshake. Yet a manager's ability to close any such bargain depends upon the ability to make good on his or her part of the deal—to produce sometime in the future that was previously promised. And when the rules change continuously, so do the manager's bargaining resources. Who wants to negotiate with someone whose commitment can be annulled by a third party's decision, particularly when that third party has established a reputation for changing its own mind frequently?[18]

Yet this instability of purpose is inherent to our conception of democ- racy. Over the last half century Americans have made some efforts to increase the stability of our democratically derived policies. For example, only two states (New Hampshire and Vermont) now elect their governors to two-year terms, and only one state (Virginia) limits its governor to one consecutive four-year term. In forty-seven of the fifty states, the governor, once in office, can hold the job for eight straight years with only one inter- vening performance review.

Nevertheless the move toward legislative term limits may well increase the instability of policy, as legislatures lose their institutional memory and oscillate even faster between different policy prescriptions: between decentralized and centralized administration, between direct service delivery and bloc grants, between command-and-control regulation and economic incentives. [19] Yet a public agency's performance may depend less on whether the administrative system for producing results is centralized or decentralized than that the agency administering the program has an opportunity to work within a consistent framework, testing and modifying whatever is chosen. And this process of experimentation, learning, and adaptation (I call it "management by groping along") requires stability of the overall policy framework. [20] "Ironically," writes Rosabeth Moss Kanter, "creating change requires stability." [21]

The Search for a Government That "Works Better & Costs Less"

Over the past decade the two federal efforts at political and administrative reform—the National Performance Review (NPR) of the Clinton administration, and the Freedom to Manage initiative of the Bush administration—have clearly tilted toward Hamilton. Both administrations have sought to improve the performance of government by suppressing the perversity of administrative rules. To "eliminate legal barriers to effective management," the Bush administration proposed the Freedom to Manage Act and the Managerial Flexibility Act. [22] And the slogan of the National Performance Review—"from red tape to results"—explicitly warns that the rules are preventing the federal government from producing results. The systemic fix suggested by this line of reasoning is obvious: contain the excesses of Madisonian protection so as to promote the opportunity for Hamiltonian performance.

Yet as Herbert Kaufman observes: "One person's 'red tape' may be another's treasured procedural safeguard." [23] When we do not like an administrative process, we denounce it as "oppressive regulation"; when we like it, we extol it as "due process."

Thus neither the National Performance Review nor the Freedom to Manage initiative have sought the wholesale abandonment of entire systems of administrative rules. Instead both combine a formal modification of some rules with a heavy emphasis on creating an organizational culture that stresses results rather than rules. For eight years Vice President Al Gore strove to convince federal civil servants that satisfying the requirements of the red tape is not enough—that every agency ought also to focus on producing results.

Indeed without such continual attention to institutionalizing a government-wide emphasis on performance (without a visible, dogged, high-level effort to change the organizational culture of the federal government), any effort to fix the administrative systems will have little impact. After all, it is much easier for a civil servant to follow the rules, and safer too. Following the rules may occasionally make civil servants look silly, but it will not get them fired or indicted.

The Temptation to Promise Lower Costs
Rather Than Better Performance

Administratively the National Performance Review was about better results; politically, however, it was about lower costs.[24] In the summer of 1993, when the Clinton administration was preparing the first NPR report and was simultaneously negotiating with Congress over the federal budget, the White House decided to link the two: The NPR would become Clinton's budget-cutting symbol. To federal civil servants the vice president may have been selling the NPR as a way to produce more and better results. But to the citizenry the president was selling the NPR as a way to have less government.[25]

In January 1994, when President Clinton delivered his first State of the Union address, he devoted only one paragraph to the National Performance Review: "Led by the vice president, we launched a campaign to reinvent government. We cut staff, cut perks, even trimmed the fleet of federal limousines. After years of leaders whose rhetoric attacked bureaucracy but whose actions expanded it, we will actually reduce it by 252,000 people over the next five years. By the time we have finished, the federal bureaucracy will be at its lowest point in thirty years."[26] Does improving government performance mean nothing more than cutting costs and people?

The NPR was designed to create a government that both "works better & costs less."[27] But when explaining to citizens what it was attempting to accomplish, the Clinton administration focused on the "costs less." The "works better" was a mere secondary consideration.

This tilt reflected both political and practical realities. After all, we can easily measure whether government costs less. We can measure it statistically, by counting up the various departments' expenditures. And we can measure it personally, by looking at our tax bill. In contrast, it is much more difficult to determine whether government actually works better. After all, what working better means to you might mean working worse to me. Still, regardless of how good or bad government works, we all want government to do this working at less cost.

What should any administration—past, present, or future—do? Should it attempt to create a government that produces better results? Or should it focus on ensuring that government costs less? And how should it explain its efforts to citizens? Should it carefully clarify how it has created a government that tastes great? Or should it simply cite some figures to document that it has become less filling?[28]

The Reality of What Is Most Fixable

What should we do? What steps should we take to improve the public service in federal, state, and local government? What would be our most effective strategy? What is wrong with trying to implement a few widely applauded management reforms? If we could swear off the costs-less rhetoric, why not adopt some of the technical fixes? Indeed, where is the flaw in the technical fix?

The logic of the technical fix is indeed alluring. Unfortunately this logic leaves out the humans. It leaves out the people who will implement the technical fix. It ignores how people have responded to previous technical fixes. It ignores the predictable ways in which the people in public agencies will respond to yet another technical fix.

The logic of the technical fix assumes that it can be imposed from above. The logic of each technical fix is that this potent instrument requires no subtlety in implementation. The logic of each technical fix assumes that the new administrative system is self-executing: You hit the start icon, and the program runs flawlessly. And yes, the technical-fix program will run. But the execution will be done by the hoop jumpers, and thus (although it may appear to run flawlessly) it may not run as intended.

The logic of the technical fix implicitly (yet unquestionably) assumes that no managerial talent is required to administer the new system. Either (1) the agency managers already possess the managerial and leadership capacity to take advantage of the benefits of the new technical system, (2) the skills required are so minimal that it is not difficult to identify a large number of employees who possess them and to give them the task of merely administering the new system, or (3) making the new system work requires absolutely no talent.

Nevertheless, despite the bluntness of traditional technical fixes, we do possess a variety of ideas about how to manage large organizations. Some of these ideas do concern systems—for example, how to create financial systems to insure that the allocated funds are, indeed, spent for their intended purposes and also to prevent, deter, and catch theft. Some of these ideas concern organizations—for example, how to streamline organizational structures to delegate authority to the lowest reasonable levels, to minimize middle-level overseers, and to enhance the applicability of local implementation.

Of course even these systems do not always work perfectly. In part this is because the people who work in these organizations are not angels. Whether the organization is public or private, the nonangels within can figure out, for example, how to evade the strictures of the financial system. In addition, even angels can make mistakes. Thus the General Accounting Office can report, year after year, that the federal government makes improper financial payments totaling billions of dollars.[29]

Sometimes, however, government finds it impossible to employ something even close to a well-established organizational principle. For example, we know a lot about the disadvantages of large bureaucracies and the advantages of lean organizations with few layers and delegated authority for both decisionmaking and implementation.[30] Yet, because public officials at all levels distrust their subordinates, they are unwilling to delegate authority. Thus government agencies are hardly lean machines. Instead they are heavy with staff—people with the responsibility for checking up on whether subordinates have made the right decisions, people with the responsibility for making decisions that could and should be made by subordinates, people with the responsibility for ensuring that subordinates have faithfully implemented blunt decisions that the subordinates could have crafted with more subtlety.[31]

We do have a variety of Hamiltonian ideas for improving the performance of government. We just possess too many Madisonian worries to be willing to really implement a large number of them.

So what should we do? Should we conclude that political and administrative constraints make it nearly impossible to improve the performance of public agencies? Such an inference seems defeatist, particularly when numerous public managers have proven otherwise.[32] Can we not learn anything from how these people survived and thrived? Can we not learn anything from how these real, human, public executives improved performance and produced results?[33] After all, they braved the same administrative and political impediments that confront any public manager. Each manager encounters a unique collection of formal administrative restrictions and informal political restraints; yet most effective leaders have overcome political and administrative obstacles that were no less oppressive than those faced by their underperforming colleagues. Can we not learn from these successes?[34]

A fundamental management principle is: Do the doable first. Before you tackle the complicated problems, solve the simple ones. In this case, the easiest thing to fix is the leadership and managerial capacity of our public managers, not the administrative apparatus of government, not the human propensities of our politics.[35] We would do best to focus on improving the capabilities and strategies of public executives, the people upon whom we citizens depend to manage the organizations that will produce the results we value. We would do best to focus on improving the ability of public executives to function effectively within the limitations and constraints imposed by the administrative apparatus and political vagaries of government. Admittedly the easiest thing to fix is not particularly easy; otherwise many more public managers would be doing an excellent job. Fixing the managers looks easy only on a relative scale.

Expanding Public Managers' Professional Repertoire

All professionals—from chess players to thermodynamic engineers, from emergency-room doctors to baseball managers—have a professional repertoire.[36] Indeed cognitive psychologists estimate that it takes about ten years to accumulate the roughly 50,000 moves that are essential to be an effective professional. When faced with a specific challenge—a decision, dilemma, problem, question, issue—an effective professional searches through a large repertoire stored in long-term memory, identifies similar circumstances, classifies and evaluates the choices made in these similar circumstances, and, from this set of relevant moves in the repertoire, matches, mixes, selects, and adapts an approach for the immediate challenge. The larger and more robust this professional's repertoire, the better catalogued the items in the repertoire, and the more explicit and accurate the cause-and-effect analytics imbedded in that repertoire, the better chance he or she has of crafting an intelligent and effective response.

Unfortunately these professionals work in what the late Herbert Simon labeled a "semantically rich domain"—circumstances "in which successful performance calls for specific knowledge as well as general problem-solving skill."[37] That is, chess players, thermodynamic engineers, emergency-room doctors, and baseball managers all need general problem-solving skills.[38]

In addition these professionals need detailed knowledge of their field. Baseball managers need to know a lot about the various combinations and permutations that can occur on the diamond (and in the clubhouse). Emergency-room physicians need specific knowledge about the many combinations and permutations of people and families that can come through the emergency-room door. These professions are so challenging because the number of possible combinations and permutations is very large indeed. To become an effective professional, a neophyte needs to build a repertoire containing a large and diverse set of moves so that he or she can respond intelligently to a large and diverse set of circumstances.

Thus it takes years to master a profession, to build a professional repertoire. Some items in that repertoire can be obtained through reading and formal study. Some items in that repertoire can be obtained through personal observation and practice. But the most resilient, the most robust, the most responsive repertoires are obtained through both intensive, analytic education and extensive, day-to-day practice. The frequent practice provides the diversity of experiences; the reflective analysis provides the theoretical linkages between cause and effect.

Well-managed business firms recognize this. To develop their future leadership cadre, these firms do two things. First, to ensure that their executives have a diversity of experiences, they assign them to a series of differing jobs with increasingly diverse and demanding responsibilities. Second, to ensure that they develop a sophisticated ability to identify and analyze different cause-and-effect theories, these firms provide their managers with a variety of educational experiences—from personal mentors to professional education. Then these firms expect each of their developing managers to evolve his or her own professional repertoire. Further these firms promote their managers based on the effectiveness and growth of their professional repertoires.

No professional ever possesses a repertoire that is complete or perfect. No professional has ever experienced (or even heard about) every possible combination and permutation in the field. Moreover the cause-and-effect theories that the professional has been taught formally or has evolved informally may be dependable enough in many frequently experienced situations but fail to hold in new circumstances.

No wonder different professionals in the same field—different baseball managers or different emergency room physicians—can make different choices when faced with precisely the same set of circumstances.[39] Nevertheless the deeper and broader a professional's repertoire, the more diverse and sophisticated will be the options from which the professional can craft an approach, the more likely this professional is to develop a strategy that is roughly on target, and the more likely he or she will be able to recognize some deviance from the predicted consequences and to make appropriate adjustments.

The Nature of the Public Manager's Repertoire

Public managers also possess professional repertoires.[40] They try things, see what works and what does not, and attempt to derive cause-and-effect lessons from these experiences. Too often, however, public managers are given little opportunity to obtain a broad and diverse range of experiences from which to evolve a robust repertoire. And they are given little opportunity to add items to their professional repertoire—or to develop explicit theories about cause-and-effect linkages—through formal study or even through deliberate mentoring. Mostly public managers develop their professional repertoires on the job.

Why do you think that many public managers are so risk averse? After all, risk aversion is not taught in graduate school, at the Federal Executive Institute, or in public management textbooks. Yet most public managers are assiduous rule followers. They meticulously adhere to the large number of rules imposed by legislatures and overhead agencies, even when such actions clearly undermine the agency's ability to achieve its mission.

Public managers added this move to their managerial repertoire from experience—perhaps through a personally painful experience, perhaps by watching the tragic experience of a colleague. When a manager bends a rule and, in the process, furthers the agency's mission, nothing much happens. At least nothing much happens because this manager furthered the mission. But if someone learns that the manager bent one of the rules, and if that someone decides to discipline the manager for doing so, that manager—and every other public servant who witnesses the punishment—will have the risk-aversion component of his or her repertoire reinforced. You do not have to spend years in the public service to add to your professional repertoire a very common cause-and-effect relationship: "If you violate a rule, someone will punish you."

Another key component of any public manager's professional repertoire is hoop jumping.[41] It is one of the bureaucratic skills that each had to master to get promoted to manage a public agency (or a division, bureau, or unit within an agency). Public managers can quickly recognize an administrative hoop and just as quickly figure out how to jump through it harmlessly:

—"Does the elected chief executive or an authorizing committee want performance measures? We'll give 'em performance measures—the more the better."

—"Does the budget office or the appropriations committee want performance measures in the budget? We'll put 'em in the budget. How many do they need? We'll give 'em twice that many."

—"Does someone want us to develop a five-year strategic plan? Fine. Let's find a strategic plan from last year that everyone liked and copy it. Even better, let's contract out the task to the same firm that produced last year's highest-rated plan."[42]

Because public managers have so many bosses—because so many elected officials, overhead regulators, and outside stakeholders think they are authorized to tell an agency manager what to do—most public managers become adept at simultaneously jumping through multiple hoops.

Dexterous hoop jumping and assiduous rule following are two key items in any public manager's professional repertoire: Follow meticulously all the rules, even the ones that get in the way of the agency's mission. Jump through all the hoops devised by various bosses, overseers, and stakeholders, though try not to let such activities absorb too much time or too many resources.

Building the Public Manager's Capacity for Leadership

Still, we do understand some concepts that can help public managers to actually be effective—some principles of leadership and management (other than risk aversion and hoop jumping) that they can employ to improve the performance of their agencies. These are not scientific formulas that when applied accurately produce precisely predictable results. Public management is not even an inexact science.[43] A public manager's professional repertoire is very difficult to codify, if only because the variables that the manager must take into account when scanning this repertoire for likely similarities are so diverse, so ill defined, so illusive.[44]

Nevertheless, every public manager, like every professional in any field, possesses a large repertoire of skills and strategies. Over years of practice, each public manager has built up his or her repertoire, sometimes consciously, sometimes unconsciously. Few may be able to explain the distinct items in their repertoire, even though they use them frequently. Nevertheless the professionals with the broadest, the deepest, and the most analytical repertoire will be the most effective; they will possess the capacity to respond most competently and creatively to a very diverse set of challenges.[45]

Thus, to fix public management, we ought to take three explicit, conscious steps to expand the capacity of the individuals who lead (and will lead) our public agencies:

—We ought to rotate public managers through a wide variety of assignments to give them the broadest possible set of experiences from which to develop a robust professional repertoire.[46]

—We ought to create a wide variety of formal learning opportunities to give public executives the chance to test and expand the cause-and-effect lessons in their repertoire and to develop a more sophisticated appreciation for the conditions under which these theoretical linkages do and do not hold.

—We ought to establish explicit mentoring relationships within every public agency (and even across agencies) to create the implicit expectation that one of the responsibilities of any public manager is to mentor subordinates.[47]

Each of these three steps is designed to broaden and deepen every public manager's professional repertoire by providing them more diverse experiences and by helping them to codify explicit cause-and-effect lessons.

Codifying Cause-and-Effect Linkages

To facilitate the ability of public managers to develop their professional repertoires—to develop analytical repertoires complete with cause-and-effect linkages—we need to provide them with some guidance. The leaders of public agencies need to understand better what contributes to high performance. They need to know when particular moves prove effective, and they need to know why. We are able to give them some guidance, but we should improve our ability to provide even more. We ought to be more systematic in identifying key components of any effective public manager's repertoire: What works, when, and why?

This is not, however, a search for the one best way. For there is no one best way. For example, many major league baseball players have rejected Ted Williams's extremely successful (and quite analytical) batting strategy, adopted one with which they were more comfortable, and been very productive.[48] Rather it is an effort to identify different strategies of public management that can work for different people in different situations, or for the same people in different situations, or even for different people in the same situation. It is a search for a variety of management strategies, tactics, concepts, and principles from which a public manager can craft a personal leadership repertoire.

Unfortunately such principles are often expressed in what Herbert Simon called "proverbs": simple rules of thumb (like, "Look before you leap") that many public managers have found helpful. Unfortunately there usually exists a competing proverb (like, "He who hesitates is lost") that other public managers have found useful. Thus these competing proverbs cancel each other.[49]

Of course, every one of these proverbs comes with some validity. None is always true. Still, none is always false. Each is valid, but in its own set of circumstances, where the number of dimensions required to specify those circumstances is very large indeed. And thus, as universally applicable rules of thumb, they have little value. They do not provide global guidance. Yes, they do apply in specific circumstances. But what, precisely, are those circumstances? When, exactly, should you look before you leap? And when, exactly, will you be lost if you hesitate? Rules of thumb do not answer this central operational question.

Codifying the circumstances under which one proverb is valid and another is not can be tedious, but it is possible. After all, our computational power continues to grow according to Moore's Law, doubling every twelve to eighteen months; thus, if we do not have the computer power today, we ought to have it in a few years or a few decades. Still, such a computer program would not be very practical. It would simply take too long to input all the necessary circumstances.[50]

A more fruitful approach would be to explain why each item does (or might) work. What is the repertoire item? What might it accomplish? And what is the causal connection between the repertoire item and its achievement? If public managers understood the if-then, cause-and-effect relationship, they would be in a better position to decide whether this move will produce the desired result in a new circumstance.

Still, to comprehend the theory of any such causal relationship, a public manager needs to see it in action. The if-then connection makes no more sense in the abstract than does a proverb. Thus these theoretical relationships can be explained only through detailed examples. Such cases need not only to provide descriptions of public management successes and failures; they also have to offer theories about why: Why did this move by the manager produce this response by employees, supervisors, peers, legislators, stakeholders, or citizens?

Managers who understand the cause-and-effect connections for the various moves in their repertoire will be much more capable of selecting the moves most appropriate to the unique circumstances that they will face.

Articulating a Mission, Managing Symbols, and Setting Performance Targets

What moves do public executives need to improve the performance of their agencies? Lots of moves, of course. Still, some are more important than others. Some have more significant cause-and-effect linkages than others. Here I will outline just three. The leaders of public agencies who have these three moves in their managerial repertoire and who use them—not necessarily brilliantly or exceptionally, just competently—can improve the performance of their agencies significantly.

First, effective leaders create a mission for their agency. Why? What is the cause-and-effect connection? A mission establishes an agency's moral imperative. It tells multiple audiences why the agency exists—what it will accomplish, what it will do to help improve the lives of citizens. To the people who work in the agency, it signals what activities are most important. To the people who are thinking about working for the agency, the mission signals why they might (or might not) want to do so. To superiors, legislators, stakeholders, and citizens, it signals what value the agency will contribute to society. The mission is one (but not the only) mechanism for recruiting resources. Nevertheless, the better the mission—the better it reflects (or leads) the aspirations of employees, potential applicants, superiors, legislators, stakeholders, and citizens—the more resources the leaders will be able to mobilize.

This mission is first expressed in words. But these words must be reinforced by symbols. Unless the agency's leaders demonstrate their personal commitment to their own words through their own deeds, no one will pay any attention. Indeed public service employees (just like their private sector equivalents) will automatically assume that the words are just that — just words. They will ignore them. They will not contemplate and then dismiss them; they will dismiss them from the beginning. Thus the second move that an effective leader must master is to reinforce the words of a mission with symbols dramatizing his or her commitment to the mission.

The most visible symbol is time. How does the manager spend his or her time? Does the parks commissioner trumpet a bold agenda for cleaning up the city's parks but spend little time developing and evaluating alternative strategies for keeping them clean? Does the public safety secretary proclaim a new program to reduce highway fatalities but have no idea how many people were killed on the state's highways last week, last month, or last quarter? People are observant. They will get the message—not the message expounded in a mission statement but the message inherent in the manager's daily schedule and personal knowledge. If the leadership team spends time pursuing the agency's mission, the rest of the employees will, too.

The second, most visible symbol is reflected in rewards. What kind of behavior is rewarded? I do not mean who gets the performance bonus or the merit raise. I do mean who is publicly recognized for what accomplishment. Did the public safety secretary visit a state troopers' barracks to publicly praise its commander for implementing an innovative and effective strategy for driving down the district's traffic deaths? Did the parks commissioner have a pizza party for the dedicated team that kept its park free of litter?

Again, the cause-and-effect linkage ought to be clear (though the behavior of many public managers would suggest that it is not). People will work to achieve results that are appreciated, not because they want or need the material reward, but because they crave the recognition that the reward provides.

What, however, should the public manager reward? How will the leader of a public agency know if a unit within the agency has accomplished anything significant? The answer is the third move in a performance-management repertoire: Set specific performance targets for these units to achieve.

What is the theoretical linkage here? Why, in addition to articulating a mission and managing symbols, does a public manager need to set performance targets? What is the cause-and-effect connection between performance targets and improved performance? Because neither the agency's leadership nor its frontline employees can use the mission statement to determine if they have done a good job this year. The performance target provides the short-term, operational definition of success. The mission statement is aspiring and transcendent; a performance target is concrete and doable. And the causal linkage psychologically potent: Give people a challenge, and the operational capacity to meet that challenge, and many people will pursue it, if only because it is there.

The causal linkage of this small, three-move subpackage of performance management is even more potent: Give people an important societal mission, a significant but attainable target, and reward them with recognition when they achieve the target, and you will motivate people to pursue both the mission and the target energetically, seriously, and innovatively.

Why should public managers be willing to believe that these causal linkages hold? Because we have seen them work repeatedly and in a wide variety of circumstances. And because what we have learned from the social sciences about human motivation supports this linkage.

Yet these moves, and the causal reasons why they work, come alive only through detailed examples. Indeed practicing managers will think about experimenting with such moves (and, if they appear to work, will add them to their repertoire) only if given a compelling example—or, even better, several compelling examples—that illustrate how the move can work in different circumstances. Moreover these examples need to not only describe the managers' moves and what happened next; they must also contain enough detail to permit people to infer (based on this example plus previous experience) their own causal linkages about why a particular move produced a particular result in a particular circumstance. Such examples, such stories or cases, make the move come alive, demonstrating that the move can work and suggesting why. These examples provide the raw material from which practicing public managers can learn lessons and ground their own management repertoire.[51]

The Illusion of Charismatic Heroes

Too often, unfortunately, the search for examples that reveal practical, replicable lessons produces only an unbelievable fairy tale, as relevant to the real world of public management as the "lessons" from managing a fantasy baseball team are to the challenge of managing a real baseball team (even in Little League let alone the majors). And at the center of this public sector fairy tale is the public manager as charismatic hero.

Indeed, every time we seek to offer potential cause-and-effect theories through the story about the trials, failures, and successes of a specific public manager, we automatically create a superstar myth—we transform a real human into a charismatic hero. We all assume that if this manager was worth using as an example, he or she must have some heroic qualities. If a public agency's leadership team is worth chronicling in an article, book, or teaching case, this group must have been something special or have done something heroic. Unfortunately this chronicle necessarily leaves out most of the messy details—the false starts, poor decisions, and disastrous mistakes. Instead the riveting story reveals how a public agency's gifted leader, or a leadership team with perfectly complementing talents, has, through unmatched intellectual brilliance and incomparable personal presence, accomplished miracles.

In reality, of course, any significant improvement in a public agency's performance does not result strictly from the personal strengths of a single individual whose astute decisions and timely actions (and perhaps a little perseverance) turn around the entire staff's individual and collective performance. More likely it evolves from what Karl Weick has called "a series of small wins." And even these small wins do not come "in a neat, linear, serial form." Rather, such wins are "fragmentary," "driven by opportunism and dynamically changing situations," and they are apt to be "scattered and cohere only in the sense that they move in the same general direction."[52]

If the chronicle of the success is to be worth reading, however, it must be neat, linear, truly coherent, and usually concise. Indeed, as Weick observes, "a series of small wins can be gathered into a retrospective summary that imputes a consistent line of development." And because this is necessarily a summary, it must leave out many of the messy details. Nevertheless, Weick continues, "this post hoc construction should not be mistaken for orderly implementation."[53]

Still, whenever we read a beautifully crafted "post hoc construction" of a public management success, we all make the same mistake. We fail to draw on our own experiences. We fail to read between the lines. We fail to extract from this neat, linear, coherent, concise saga our own sense of how chaotic the whole episode must have been. Instead, we accept that the author has judged this story to be worth retelling precisely because it is different from anything that we have ever experienced. This must be the story of a dazzling, charismatic superhero who managed through brilliant strategy, clever tactics, decisive action, and force of personality to tame the public bureaucracy dragon.

Thus we promote yet another real (if creative, resourceful, and certainly dedicated) mortal into the pantheon of charismatic but unreal heroes. And then we each implicitly take the next logical step: I cannot possibly be like him, her, or them.[54]

Suppose this implicit reasoning is correct. Suppose most mortal managers (when faced with the standard surplus of administrative and political constraints) are simply unable to improve a public agency's performance. Suppose public service leaders are born, not made. Then, to improve the public service, we would need to identify and recruit the few superheroes. Then the task of improving the performance of public agencies in the twenty-first century would be the task of finding people with charismatic leadership skills wired into their DNA. Then the challenge would be to develop mechanisms for identifying and for attracting to public service those rare individuals who possess the precise combination of innate smarts, instinctive savvy, and natural charm necessary to command the loyalty and dedication of public employees and, thus, to convert lethargic bureaucracies into high-performance machines.

If we believe that leadership comes purely from natural talents, we ought to search diligently for people with these innate skills (and for ways to attract them to public service). If, however, we accept that the professional repertoire required to lead public agencies to accomplish public purposes is neither enigmatic nor inherited but can be acquired by normal people, then we ought to concentrate on helping public managers, and public managers in training, to develop their own repertoires.

Moreover, if leadership skills can indeed be acquired, the purpose of identifying and describing examples of effective public management is not to glorify a few mythical public management gods whom no reasonable person would ever take as a role model. Rather the challenge is to use such examples to define and codify lessons that can be incorporated into managerial repertoires, to illustrate cause-and-effect relationships that are widely applicable, and to specify the circumstances under which such cause-and-effect relationships hold.

Expanding Every Public Manager's Repertoire

No technical fix obligates public managers to take seriously the necessity of establishing performance targets. The legislature or the elected chief executive can of course require agency managers at all levels to do so. But they cannot force them to set significant targets that challenge and stretch the agency's employees. The legislature or the chief executive can require every agency manager to jump through the performance-target hoop (just as they can require these managers to jump through the performance-budgeting hoop, or the strategic-planning hoop, or the pay-for-performance hoop).[55] And these agency managers will perform the requisite hoop jumping. And while they do this, they will subvert the hopes that the elected officials or overhead regulators had when they constructed their new, improved hoop.

Moreover, in requiring strict, inflexible, across-the-board implementation, the legislature or overhead body can actually subvert the strategic purpose of the technical fix. First, because the technical fix is imposed from above, with little explanation, training, or support, it is often implemented badly. Second, the inflexible requirements of the technical fix inhibit the ability of thoughtful managers to use it discerningly and subtly—to adapt the general concept to the unique needs of their agency. Third, this mindless, artless (and thus inevitably flawed) implementation undermines the credibility of the concept itself. "See," the critics and the cynics will observe, "it doesn't work."

The three core tasks of performance management are not all that effective public managers do. Articulating a mission, managing symbols, and setting performance targets are not the three simple steps that will transform the performance of our public service. They are necessary but not sufficient. Indeed, with a professional repertoire of 50,000 moves, public managers obviously need to be able to do a large number and variety of other things. They have to monitor progress, create organizational capacity, reward success, and check to ensure that, as the agency achieves its performance targets, it is also helping to realize its mission.[56] They have to know how to do these things under a wide variety of circumstances. They need a large leadership repertoire. They have to know how to deal with the goof-off employee, the insufferable legislator, and the harassing journalist. And in the process of deploying their repertoire, they have to understand the underlying theoretical linkages so they can be creative in crafting each move to match the unique circumstances of their organization and its political environment. Abstractly these tasks seem simple. But implementing any of them analytically, discerningly, and subtly is a significant challenge.

Indeed, performance management is not easy. There exist a variety of psychological barriers that keep public managers from doing the various tasks (particularly setting explicit performance targets).[57] It is not that we lack some understanding of what it takes to drive the performance of public agencies. Rather it is that those strategies require a lot of adaptation, a dollop of creativity, a measure of self-confidence, and a little chutzpah. And there is no technical fix to our administrative or political systems that will make public executives more analytical, more creative, more self-confident, or more daring. Public managers only acquire these qualities as they expand and evolve their own repertoire.

Preparing Public Managers for the Twenty-First Century

Different people are born with different aptitudes, and, by the time they are adults, they have acquired different skills. But through effective teaching, dedicated study, and hard work, any professional can improve his or her skills. Not everyone can hit like Ted Williams, but all baseball players (young and old) can learn to be better hitters—or at least every reasonably dedicated player can. Similarly all dedicated public managers can increase their managerial batting average.

Moreover, in helping every public manager improve his or her own management repertoire, we are trying to do precisely that: We are trying to improve every manager—every cabinet secretary and every frontline supervisor. Our objective is not to create a few public management stars—a few Michael Jordans of public management who soar high above everyone else, winning performance championships in a single bound. Rather our objective is to ratchet up every public manager a notch or two. If we could do that, if we could improve every public manager's repertoire, we would achieve much more than if we created even a dozen superstars.

We need more than a few outstanding public managers; we need to improve every public manager. In its minor league operations, a major league baseball team does not concentrate its teaching on only a few hand-picked potential superstars. It tries to ratchet up the quality of every player in its organization. It knows that only by teaching, coaching, and improving all the players throughout its system—by playing thousands of games, each of which creates its own unique collection of circumstances—can it produce a successful major league team.[58] Similarly, if we are serious about improving public management, we have to be serious about educating all public managers.

Unfortunately, despite our political rhetoric about making government more businesslike, we have rarely been willing to establish in government the kind of personnel development and training programs that are standard in business (and in baseball). If we truly want better public managers, we will have to do what business does (and what Branch Rickey did when he invented baseball's farm system)[59]—invest in developing our future leaders. A business that seeks to have competent leaders available to manage its divisions in the future recognizes and accepts the environment within which these managers must function and then makes a major investment in helping their managers learn how to be effective in that environment. The public sector needs to do the same. Instead, however, we seek simple, self-executing technical fixes while neglecting the need to enhance the capacity of public managers to lead their agencies.

This is not a heroic search for superstars nor a defeatist acceptance of the suboptimal. It is simply the best way to prepare many people to lead the future public service, to prepare public managers for the demands of leading public agencies. For the twenty-first century the challenge of public management is to produce the results that citizens value.

This does not mean removing the formal administrative constraints and informal political restraints that inhibit better performance. Yes, it might be helpful if some of these were lessened. And indeed we may see a slight swing of the Madisonian-Hamiltonian pendulum from near the Madisonian apogee to something closer (at least) to the perigee. And yes, it would certainly be helpful if someone would discover a clever technical fix that would permit us to fully satisfy both our Madisonian and Hamiltonian desires (though I do not think we should devote many resources to this search).

Until then, however, we ought not to despair. Rather we ought to exploit what we have already learned about how to improve the performance of public agencies. We ought to make sure that public executives have a broad repertoire—that they recognize the potency of (among other things) articulating a mission, managing symbols, and establishing performance targets. We ought to give every public manager the opportunity to expand his or her professional repertoire. If we do, maybe our public service will be able to meet the challenges of the twenty-first century.

Notes

1. In 1977 and 1978, the Carter administration devoted a lot of resources—particularly the energies and intelligence of some of the most talented people it recruited to public service—to reorganizing the federal government. Yet, are our nation's youth really better educated today because the Carter administration created (out of the old Department of Health, Education, and Welfare) a new Department of Education?

2. Karl R. Popper, *Conjectures and Refutations: The Growth of Scientific Knowledge* (Basic Books, 1962), p. 25.

3. One study found that 15 percent of citizens surveyed had encountered "difficulties" or "problems" with four different "control agencies" concerning taxes, drivers' and vehicle licenses, traffic violations, and police interference. It further found that, of those who sought one of seven different kinds of government services (from job training to welfare to retirement), about an eighth were "very dissatisfied" and another eighth were "somewhat dissatisfied" with how the agency handled the problem. Twenty-two percent of these people rated their solution "unfavorable," and an eighth thought they were treated "unfairly." Ten percent thought that the office with which they dealt was "very inefficient." Daniel Katz and others, *Bureaucratic Encounters: A Pilot Study in the Evaluation of Government Services* (Survey Research Center, Institute for Social Research, University of Michigan, 1975), pp. 23, 64, 65, 69, 68. These data hardly suggest that every individual citizen can tell a horror story about his or her personal interaction with government. But they do suggest, given the number of acquaintances that each of us has, that we all know some who can.

4. Sometimes the technical fix is not something that we require every public agency to do but something that we do to every public agency.—"If only public agencies would have their performance publicly graded. Then these agencies would be publicly embarrassed by their grades and, as a result, motivated to improve their performance. Thus let's grade all public agencies." Like all the technical fixes, however, the grade-the-agencies fix does nothing to improve the capacity of the agencies' managers to respond to this very public kind of "negative psychological KITA" (as Frederick Herzberg called it in "One More Time: How Do You Motivate Employees?" *Harvard Business Review*, vol. 46, no. 1 [January–February 1968], p. 54).

5. In *The Federalist Papers,* Hamilton took on the major responsibility for explaining why, under the existing Articles of Confederation, the government was too weak, while Madison accepted the task of explaining why, under the new Constitution, the government would not be too strong. Jay wrote the other six, which focused on defense and international relations. See Alexander Hamilton, James Madison, and John Jay, *The Federalist Papers,* edited by Garry Wills (Bantam Books, 1982).

6. Hamilton in *Federalist* No. 70, Madison in *Federalist* No. 51, in Hamilton, Madison, and Jay, *Federalist Papers,* pp. 355, 261.

7. Elsewhere I call this the "accountability dilemma." To the extent that we employ rules to prevent the abuse of power (to ensure that public officials are accountable for the handling

of public finances and for treating all people fairly), we can hinder government's performance. At the same time, I argue, if we are willing to rethink the nature of democratic accountability and the processes by which we create it, we might be able to eliminate, or at least mitigate, this tradeoff. This would not be, however, a technical fix. Rather it requires an intellectual metamorphosis, a fundamental rethinking of our approach to government. See Robert D. Behn, *Rethinking Democratic Accountability* (Brookings, 2001), pp. 10–12, 120–40.

8. Madison's winning streak is the envy not just of the Boston Red Sox but even of Red Auerbach's Boston Celtics.

9. I distinguish between the abuse of power that troubled Madison and the corruption that worried the Progressives. Both can occur because, when public officials do their job, they have to exercise discretion. The Progressives' corruption occurs when a public official exercises this discretion for personal benefit. Madison's abuse of power occurs when a public official exercises this discretion so as to deny a citizen his or her liberty or other constitutional right. Robert D. Behn, "Government Performance and the Conundrum of Public Trust," in John D. Donahue and Joseph S. Nye Jr., eds., *Market-Based Governance: Supply Side, Demand Side, Upside, and Downside* (Brookings, 2002), pp. 323–48.

10. Actually the Progressives believed that their administrative reforms would improve efficiency. See, for example, Woodrow Wilson, "The Study of Administration," *Political Science Quarterly,* vol. 2, no. 2 (1887), pp. 197–222; Frank Goodnow, *Politics and Administration: A Study in Government* (Russell & Russell, 1900).

11. There may be systems that are effective in preventing the abuse of government power and also do not reduce efficiency. Unfortunately we do not appear to have discovered many such systems.

12. For a discussion of the historical relationship between the abuse of government authority, the corruption of public officials, discretion, and trust, see Behn, "Government Performance."

13. Both Massachusetts and New Hampshire still have an elected Governor's Council, a body originally designed to watch out for the misdeeds of the king's governor.

14. Hamilton, Madison, and Jay, *Federalist Papers,* p. 262.

15. For a discussion of the link between trust and discretion, see Behn, *Rethinking Democratic Accountability,* pp. 81–102.

16. Of course this constancy of purpose was not the only advantage that NASA possessed during the 1960s as it sought to land a man on the moon. It had very few stakeholder groups who believed they had the right and obligation to tell the agency how to do this. As one wag observed, no one cared where on the moon this man would land.

17. For example, at the Massachusetts Department of Public Welfare, Commissioner Charles M. Atkins created an "implicit contract" with his staff. If the department's employees would get the error rate down and the employment rate up, Atkins would get them higher job classifications, lower caseloads, and better offices. Robert D. Behn, *Leadership Counts: Lessons for Public Managers* (Harvard University Press, 1991), pp. 63–64.

18. This explains why the Department of State prefers to negotiate with a dictatorship and why nations dislike signing treaties with the United States, which has a Constitution requiring all treaties to be ratified by another, cantankerous group, the Senate.

19. The term limitation movement has also reduced the ability of governors to succeed themselves. But all such recent term limits have permitted governors to serve at least two successive four-year terms.

20. Robert D. Behn, "Management by Groping Along," *Journal of Policy Analysis and Management,* vol. 7, no. 4 (Fall 1988), pp. 643–63; Behn, *Leadership Counts,* chap. 7.

21. Rosabeth Moss Kanter, "When a Thousand Flowers Bloom: Structural, Collective, and Social Conditions for Innovation in Organizations," *Organizational Behavior,* vol. 10 (1988), p. 195.

22. Office of Management and Budget, "President Bush Proposes Legislation to Improve Management of Federal Agencies," Press Release 2001-47, October 15, 2001, p. 1.

23. Herbert Kaufman, *Red Tape: Its Origins, Uses, and Abuses* (Brookings, 1977), p. 4.

24. For example, the 1995 NPR report emphasizes these savings: "$58 billion of NPR's $108 billion in savings proposed in 1993 are already locked in." Al Gore, *Common Sense Government: Works Better & Costs Less* (Government Printing Office, 1995), p. 3.

25. Do we now have less government? We do have fewer federal employees. In 1996, reports Paul Light, federal civilian employment was 1.9 million, down by nearly 400,000 (or more than 15 percent) from its high in 1968. But Light calls this an "illusion of smallness," for he observes that there are three other kinds of workers who help do the federal government's business: people employed by organizations with federal contracts, people employed by organizations with federal grants, and people employed in state and local governments who do work mandated by the federal government. And in 1996, estimates Light, these three employers accounted for 12.7 million full-time job equivalents. See Paul C. Light, *The True Size of Government* (Brookings, 1999), p. 1. The analytical methods employed to produce Light's estimates have been critiqued. Nevertheless the general point still holds: Counting the people who receive a paycheck directly from the federal government does not produce an accurate picture of the number of people doing the federal government's work.

26. "Clinton Stresses Welfare, Health-Care Reform," *Congressional Quarterly Weekly Report,* vol. 52, no. 4 (January 29, 1994), p. 194.

27. The phrase "works better & costs less" was featured in the title of the first (and several subsequent) reports of the National Performance Review. Al Gore, *From Red Tape to Results: Creating a Government That Works Better & Costs Less* (Government Printing Office, September 7, 1993).

28. Any administration could, of course, make both arguments: "We have created a government that tastes great and is less filling." Still, it is the filling that can be measured with a widely accepted yardstick, while (as the cliché goes) there is no accounting for taste. Moreover, will people accept that government *can* work better and cost less? Will they believe that a specific government does work better and cost less? Is it not as difficult to find a government that possesses these two characteristics as it is to find a beer that both tastes great and is less filling? Are these two concepts not completely contradictory? Maybe not. Maybe citizens will be willing to believe that government can both work better and cost less. Maybe, however, this requires too many mental gymnastics. After all, as F. Scott Fitzgerald once observed, "The test of a first-rate intelligence is the ability to hold two opposed ideas in the mind at the same time and still retain the ability to function." "The Crack-up," *Esquire,* February 1936.

29. See these reports from the General Accounting Office: "Financial Management: Increased Attention Needed to Prevent Billions in Improper Payments," GAO/AIMD-00-10, October 29, 1999; "Financial Management: Billions in Improper Payments Continue to Require Attention," GAO-01-44, October 27, 2000; "Financial Management: Improper

Payments Reported in Fiscal Year 2000 Financial Statements," GAO-02-131R, November 2, 2001; and "Financial Management: Coordinated Approach Needed to Address the Government's Improper Payments Problems," GAO-02-749, August 9, 2002.

30. Both bureaucratic and lean organizations have advantages and disadvantages. Thus any effort at organizational design seeks a balance, attempting to obtain the advantages of the bureaucratic and the lean, while minimizing their disadvantages. The design of many government agencies, however, is tilted strongly toward the bureaucratic and away from the lean.

31. When Alan K. ("Scotty") Campbell left public service for the private sector, he was immediately struck with one big difference: Business executives have many fewer staff assistants than those in government. Private firms are willing to delegate authority; indeed, they believe it is essential to do so. And they do not keep a lot of extra staff around to check up on the decisions made by their subordinates.

32. Are these effective managers much rarer in the government than in business? Maybe not. Hogan and his colleagues "estimate that somewhere between six and seven out of every ten managers in corporate America are not very good as managers." Robert Hogan, Robert Raskin, and Dan Fazzini, "The Dark Side of Charisma," in Kenneth E. Clark and Miriam B. Clark, eds., *Measures of Leadership* (West Orange, N.J.: Leadership Library of America, 1990), p. 347.

33. For examples of some particularly effective public managers, see the winners of the Harvard University, Ford Foundation awards program for Innovations in American Government, some of which are chronicled in John D. Donahue, ed., *Making Washington Work: Tales of Innovation in the Federal Government* (Brookings, 1999). See also Norma M. Riccucci, *Unsung Heroes: Federal Execucrats Making a Difference* (Georgetown University Press, 1995); and Behn, *Leadership Counts.*

34. Yes. One explanation for the success of any manager—public, private, or nonprofit—is luck. This individual was lucky. Jupiter was aligned with Mars. In fact, however, luck is recognizing it. Every one of us, including every public manager, is lucky. The question is: Do we recognize our luck? And, once we do, are we smart enough to exploit it?

35. Public managers have a spectrum of responsibilities. At one end of this spectrum is the administrative chore of ensuring that the various systems and processes of the agency function efficiently and effectively. At the other end of the spectrum is the leadership challenge of motivating the individuals in the agency to pursue their mission energetically and intelligently. Public managers have responsibilities that range from seemingly mundane administrative chores to compelling leadership.

36. For a discussion of problem solving in chess, see William G. Chase and Herbert A. Simon, "Perception in Chess," *Cognitive Psychology,* vol. 4, no. 1 (January 1973), pp. 55–81; Herbert A. Simon and Kevin Gilmartin, "A Simulation of Memory for Chess Positions," *Cognitive Psychology,* vol. 5, no. 1 (July 1973), pp. 29–46; and William G. Chase and Herbert A. Simon, "The Mind's Eye in Chess," in William G. Chase, ed., *Visual Information Processing* (Academic Press, 1973), pp. 215–81. For a discussion of professional problem solving in thermodynamic engineering, see R. Bhaskar and Herbert A. Simon, "Problem Solving in Semantically Rich Domains: An Example from Engineering Thermodynamics," *Cognitive Science,* vol. 1 (1977), pp. 193–215. For an example of how an emergency room doctor developed one rule of thumb in her professional repertoire ("Be

suspicious of parents with an injured child who want to leave quickly"), see Pamela Grim, "Taking a Stand," *Discover*, July 1997, pp. 36, 38, 40–41.

37. Herbert A. Simon, "Information Processing Models of Cognition," *Annual Review of Psychology*, vol. 30 (1979), p. 369.

38. Some of these professionals also need interpersonal skills, though some (baseball managers) need them more than others (chess players).

39. There is no reason to assume that every management challenge has one optimal answer, with every other option being clearly suboptimal. In fact a number of quite different solutions may be almost equally effective. See Robert D. Behn, "Case-Analysis Research and Managerial Effectiveness: Learning How to Lead Organizations Up Sand Dunes," in Barry Bozeman, ed., *Public Management: The State of the Art* (Jossey-Bass, 1993), pp. 40–54.

40. For a discussion of the public manager's professional repertoire, see Robert D. Behn, "The Nature of Knowledge about Public Management: Lessons for Research and Teaching from Our Knowledge about Chess and Warfare," *The Journal of Policy Analysis and Management*, vol. 7, no. 1 (Fall 1987), pp. 200–12.

41. You could argue that risk aversion and hoop jumping are really the same move. After all, why jump through all the hoops? Because you are risk averse. Both risk aversion and hoop jumping are managerial responses to requirements imposed from above. Still, hoop jumping is slightly different from risk aversion.

If the requirement reflects a broad societal norm ("public officials should not steal"), the manager needs to deploy the risk-aversion move. In this situation the manager needs not only to follow all the associated rules assiduously but also needs to be alert for additional ways that employees can, while still following all the rules, nevertheless violate the societal purpose behind them. Indeed this may require the manager to create additional (nonofficial, nonimposed) rules, just to be sure that nobody violates the societal norm and gets the agency in trouble.

If, however, the requirement merely reflects some theory about how government should function, if it does not reflect a widely accepted societal norm, then the public manager deploys the hoop-jumping move. This theory—be it in the brain of an academic, a stakeholder organization, an elected executive, or a legislator—is imposed through some rules. There is, however, a difference: These rules are backed not by a strong societal norm but only by some administrative theory. In this case the hoop-jumping manager again abides by the rules—but just by the letter of these rules. The manager and the agency can get in trouble with various superiors and overseers if they fail to follow the rules. But failing to do more than is required will not subject them to a journalistic exposé or a legislative grilling.

Risk aversion and hoop jumping are two separate moves. In organizing his or her professional repertoire, however, a manager may think of these two moves as belonging to a single class of moves—the class that contains all the moves designed to keep him or her, and the organization, out of trouble.

42. At the Visions conference that led to this volume, a participant, noting that one federal agency had contracted out the development of its strategic plan, asked incredulously why a public agency would contract out such a core activity. Answer: because the managers of this agency did not see the task of creating a strategic plan to be a core activity. Rightly or wrongly, they did not believe that a new strategic plan would help them cope with the

challenges that they faced. And thus they decided to contract out this activity to a firm that had demonstrated the ability to produce a strategic plan that would make whomever ordered the strategic plan happy. It's Hoop Jumping 101.

43. Elsewhere I have argued that the profession of public management is closer to engineering than it is to either science or art. Robert D. Behn, "Public Management: Should It Strive to Be Art, Science, or Engineering?" *Journal of Public Administration Research and Theory*, vol. 56, no. 1 (January 1996), pp. 91–123.

44. Why do business executives often fail when they become public executives? Because the professional repertoire that they were explicitly taught and that implicitly evolved reflected a different set of circumstances. And one of the major differences in those circumstances concerns the nature of the two sectors' stakeholders. Public managers have to pay attention to a greater number of stakeholders with a greater diversity of interests. Thus, when many business executives make the move to government, they believe they can ignore many of these stakeholders; this can quickly get them into trouble. We would not expect a great football coach to be immediately successful in baseball. Why do we assume that a successful business executive automatically possesses the complete professional repertoire necessary to effectively lead a public agency and to improve its performance?

45. Many items in a professional's repertoire are simple rules of thumb: When this, do that. When that, do not do this. For example, take one of the rules of thumb in baseball: Never make the first or third out at third base. Simple enough. But if you do not understand why, if you do not understand the causal linkage in the rule, you are apt to forget it, or to use it in a situation for which the simple rule of thumb does not make sense.

46. Note that the military services have created such a system of conscious career rotation. After all, the services must develop their leaders internally; the navy cannot recruit a vice president from Microsoft to be the chief of naval research. Because the national Forest Service faces the same constraint, because it too must develop its leaders internally, it has also developed a system of career rotation. See Herbert Kaufman, *The Forest Ranger: A Study in Administrative Behavior* (Johns Hopkins University Press, 1960).

47. When mentoring subordinates, a public executive will, almost by definition, be forced to be much more explicit about the cause-and-effect linkages in his or her own professional repertoire.

48. Robert D. Behn, "Baseball Management and Public Management: The Testable vs. the Important," *Journal of Policy Analysis and Management,* vol. 11, no. 2 (Spring 1992), pp. 315–21; Robert D. Behn, "The Futile Search for the One Best Way," *Governing* (July 1996), p. 82.

49. Herbert A. Simon, "The Proverbs of Administration," *Public Administration Review,* vol. 6 (Winter 1946), pp. 53–67.

50. Such artificial intelligence systems are being created in medicine. But in this profession it is easier (though only on a relative scale) to specify the patient's most important circumstances. These circumstances include the standard medical data that are well specified (temperature, blood pressure), some medical information that is not so easy to specify (energy and attitude), and other patient circumstances that may be relevant in some cases (family situation, job stress). But there is nevertheless some agreement that these circumstances are all potentially relevant. In public management however there is little agreement about which are the most potentially relevant circumstances, let alone any understanding of how to specify them.

51. For examinations of how managerial expertise and repertoire moves are conveyed through such cases, see Stephen W. Maynard-Moody and Marisa Kelly, "Stories Public Managers Tell about Elected Officials: Making Sense of the Politics-Administration Dichotomy," in Barry Bozeman, ed., *Public Management: The State of the Art* (Jossey-Bass, 1993), pp. 71–90; and Michael Barzelay, *The New Public Management: Improving Research and Policy Dialogue* (University of California Press, 2001).

52. Karl E. Weick, "Small Wins: Redefining the Scale of Social Problems," *American Psychologist*, vol. 39, no. 1 (January 1984), p. 43.

53. Ibid.

54. As an important quality of leaders and managers, charisma is overrated. Yet, because we often accept that it is essential to effective management and leadership, it serves as a expedient excuse: "I could be a more effective manager, a more influential leader, but I can't help it; I'm just not charismatic." To the extent that everyone accepts that charisma—personal charm, mystical magnetism, professional dynamism, a commanding presence—is necessary to get large public agencies to improve performance, it provides a convenient excuse for every mortal human. Yet our ability to improve the performance of the public service and of government depends not on the charisma of heroes but on the skills of ordinary humans. Moreover, charismatic managers can actually harm an organization. Beware of "the dark side of charisma" warn Hogan, Raskin, and Fazzini: "Certain kinds of people with identifiable personality characteristics tend to rise to the tops of organizations, and these people are potentially very costly to those organizations." Who are these certain kinds of people, who "have little or no talent for management"? Hogan and his colleagues suggest that they come in three varieties: (1) The High Likeability Floater, who is "congenial but unambitious"; "little happens under their guidance beyond the maintenance of good morale." (2) Hommes de Ressentiment, who possess "a deep strain of resentment, smoldering hostility, and a desire for revenge"; they "always do well in interviews" because they possess "the ability to appear charming, bright, and leaderlike." (3) The Narcissist, who is "self-confident, assertive," and "exploits his or her subordinates while currying favor with his or her supervisors"; they "are strongly motivated by needs for recognition and pleasure and less so by needs for achievement and success." Hogan, Raskin, and Fazzini, "Dark Side of Charisma," pp. 343, 346, 348–49, 352, 350–51.

55. In early 1970s, the Nixon and Ford administrations implemented Management by Objectives. But what kind of objectives did the various federal departments establish? *National Journal* reported that "some goals are so vague as to appear meaningless and others are so minute they appear picayune." For example, the Department of Energy created a number of goals including both the vague ("Reduce energy consumption without damaging the state of the economy") and the minute ("Help implement the 1974 Energy Supply and Environmental Coordination Act"). For experienced public managers, jumping through this new MBO hoop was easy. Joel Havemann, "Executive Report: Ford Endorses 172 Goals of 'Management by Objective' Plan," *National Journal*, vol. 6, no. 43 (October 26, 1974), pp. 1597, 1602.

56. An explicit performance target is never precisely the same as the mission. Most organizations can find ways to achieve their precise performance targets and still not really accomplish their mission. At the same time, because the mission is inherently vague, it cannot provide specific guidance about what should be done this year, this quarter, or this month. Consequently the manager of the organization has to repeatedly verify that, in the

process of meeting its performance targets, the agency is also contributing to its mission. Behn, *Leadership Counts,* pp. 74–76.

57. Robert D. Behn, "The Psychological Barriers to Performance Management: Or Why Isn't Everyone Jumping on the Performance-Management Bandwagon," *Public Performance and Management Review,* vol. 26, no. 1 (September 2002), pp. 5–25.

58. Okay, so the Boston Red Sox have not learned this.

59. Robert D. Behn, "Branch Rickey as a Public Manager: Fulfilling the Eight Responsibilities of Public Management," *Journal of Public Administration Research and Theory,* vol. 7, no. 1 (January 1997), pp. 1–33.

12

ALEXANDER KEYSSAR
ERNEST R. MAY

Education for Public Service
in the History of the
United States

EDUCATION FOR PUBLIC SERVICE in the United States has evolved as public service itself has evolved. Schooling intended to prepare men and women to serve in the public sector has necessarily reflected both prevailing beliefs about government and prevailing beliefs about teaching and learning. Not surprisingly the education of Americans for public service has for the most part followed obsolescing principles and aimed at preparing people to work in a present that was fast vanishing into the past. The utility of a chapter here on this history is to emphasize how hard it is and always has been to provide professional education for a future almost certain to be different from either present or past.

Without getting into the mucky debate about American exceptionalism, it can be noted that education for public service in the United States has differed from such education in most if not all other parts of the world. In continental Europe, Roman law created a tradition of intensive training in methods of discovering and applying administrative rules. Though the British developed a distinctive common law tradition, England and Scotland were influenced by Europe's Roman past and by their need to transact business with European states. Hence they too became accustomed to entrusting public business to experienced, long-service administrators who commanded the languages and knew the precedents of government. John Locke and Samuel Pepys are famous examples.[1]

England in fact marched ahead of continental Europe in creating a formal civil service with associated educational requirements. By the eighteenth century the English administrative service had become larded with appointees chiefly qualified by family connections. This bureaucracy was assigned partial blame (and rightly so) both for provoking the American war for independence and for losing the war once it had started. Scandals in India (still ruled by a chartered company) then led to the creation of a formal school for training administrators. Regarded as a great success, the Indian civil service became a model for a domestic civil service, with the difference that the Oxbridge liberal arts curriculum was presumed to provide all the requisite preparation. As was argued by the historian Thomas Babington Macaulay, who had a large hand in shaping the British civil service: "Early superiority in literature and science generally indicates the existence of some qualities which are securities against vice—industry, self-denial, a taste for pleasures not sensual, a laudable desire of honorable distinction, a still more laudable desire to obtain the approbation of friends and relations." As Herman Finer contends in his classic study of the British civil service, the creation of an administrative elite owed much to the fact that Britain was governed at Westminster by aristocrats and members of the upper middle class, who thought of themselves as secure in ownership of the home islands and empire and simply wanted their property to be well managed.[2]

The United States, in contrast to continental Europe and the United Kingdom, had not only no tradition of service to the state but active abhorrence of the *idea* of the state. The Americans of 1776 had rebelled against the British state in all its forms—not only the monarchy in London but every governor and appointed council in every colony. Though they mostly used the term *state* for the new entities they created, they insisted that their governments were to be agents of their citizenry and nothing more.

The founding fathers believed that education for public service consisted essentially in study of past experience, especially that of the ancient world and modern Britain. While historians quarrel about the extent to which the founders relied on Greek and Roman classics themselves or on summations handed down by British Whigs and Commonwealthmen, no one who has leafed through records of the Continental Congress, the Constitutional Convention, or the pamphlet war preceding ratification can take issue with the conclusion in Carl Richards's *The Founders and the Classics* that "the most remarkable aspect of the debates . . . was not the Federalists' narrow victory over the Antifederalists, but the classicists' rout of the anticlassicists."³ Victory commonly went to the orator or pamphleteer with the largest arsenal of classical citations or quotations.

This concept of education for public service did not long survive. Gordon Wood argues in *The Creation of the American Republic* and later works that, immediately after ratification of the Constitution, there was a popular reaction against the elitist classicism prevailing in the Federalist-Antifederalist debates. Ratification, Wood asserts, marked the "end of classical politics." Other historians see the shift as occurring later, perhaps even after the War of 1812.⁴ But there can be no question that, by the time of Andrew Jackson, the idea that classical education provided special fitness for public service had fallen into total disrepute. Indeed the idea of any linkage between education and employment came into question, with the ministry the best barometer. Whereas the churches of colonial and early national America had had learned clergy (comparatively speaking), the evangelical churches that mushroomed in nineteenth-century America set no such requirement.⁵

At the time when Britain's governing classes decided that their properties needed educated managers, the United States was becoming the world example of democracy: a nation (or collection of nations) governed by a mass electorate. The ruling principle was President Andrew Jackson's, that "the duties of all public officers are, or at least admit of being made, so plain and simple that men of intelligence may readily qualify themselves for their performance." One corollary was the famous maxim of Senator (later secretary of state) William Learned Marcy of New York that, after an election, "to the victor belongs the spoils of the enemy." A more high-minded corollary was that amplified in Frederick Grimke's book of 1848, *The Nature and Tendency of Free Institutions*: "It is of the greatest importance, in a country where the electoral franchise is extensively enjoyed, that as large a number of citizens as practicable should be initiated into the mode of conducting public affairs, and there is no way by which this can be so well effected as by a rotation in office."⁶

These Jacksonian notions even led to attacks on the one national institution that had already been erected to provide education for a branch of public service: the academy to train army officers at West Point. Established in 1802, the academy satisfied both Federalists, who thought the nation should have a professional army, and President Thomas Jefferson, who was interested primarily in having a school for engineers. Jacksonians criticized the academy, arguing that the nation needed only citizen soldiers, but those attacks were rebuffed, and in the late 1840s a naval academy was added to provide on land some of the professional training that had long been given at sea to midshipman officer candidates.[7]

Alexis de Tocqueville, whose *Democracy in America* was based on observations made during the Jackson era, commented with wonderment on the absence in America of even the most basic level of formal governmental administration. "The public administration is, so to speak, oral and traditional," wrote Tocqueville,

> no one cares for what occurred before his time: no methodical system is pursued, no archives are formed, and no documents are brought together when it would be very easy to do so. Where they exist, little store is set upon them. I have among my papers several original public documents which were given to me in the public offices in answer to some of my inquiries. In America society seems to live from hand to mouth, like an army in the field. Nevertheless, the art of administration is undoubtedly a science, and no science can be improved if the discoveries and observations of successive generations are not connected together in the order in which they occur. One man in the short space of his life remarks a fact, another conceives an idea; the former invents a means of execution, the latter reduces a truth to a formula; and mankind gathers the fruits of individual experience. . . . But the persons who conduct the administration in America can seldom afford any instruction to one another; and when they assume the direction of society, they simply possess those attainments which are widely disseminated in the community, and no knowledge peculiar to themselves. Democracy . . . is therefore prejudicial to the art of government.[8]

Tocqueville saw lawyers as America's governing class. "If I were asked where I place the American aristocracy," he wrote, "I should reply without hesitation that it is not among the rich, who are united by no common tie, but that it occupies the judicial bench and the bar."[9] The public at large learned how to exercise its own governing power, Tocqueville thought, chiefly through the discipline of service on juries.[10]

In roughly the period in which Tocqueville wrote, efforts commenced to give Americans formal schooling in how to govern their democracy. For the mass public, sponsors of public education such as Horace Mann, Noah Webster, and Benjamin Rush sought a curriculum that would, in Rush's phrase, "convert men into republican machines."[11] For the elites this meant training in law. At the time lawyers did not qualify to be lawyers through academic study. As in England, they served apprenticeships, not in centrally located inns of court but, as a rule, trailing after lawyers who followed judges roving their circuits. The transition from being an apprentice to being a lawyer lacked formality. As a distinguished Wisconsin lawyer explained,

> When one desired to be admitted to the bar in those days he got a lawyer to move the court to appoint a committee, and of course the court appointed the mover of the proposition and whoever the mover and the judge might select, and then the duty of the applicant, according to this tradition of the bar, was to invite this committee to a wine supper. . . . The examination took place after supper.[12]

Law schools were set up in association with colleges as, in effect, academic departments designed to give college students enough knowledge of law to understand what lawyers did.

Between 1850 and 1900, as the United States grew in population and became increasingly industrialized, the demand for public services of one type or another accelerated rapidly. The challenges first appeared at the municipal level. The rate of urbanization was high, and the escalating cost of basic services began to stress municipal budgets and distress the payers of property taxes. In addition, urban problems, such as public health (epidemics were epidemic), sanitation, street engineering, and public transportation, acquired increasingly technical dimensions. In this context the need for trained and capable public servants—with something more than general intelligence—seemed more evident, even pressing. Indeed one might see in the late nineteenth and early twentieth centuries the emergence of the notion of public service as a profession—which of course accompanied the rise of the "professions" more generally and the proliferation of professional schools (and standards) in law, medicine, engineering, and even public health. It is in this period also that the notion of a career in public service begins to emerge.[13]

A concern for a competent and efficient public service fueled the creation of state civil service programs as well as congressional passage of the Pendleton Act in 1883, creating a national civil service. Consequently entrance into some public service occupations (the proportion of public jobs covered by the legislation varied over time) was determined by competitive examinations. The educational levels required for entrance were not high: The exams suggest that basic literacy and numeracy were key, as were a rudimentary knowledge of accounting and some constitutional history. Not surprisingly then the Pendleton Act and other similar reforms did not generate any significant developments in the educational arena, although some universities (particularly public universities) began to offer courses with an eye toward public service.[14]

New pressures also appeared on the international front, as the United States became actively involved in global affairs. The profession of diplomacy escaped all professionalization until the beginning of the twentieth century, when Congress established examinations for entry into the consular corps, the controlling argument being that consuls had to be prepared to promote foreign trade. Diplomats as distinct from consuls were not required to pass examinations until the mid-1920s, and then as now the higher diplomatic posts remained "spoils." No particular educational background was ever required for consular or diplomatic service (though the Foreign Service exams were often accused of being tailored for Ivy League liberal arts graduates).[15]

It was thus in the late nineteenth and early twentieth centuries that a loosely defined field of public administration began to take shape. By then the American system of government, likened by Tocqueville to an army in the field and characterized by recent scholars as an assembly of "courts and parties," had clearly become inadequate for coping with public needs.[16] At every level, from the township up, Americans turned to the expedient of creating administrative agencies to take the place of courts in implementing legislation, such as that on freight rates or zoning. Because this was somewhat imitative of practice in Roman law countries, because these new agencies were assuming functions previously performed by judges, and because the period was one in which formal law schooling became practically the only route into the legal profession, it would have seemed logical for law schools to make themselves the central vehicles for providing education at least for public administration and perhaps for public service more broadly.

Yet this did not occur. As William C. Chase explains in his elegant monograph, *The American Law School and the Rise of Administrative Government*, law schools failed to become explicit providers of education for public service because, just at this period in their history, teachers in law schools began to think of themselves as scientists advancing a branch of basic knowledge, rather than as trainers of practitioners. In the Harvard

Law School, Christopher Columbus Langdell advocated case-method teaching, on the theory that close examination of judicial opinion permitted the discovery of eternal principles, just as observation of nature permitted physicists to discover laws of nature. "If law be not a science," Langdell declared, "a university will consult its own dignity in declining to teach it." In fact, he said, law was "one of the greatest and most difficult of the sciences."[17]

Though the notion of law professors rooting out of Supreme Court reports the equivalent of a second law of thermodynamics proved to be short-lived, case-method teaching concentrated on judicial opinions came to dominate legal education, the new rationale being the ability thereby to teach, in the words of Langdell's star pupil, James Barr Ames, "the power of solving legal problems."[18] Consequently administrative law became a specialty in law schools (taught at Harvard by Felix Frankfurter), but it was not the kind of administrative law taught in Roman law countries. It was instead inquiry into the legal principles underpinning court decisions on the actions of administrative bodies. In choosing this path, law schools in the United States were effectively declining to offer education specifically for public service.

Other branches of the established universities also faltered in facing this challenge. At Columbia, Frank Goodnow attempted to create European-style study of administrative law, basing himself both in the law school and in a department of political science. But his undertaking failed, condemned from the law school side as not "strictly legal" and from the political science side as too "legalistic."[19] Harvard at the turn of the century considered creating a school of diplomacy and public service but decided that there was little demand for such an education and founded the business school instead.

Indeed the first successful effort to develop training that would combine general administrative skills and knowledge (finance, accounting, personnel management), technical knowledge where relevant, and some knowledge of the social sciences came not at a university but at the Training School for Public Service, founded in 1911 by the New York Bureau of Municipal Research, itself founded in 1906. Funded largely by Mrs. E. H. Harriman and led by historian Charles Beard, the school sought to provide both academic and in-the-field training for those who would work in city governments. Its stated aims included "to train men for the study and administration of public business," to qualify men "competent to test and improve" methods and results of municipal service, to engage in research, and to "furnish . . . a connecting link between schools and colleges and municipal or other public departments for practical field work."[20]

The founding of the Training School for Public Service was followed by the first wave of formal programs, based in universities, for the study of public administration and the education of men and women for public service. (The TSPS itself moved to Columbia University in 1931, while some of its programs went to the Maxwell School at Syracuse.) The demand for graduates of such programs was fueled by the expansion of government at all levels, by the growth of the executive branches of state governments, and notably by the spread of home rule and city manager forms of municipal governance. The need for such programs at universities was pressed repeatedly by the American Political Science Association.[21]

Between 1914 and 1930 programs in public administration or municipal administration were created at several dozen institutions, including Michigan, UC Berkeley, Stanford, Syracuse, Cincinnati, University of Southern California, Minnesota, Columbia, Chicago, and the newly renamed Brookings Institution. The programs were generally small and varied in their curricula, but most tended to have a blend of the following elements: the study of history, government, and public affairs, in a general liberal arts context; the more specialized study of a social science, for example, sociology (a new field), political science, and economics; the general study of administration, with a clinical component; and in some cases administrative training for specialized experts who sought to become more involved in policy (for example, physicians, engineers, agronomists, or teachers). The study of public administration per se was developed with particular strength at the Maxwell School at Syracuse, under the guidance of its pioneering dean, William Mosher.[22]

Not surprisingly the Great Depression and the New Deal spawned the next major surge in educational programs for governance and public service. Between 1933 and 1941 programs were created in more than two dozen universities, including major national institutions such as Harvard and Yale. At these institutions (and to some degree elsewhere as well) the programs were designed expressly to train people for service in the national government: The 1930s in effect witnessed the nationalization of the impulses that had centered on municipal and state issues during earlier decades. One symbolic indicator of this shift was the creation of the National Institute for Public Affairs, which provided nine-month training internships in federal offices in Washington. The programs of the 1930s placed more emphasis on subject matters (such as economics and social policy) that appeared to be the domain and concern of national policy. At the same time law schools began to pay greater attention to administrative law, while the ties between the social sciences and public administration deepened, symbolized by the Social Science Research Council's creation of a committee on public administration in 1934. The government Reorganization Act of 1939 also prompted (and reflected) new thinking about the nature of large organizations.[23]

According to a study conducted under the auspices of the SSRC and published in 1941, the content of the programs of the 1930s tended to vary in several respects: in the degree to which there was coursework in addition to clinical or field experience; in the degree to which they stressed public administration per se as a field rather than the social science disciplines (the Maxwell School at Syracuse put the greatest stress on administration); and in precisely where they were housed within universities (as separate schools, as programs linking courses in various departments, as parts of political science departments, or even as programs within business schools, as at Wharton).[24]

World War II, despite its immense challenges, does not seem to have prompted any immediate changes in education for public service. After all, most of the potential students were in uniform, and urgent matters at hand took precedence over curricular innovation. Notably however the war drew large numbers of academics, particularly from the social sciences, into government service, in both policy and administrative positions. (This wartime migration was even larger than it had been during the New Deal: One analyst referred to it as the largest program in postdoctoral education for faculty in the nation's history.) As a result universities after the war contained numerous academics who had returned to university life after having gained years of hands-on experience in public service and governance. The war also had the effect of introducing large numbers of lawyers to public management problems that few had previously encountered—for example, allocating scarce materials, regulating prices and wages, or establishing civil administration in liberated or occupied areas abroad.[25]

The postwar period, however, saw some tumult in the educational arena. On the one hand the experiences of many academics led to a new pragmatism in teaching that included a growing pedagogical focus on case studies. (An interuniversity consortium on case studies was launched in 1948.) On the other hand social scientists (particularly political scientists) began to question many of the intellectual presumptions of the field of public administration and indeed to question whether there was such a field. Could administration really be separated from policy, as many had claimed during the interwar years? Could public administration be studied without respect to a theoretically sound and sophisticated understanding of human behavior on the one hand and political contexts on the other? If there was no distinctive field of public administration, then what should prospective public servants study: political science, decision theory, or what? Institutions training students for public governance stopped proliferating and began either reaching out more to the social sciences or hunkering down to protect themselves from social science criticism. At the same time American dominance in the postwar world, coupled with the cold war, led to a new emphasis on knowledge of world affairs.[26]

By the 1960s and early 1970s these intellectual tensions had contributed to a redefinition of the educational field—from "public administration" to "public policy." At the heart of this shift was a growing faith in the power and prestige of economics as a field, a method, and even a science. In addition to the apparent triumph of macroeconomists over the vagaries of the business cycle, economists, heavily dependent on tools developed by mathematicians, also appeared to have come up with solutions for the awful intellectual problem of how to manage international relations in an era of nuclear plenty. In and around Robert McNamara's Department of Defense, economists put into practice techniques of program analysis and benefit-cost measurement, which President Lyndon Johnson then forced on all domestic departments involved in building his Great Society. (One scholar tells of visiting the office of a cabinet secretary in order to explain to him a several-hundred-page booklet on policy planning budget systems, one of the hallmark techniques of the era. He came upon the secretary fingering the booklet and asking, "What is this piece of shit?" He had the pleasure of responding, "That piece of shit, sir, is what the president of the United States has directed that you introduce into your department.") Harvard's Kennedy School came into being at precisely the period when the key to preparation for public service seemed to be mastery of the principles and techniques of economic analysis, and the Kennedy School was hardly alone in sprinting down this path.

Yet the Vietnam War took some of the luster off the accomplishments of McNamara and his "whiz kids," while the apparent failure of many Great Society policies also cast doubt on the power of the new techniques of policy analysis. Indeed the Nixon administration and most of its successors paid much less attention to economists or economic analysis than had the Democratic administrations of the 1960s. Rather quickly the new shibboleth in education for public service became "public management," which promised to train students to implement as well as select policies. Programs at Wharton, Stanford, and Yale accordingly placed less emphasis on economics than had (or did) the Kennedy School. Yet, as promising as this new approach seemed to be, public management proved to be as hard to define and teach as had the subject of public administration several decades earlier.[27]

This brief historical sketch, brought to a merciful close even before scanning the more familiar vicissitudes of the past two decades, makes clear that education for public service has not evolved in any simple or unidirectional way over the past two centuries. Public service itself has changed along many different axes, as have common values and ideas about economies, societies, and political institutions: Educational programs for public servants have reflected all of those changes, sometimes after a substantial lag time. The certainties of one decade have rarely seemed so certain two or three decades later. The tools that seemed appropriate to face one era's challenges often appeared clumsy not long thereafter. On occasion a long-forgotten wheel has been reinvented to great applause.

This history also makes one other fact quite visible: Throughout American history most public servants have not been trained expressly for public service. The scale of programs for education for public service has always been small in relation to the total number of persons working for municipal, state, and federal governments. Whether this has had a deleterious effect on the conduct of public business is impossible to determine. It is however consistent with the values of a nation that has embraced the notion that true power lies with the people as a whole, and that consequently the most important education for public service comes through civics courses in public schools and through popular participation in politics.

Notes

1. Frederick C. Mosher, *Democracy and the Public Service,* 2d ed. (Oxford University Press, 1982), pp. 29–40.

2. Herman Finer, *The British Civil Service* (Allen and Unwin, 1937). The quotation from Macaulay is from Mosher, p. 69.

ALEXANDER KEYSSAR AND ERNEST R. MAY

3. Carl J. Richards, *The Founders and the Classics: Greece, Rome, and the American Enlightenment* (Harvard University Press, 1994), p. 233.

4. Gordon Wood, *The Creation of the American Republic, 1776–1787* (University of North Carolina Press, 1969), p. 606. See also his later book, *The Radicalism of the American Revolution* (Knopf, 1992); and, for a later dating of the classics' loss of persuasive power, Joyce O. Appleby, *Liberalism and Republicanism in the Historical Imagination* (Harvard University Press, 1992); and Edwin A. Miles, "The Young American Nation and the Classical World," *Journal of the History of Ideas,* vol. 35 (April–June 1974).

5. Mosher, *Democracy and the Public Service*, pp. 41–47; Paul P. Van Riper, *History of the United States Civil Service* (Westport, Conn.: Greenwood Press, 1976), pp. 11–52.

6. See Leonard White, *The Jacksonians: A Study in Administrative History, 1829–1861* (Macmillan, 1954), pp. 552–67; Van Riper, *History of the United States Civil Service*, p. 36.

7. Allan R. Millett and Petger Maslowski, *For the Common Defense: A Military History of the United States* (Free Press, 1984), pp. 99–100, 129.

8. Alexis de Tocqueville, *Democracy in America* (Knopf, 1945), pp. 219–20.

9. Ibid., p. 288.

10. Ibid., p. 296.

11. Benjamin Rush, "Thoughts upon the Mode of Education Proper in a Republic," quoted in William R. Johnson, *Schooled Lawyers: A Study in the Clash of Professional Cultures* (New York University Press, 1978), p. 7.

12. James G. Jenkins, speaking in 1906, quoted in ibid.

13. Alice B. Stone and Donald C. Stone, "Early Development of Education in Public Administration," in Frederick C. Mosher, ed., *American Public Administration: Past, Present, Future* (University of Alabama Press, 1975), pp. 17–25.

14. Van Riper, *History of the United States Civil Service*, pp. 96–168; Stone and Stone, "Early Development," p. 25.

15. Warren F. Ilchman, *Professional Diplomacy in the United States, 1779–1939: A Study in Administrative History* (University of Chicago Press, 1961).

16. See Stephen Skowronek, *Building a New American State: The Expansion of National Administrative Capacities* (Cambridge University Press, 1981).

17. William C. Chase, *The American Law School and the Rise of Administrative Government* (University of Wisconsin Press, 1982), p. 29.

18. Ibid., p. 37.

19. Ibid., pp. 48–49.

20. Stone and Stone, "Early Development," pp. 28–29; quotation from the Bureau of Municipal Research, *Training School for Public Service, Announcement–1911* (New York, 1911), p. 2.

21. Stone and Stone, "Early Development," pp. 26–32.

22. Ibid.

23. Rowland Egger, "The Period of Crisis," in Mosher, *American Public Administration*, pp. 49–96. A comprehensive survey of the developments of the 1930s is presented in George A. Graham, *Education for Public Administration: Graduate Preparation in the Social Sciences at American Universities* (Chicago: R. R. Donnelly and Co., 1941). See also *Training for the Public Service Occupations, 1937,* Vocational Education Bulletin 192 (Government Printing Office, 1938).

24. Graham, *Education for Public Administration*, pp. 135–317.

25. Egger, "Period of Crisis," pp. 83–92.

26. James W. Fesler, "Public Administration and the Social Sciences: 1946–1960," in Mosher, *American Public Administration,* pp. 97–125.

27. On the 1960s and 1970s (and thereafter), see Donald E. Stokes, "The Changing Environment of Education for Public Service," *Journal of Policy Analysis and Management,* vol. 15, no. 2 (1996), pp. 158–170.

13

IRIS BOHNET
SUSAN C. EATON

Does Performance Pay
Perform?
Conditions for Success
in the Public Sector

I N THE PAST ten years the potential for introducing elements of pay for
performance into government work has become a hotly debated issue in
Washington. Based on the approach called new public management in
Britain, Canada, and New Zealand, Vice President Albert Gore presented
a proposal to transform federal agencies into performance-based organizations in March 1996. The proposal identified ten organizations, accounting for about 2 percent of the federal civilian work force, as candidates for
the reform.[1] Some supporters argued that up to 75 percent of the federal
bureaucracy could be transformed into performance-based organizations
and that the proposal could cut operating costs by $25 billion by 2004.[2]
One key reform to be made was to liberalize civil service rules on employee
pay so that discretionary pay could motivate employees to work more effectively, and managers could clearly single out good performance.

This chapter offers a framework for deciding whether, and under what
conditions, pay should depend on output to increase incentives for performance. While the conditions for success we present also apply more gen-

We thank our discussants, Nancy Katz and Joseph Newhouse, for their helpful suggestions, and the participants of the 2002 Visions meetings for their comments. Financial support from the Visions of Governance for the Twenty-first Century project is appreciated.

erally, we focus on the public sector, specifically on the federal level in the United States. We acknowledge that many other attributes of organizations, including monetary and nonmonetary incentives (promotion, training and travel opportunities, or awards such as employee-of-the-month) may affect performance, but we concentrate on the payment system here. This chapter weaves together analysis based on economics, human resource management, and social psychology to demonstrate not only what "should" happen according to economic theory but what we know can and does happen when human beings are involved, with all their deviations from the rational, money-maximizing "economic man."

Pay-for-Performance Logic

Our reference point from economics is a fairly straightforward payment scheme, where an employee's pay is tied to output in a proportional way, so that the more output, the higher the pay. This is commonly known as a piece rate system, and simple examples are found in garment factories, home production arrangements, and on farms, where the employee is paid a specified amount of money for each piece of work completed. However, typically the piece rate is combined with some base wage that is not contingent on performance, so that actual pay is equal to the base wage plus the piece rate. Hourly wages or salaries supplemented with a per-piece rate for production above a required minimum are an important part of any performance-based organization plan. This is in part because the employee needs to be assured of a minimum wage as well as the employer of minimum production. The concept arises directly from Taylorist scientific management, where there is a most efficient way to do each job, and the employee has to be motivated by external forces to do the job more efficiently.[3]

Such payment systems are reported to have become more prevalent in the private sector in recent years. Ninety percent of Fortune 1000 companies report that they rely on incentive schemes that tie pay to some measure of output. More than 75 percent of all U.S. companies say at least some part of pay is pegged to performance, and 93 percent of the largest 460 European firms indicate that performance-based pay gained in importance during recent years. Unfortunately the specifics of performance pay in these companies are poorly documented. Only rarely do we know how large the fraction of pay that depends on performance actually is, and recent surveys suggest that it is typically less than 10 percent.[4]

State of the Empirical Research

The existing empirical evidence in economics is summarized by Avinash Dixit, Robert Gibbons, and Candice Prendergast.[5] These surveys stress that the few empirical studies on the effect of performance pay all focus on simple jobs, where a measure of performance is easily available. The empirical studies find a positive effect of pay for performance on productivity, although the magnitude varies substantially. One detailed investigation of the impact of piece rates on performance has been undertaken by Edward Lazear.[6] He studied auto windshield installation at Safelite Glass to measure productivity changes after a switch from fixed hourly wages to piece rates. He found that productivity rose by approximately 35 percent after the change in incentive schemes, with wages increasing by about 12 percent. He showed that approximately one-third of the impact was due to turnover, where the less able were replaced by more talented workers.[7]

A more recent study on the effect of performance pay on productivity was conducted by Iris Bohnet and Felix Oberholzer-Gee.[8] They investigated the effect of financial incentives on the number and quality of suggestions for improvement submitted to about a thousand firms over ten years. There are two differences in this work compared with the earlier empirical studies: Employees were confronted with a complex project rather than a simple task, and they were charged with more than one task (their regular job plus the creation of ideas). The authors found that higher piece rates increased the number but decreased the quality of suggestions produced and had a negative effect on performance overall.

It is difficult to find empirical studies on the effectiveness of performance pay in the public sector. Anecdotal reports suggest that the Next Steps Initiative (NSI) in Britain was a success, but there is hardly any empirical evidence to support this impression.[9] Alasdair Roberts summarizes the main reasons for the missing research studies in Britain, which was among the first countries to strengthen pay incentives: "One difficulty is the lack of performance data for executive agencies for prereform years. A second problem is a lack of consistent performance data for postreform years: Agencies have often added, removed, or modified measures from one year to the next. A third problem is uncertainty about the effect of other reform initiatives undertaken after NSI."[10]

Some would argue that the lack of a definitive evaluation of performance pay is no accident. Alan Blinder, introducing a collection of essays on pay for performance, notes that "rising and falling tides of interest in the various incentive plans have more to do with changing social, political, and economic fashions than with accumulating scientific evidence on how well the plans work."[11]

We argue that the conditions for success of any pay-for-performance plan depend on three main factors: the kind of output produced, the people producing the output, and the organizational setting in which the people produce the output. We suggest that the conditions for success are generally not met in the private sector, and even less so in the public sector.

Output

The type of output appropriate to pay-for-performance arrangements has three key characteristics: It is a single task, clearly measurable, and linked to a single individual.

Pay for performance works best if employees have to complete one well-specified task

Most employees are charged with not one but multiple tasks. If high-powered incentives for output are used for one task alone, others will be neglected.[12] Because some tasks tend to be more easily observable and measurable than others, using different payment rates for different tasks may be tempting for employers but will often cause employees to reallocate effort in undesirable ways.

An example is the quantity-quality trade-off. A worker may pick more lettuce if paid by the head, but she will not necessarily ensure that all the lettuce is of high quality, unless the pay system incorporates quality. Research suggests that firms are aware of the ubiquity of multitasking and are less likely to use piece rates when an employee undertakes more than one task.[13] In contrast to the single task of the auto windshield shop, computer programmers, nurses, and intelligence agents, for example, are charged with multiple tasks.

Most organizations, especially public agencies, are faced with multi-tasking problems, making it more likely that their agents will focus on the task that is most easily measurable. OSHA, the Occupational Safety and Health Administration, for example, enforces laws to protect worker safety and health. The statistics show that industrial hazards present a greater threat to worker health than to safety. Despite this, OSHA has focused on safety rather then health concerns. As James Q. Wilson writes:

> Regulation-writers find it much easier to address safety than health hazards. The former are technically easier to find, describe, assess, and control than the latter. A worker falls from a platform. The cause is clear—no railing. The effect is clear—a broken leg. The cost is easily calculated—so many days in the hospital, so many days of lost wages, so much to build a railing. The directive is easy to write: "Install a railings platform." But if a worker develops cancer fifteen years after starting work in a chemical plant, the cause of the cancer will be uncertain and controversial. The cost of the disease will be hard to calculate. The solution will be hard to specify.[14]

Similarly the Internal Revenue Service found after implementing its pay-for-performance plan, in which it rewarded agents for the amount of monies collected, that some agents were becoming belligerent with tax-payers in order to increase the amount of their collections.[15]

Pay for performance works best if output due to effort can be distinguished from output due to luck

If an employee's performance is not verifiable, what economists call moral hazard arises. Rather than being able to directly pay for performance, the employer has to pay for a random outcome that is related to the employee's effort. The conditions for an incentive scheme to be optimal under these circumstances are very restrictive. Generally speaking the base wage becomes larger and the incentive portion smaller if it is difficult to determine how closely effort and outcome are related.

Studies suggest that, in practice, pay-for-performance systems for non-professional employees are used where the output can be easily measured—for instance, the number of phone calls answered in a given time, the number of lettuce heads picked, the number of keystrokes made, or the number of windshields installed. At the same time performance pay is prevalent for the highest-level employees, namely chief executive officers, whose effect on output often is hard to control or measure. It has been common to reward CEOs with stock options to make sure that they act with the owners' interests in mind. Even before the scandals of 2002, CEO compensation studies found that incentive pay is not properly calibrated to measure performance and therefore cannot be working as planned.[16] A recent study finds that CEOs are effectively rewarded for luck.[17] These researchers also report that pay for luck is strongest among poorly governed firms, and that adding a major shareholder to the board decreased the pay for luck by 23 to 33 percent.

Output in the public sector is more likely to be vaguely defined than in the private sector. For example, the Department of State is asked to "promote the long-range security and well-being of the United States," and the Bureau of Indian Affairs to "facilitate the full development of the human and natural resource potential of Indian and Alaska Native people." Output measurement is further complicated by the fact that many services provided by public agencies benefit the community at large rather than separate individuals. The value of such public goods is harder to measure than the value of private goods. Such goods are not traded on the market, so it is hard to set an appropriate price.

Pay for performance works best if output can be attributed to one person's effort

The provision of public goods often requires cooperation and coordination within and across agencies. Team production is not a problem if the employer cares only about the sum of the individual employees' efforts and if each effort can be evaluated separately and has no relationship to the efforts of others. Typically this is not the case, however, and an incentive system for the whole team must be designed to reinforce people's willingness to share and to work together with others.

However, performance pay distributed as a reward for team performance also creates incentives to free-ride, or to slack off and let other people do the work. Joseph Newhouse found that group incentives in a medical practice led to a rise in overhead costs and to doctors working fewer hours, as the fraction of revenues shared with others increased.[18] Investigating the effect of team-based compensation on individual productivity for telephone operators in a large financial company, Daniel Hansen reported a negative effect on the formerly more productive and a positive effect on the formerly less productive employees.[19] While Hansen's first finding supports the idea that some people are free-riding, the second suggests that perhaps peer pressure may have induced the formerly less productive to increase their productivity.

Measuring team output and arranging pay systems that avoid the problem of free-riding and coworker resentment are complicated. While some such schemes have been devised, most pay for performance is implemented on an individual basis and thus does not fit well with today's team-oriented workplace. In the unusual case where group rewards are used, they function best if the entire work organization is aligned with the rewards; hybrid arrangements, which combined individual and group rewards, were less effective than either individual rewards (for truly individual work) or group rewards (where the work was truly interdependent).[20] In these instances the size of the group is important (small groups generally function better than large ones), the composition of the group is important (the group must have all the skills required), and the support, both material and in leadership and coaching, that the group gets is critical to its success.[21] Pay is only one component of a much larger and more complicated set of factors that require alignment to get good results.

People

The characteristics of the people who do the work are germane to the suitability of pay-for-performance arrangements. Relevant lessons can be drawn from extensive bodies of research on human psychology and the sociology of organizations. It is important to identify and critically scrutinze assumptions behind any pay plan. These include assumptions about how people are motivated, what makes them work harder, and how they wish to be treated or viewed, as well as how they view themselves. We focus on two characteristics crucial for the success of pay for performance: people solely motivated by income and, more specifically, people motivated by absolute rather than relative income (those who do not care how much others are paid).

Pay for performance works best if employees work primarily for money

Pay-for-performance systems generally deliver rewards primarily in the extrinsic form of money. If people are not only interested in the income they earn but also are motivated by other components of their job, for example, satisfaction from task completion or challenging work, then increasing pay may either have a small positive, zero, or even negative effect on performance. Most social psychological research suggests that people do not want to believe they work primarily for money, and studies show that public servants are much less likely than employees in business to value money over other goals in work and life.[22] In some professions, as in the case of a religious vocation, a military career, or social service delivery, other components may be so important that money does not make up a critical portion of the benefits derived from work. Such individuals can be offended when they are treated as if they were responsive only to money. Sometimes pay-for-performance plans are referred to as "bribes" by employees and are taken to mean that management does not respect their devotion to the mission itself. Commitment to the job and employer has been shown to be strongly related to performance and is closely tied to workplace motivation, perceptions of fairness, and relationships with coworkers and supervisors rather than to pay levels.[23]

Essentially the assumptions behind pay for performance rest on a theory about people that is grounded in what Douglas McGregor calls Theory X, which holds that employees are averse to effort and would prefer not to work if they could get away with it. McGregor argues that in reality most employees would benefit from Theory Y management, which assumes that most people like to work, gain psychic as well as financial rewards from working, and want to do a good job.[24] William Ouchi adds, in his Theory Z, the concept that people typically enjoy working in teams and groups; thus they gain benefits from social interaction at work and do not function best if treated solely as independent agents.[25]

Clayton Alderfer presents a theory and evidence that all people require "existence, relatedness, and growth."[26] This is a response to Abraham Maslow's hierarchy of needs, which asserts that material needs come before any such concerns as belonging, self-esteem, or self-actualization. Alderfer, in contrast, argues that the three fundamental human needs coexist simultaneously, so that pay helps with "existence" needs but not with social or growth needs. A supportive structure of work, good management, and well-designed organizations is required for employees to have successful group or team experiences (for relatedness) and for continuous lifelong learning (for growth) as well as for a feeling of accomplishment. Thus a pay-for-performance advocate is implicitly putting emphasis on the material needs of employees and must be wary of ignoring or underestimating other needs, like social relationships or learning.

Performance pay can even decrease performance if it undercuts employees' intrinsic motivation. Rewards have been found to undermine intrinsic motivation if they are perceived to be controlling.[27] In many situations firms must rely on their employees' judgment, trusting that workers have the interest of the company in mind, even if their behavior can neither be precisely observed nor rewarded. If employees are intrinsically motivated, they will try to meet their obligations, even when they cannot be contractually required to do so, and indeed even when their performance cannot be verified. Remember also that precise monitoring is not only difficult and expensive, but it may create an adverse reaction in employees who feel they are not trusted. If performance pay undermines intrinsic motivation, overall productivity can be negatively affected.

In a similar vein Frederick Herzberg calls salary a "hygiene factor" or a "dissatisfier" in an article that has become a classic.[28] He argues that salary levels predominantly generate negative feedback to an organization, no matter how high or how constructed, especially when compared to intrinsically motivating factors like the meaning of the job, a sense of satisfaction at the accomplishment of valued tasks, and the engagement with one's values. These are factors that managers can control without performance-based pay. Alfie Kohn agrees, suggesting that managers should "pay people well, pay people fairly, and then do everything possible to get money off their minds."[29]

If motivation because of the inherent value or worth of the job is more important in the public sector than in the for-profit sector, the reduction of intrinsic motivation through performance-based pay will be a correspondingly bigger problem. Various studies have shown that those who choose to work for the public sector are more inclined to value public service and their ability to work for the public good than those who work for private businesses.[30] These differences, which were consistently documented in the 1960s through the 1970s, apparently began to decrease in the early 1980s but then were reconfirmed by later studies.[31] Some studies have tried to identify a specific factor, called public service motivation, and in a 1999 study of 10,000 federal employees this motivation was positively associated with performance.[32] While we do not have a definitive answer yet, it is reasonable to think that many public employees value the nature of their work for its own sake more highly than do their private sector counterparts.

James Heckman, Jeffrey Smith, and Christopher Tabor discuss an interesting example of intrinsic motivation related to the Job Training Partnership Act of 1982, where the absence of performance pay for caseworkers produced the desired outcome, namely to help the most disadvantaged, while the presence of performance pay created adverse incentives for the management.[33] The stated aim of the Job Training Partnership Act was to improve employment prospects and earnings of the disadvantaged. About 600 training centers all over the United States were charged with this task. Their funding included performance-based incentives. While only families below the poverty line or unemployed were eligible, centers had some discretion in accepting applicants. Because employment status and earnings after completion of program were used as performance measures, and because incentive pay went to the centers and not to the caseworkers, the centers had an incentive to select the most qualified applicants whose prospects looked good. Caseworkers, on the other hand, were intrinsically motivated to help the least well-off and tended to admit the least employable applicants. While caseworkers' preferences are more aligned with those of the general public (Congress) than with those of the managers, this alignment gave their centers a worse placement record and reduced the performance payment received.

Pay for performance works best if employees only care about absolute pay

If people evaluate compensation relative to some reference point, for example, other comparable employees' salaries or the organization's profits, then pay for performance may not work well. While relative income is rarely considered by economists to be a major concern, many people care more about changes than levels.[34] More importantly changes for the better are valued less than changes for the worse. Whether a change is perceived as a gain or as a loss depends on the reference point.

The most obvious reference point that workers use when evaluating their compensation is their past salary, which has recently been supported by an interesting study by Truman Bewley entitled *Why Wages Don't Fall during a Recession*.[35] The book investigates why salaries rarely decline during economic downturns and asks: Why do labor markets not behave like product markets, where excess supply typically leads to a fall in prices? Bewley found an answer to this question in interviews with 336 managers, labor leaders, and employment counselors in Connecticut in 1992 and 1993: Employees feel losses with disproportionate intensity, and managers know this. A wage cut, say of 5 percent, hurts employees much more than a 5 percent wage increase pleases them. A cut negatively affects employees' morale, productivity, effort, creativity, and cooperativeness.

Comparisons with peers, or social comparisons, are a second reason why performance pay may not work; they involve considerations of both procedural and distributive justice. This simply means that for a pay system to enjoy legitimacy and acceptance (both are required for effectiveness), employees must see it as fair in terms of process and outcomes. Recent research suggests that, even if outcomes are agreed to be fair, performance can be negatively affected if the process through which the outcomes are achieved is perceived as unfair.[36]

Human psychological processes make differentiation among close co-workers extremely controversial. Garrison Keillor's description of Lake Wobegon as a town where "all the children are above average" resonates in part because it also describes any given adult work force—at least their view of themselves. Very few people wish to perceive themselves as in the bottom tier of performers; in fact research shows that 80 percent of individuals feel that they fall into the top 30 percent of ability.[37]

Even though the simple performance-based pay scheme does not provide tournament-style incentives, in which some win and others lose, employees often perceive piece-rate pay as doing just that. Not everyone can be a top performer, but everyone would like to be a winner. Highly qualified people can be discouraged and leave the organization if they do not win. The silver-medal syndrome, based on a study of Olympic champions, shows that the most disappointed people are those who come in second in a competition, having hoped that they would be first.[38] Robert Behn agrees: "Any system that guarantees most people are likely to lose is a poor system for motivation," he notes. "You want to set a reward that everyone can achieve—you do not want only the top 20 percent of people to succeed."[39]

Studies of social comparison effects show that employees receiving bonuses are likely to find ways to share them with their work group, to alternate or rotate who receives them, or to do almost anything to reduce distinctions among group members. This has been documented in the federal and state sector, as in the case of a group of Wyoming public sector workers who decided to hold a party with the annual bonus rather than endorsing the distinctions it was intended to promote.

What is perceived as fair? In some cases there may be differences between the public and the private sector. For instance, more than 40 percent of U.S. public employees are unionized and are familiar with a system that reduces inequality between the lowest- and highest-paid employees. Pay increases are typically a result of an increase in responsibility or seniority. This system has a high degree of perceived procedural justice, at least for those who have known nothing else since being hired. Removing the promise of increased pay after acquiring more experience or skills would be a major culture and morale shock. In addition unions typically oppose merit pay unless there are clear criteria for merit and all employees potentially can earn such pay. Unions express serious concerns about the potential for favoritism and oppose what they see as subjective evaluations that serve to divide employees who must work together.

Managers sometimes argue that the carrot-and-stick method of dealing with employees at all levels is best. A well-known Harvard Business School professor always asked his audience to imagine what kind of creature is usually depicted between the carrot and the stick.[40] He then describes what he calls the great jackass fallacy, which he suggests results in self-fulfilling behavior by employees. Further, pay for performance is probably most effective if salaries are not public, which is often the case in private business firms able to avoid exactly the kind of social comparisons we describe above. However, most U.S. government salaries are public as a result of legislation or public disclosure laws, such as the Freedom of Information Act. This would be another barrier to meeting the ideal conditions for pay-for-performance plans in the public sector.

Organization

One key organizational factor that affects the conditions under which pay for performance can be successful is the degree to which employees know what to do and whom to serve. This often relates to the problem of multi-agency, that is, the fact that some employees have many masters.

Pay for performance works best if the employees know which output to produce

Knowledge of an organization's objectives and goals is not a given for employees. Often the absence of clear goals can be attributed to multiple or changing leaders or managers with different objectives. In the private sector we often assume that a firm is a top-down hierarchy with the CEO as principal and the top managers as her agents. While this is not always accurate for a private firm, it reflects the public sector reality even less well. Typically any public servant's effort will affect many people higher in the organization who may not be able to agree on one output to be produced because of political or programmatic differences.

The problem economists call multiagency is especially pronounced in the United States because the legislature has more influence in shaping the priorities of government agencies than, for example, in the United Kingdom. "Senior executives in a congressional system of government are compelled to serve many masters," writes Alasdair Roberts.[41] He reports that Congress is indeed reluctant about performance-based reforms: "A provision to negotiate annual performance agreements had been included in the Clinton administration's bill to reorganize the Patent and Trademark Office as a performance-based organization. The U.S. Patent and Trademark Office's user groups strongly opposed the administration's plan, arguing that it would give the Commerce Department too much influence over the organization (American Intellectual Property Law Association, 1995). The House subcommittee on intellectual property agreed."[42]

The National Performance Review seems to have been aware of multiagency problems because it included only those departments in its reform program that "have a clear mission with broad-based support from its key 'stakeholders'—both internal and external to the agency—regarding its mission."[43] Excluded from the very beginning were those organizations in which public servants also cater to reference groups outside of politics, such as economists and lawyers in the Federal Trade Commission or economists on the Council of Economic Advisers.

Conclusions

Pay for performance as outlined in economic theory and in human resource management research requires the existence of certain conditions to be an effective system for high motivation and outcomes. These conditions include key assumptions about the output desired, the people providing the output, and the organizational context of the workers. However, these conditions are often not met in the public sector, in part because of the complexity of the typical government product, the nature of public goods, the increasing role of teamwork and cross-agency collaboration, and the social comparisons and internal motivational dynamics of employees in general and public employees in particular.

Performance pay in the public sector can be effective under specific conditions, met, for example, by many of the national research laboratories.[44] We suggest that managers examine whether their organizations, their employees, and the jobs they supervise meet the conditions for success identified here before introducing even simple pay-for-performance schemes. We do not argue that contingent incentives are not effective under the right conditions, only that the ideal conditions are rarely met by empirical reality. Unfortunately the current literature does not allow us to give practical advice about the costs and benefits of pay for performance in a less than ideal world. All we can say with confidence is that the less well the conditions presented here approximate reality, the larger the base pay and the smaller the piece rate should be.

Managers will have to either turn to more complex monetary incentive schemes or consider adding or substituting nonmonetary incentives to motivate their employees. While beyond the scope of this chapter to describe in detail, many opportunities exist to recognize and reward positive performance in public and private organizations. These include programs such as public recognition, training and education opportunities, development assignments that are challenging, cross-functional or career-building assignments, travel to desirable places, extensive autonomy and flexibility, and others.[45] These, along with the opportunity for public service, can help employees feel that their jobs make their own lives better and contribute to the effectiveness of the work and the social goals they value.

Notes

1. These include, in chronological order of the date the proposed transformation was announced, the Patent and Trademark Office, the National Technical Information Service, the Defense Commissary Agency, the Animal and Plant Health Inspection Service, the Federal Housing Administration, the Government National Mortgage Association, the Office of Retirement Programs, the St. Lawrence Seaway Development Corporation, the Mint, and the Seafood Inspection Program. Alasdair Roberts, "Performance-Based Organizations: Assessing the Gore Plan," *Public Administration Review*, vol. 57, no. 6 (1997), p. 466.

2. David Osborne, "Reform and Invest: Reinvention's Next Steps," in Walter Marshall, ed., *Building the Bridge: Ten Big Ideas to Transform America* (Lanham, Md.: Rowman & Littlefield, 1997), pp. 93–109.

3. *Taylorist* here refers to the standard time-and-motion study approach to work efficiency pioneered by Frederick W. Taylor in the 1910s. Many human resource management

scholars cite Taylor's *Principles of Scientific Management* (Harper and Row, 1911) as a basis for early management approaches to getting workers to produce more output.

4. A recent review on pay for performance concludes: "Despite the frequent use of pay for performance as an incentive motivator because of presumed value of money to employees, many lingering doubts remain regarding the effectiveness of this approach. . . . In particular, with but a few exceptions . . . most of the evidence regarding the effectiveness of pay for performance is based on anecdotal testimonials and one-time company cases, rather than on methodologically more rigorous empirical studies." Alexander D. Stajkovic and Fred Luthans, "Differential Effects of Incentive Motivators on Work Performance," *Academy of Management Journal,* vol. 4, no. 3 (2001), p. 582.

5. Avinash Dixit, "Incentives and Organizations in the Public Sector: An Interpretative Review," Department of Economics, Princeton University, 2001; Robert Gibbons, "Incentives in Organizations," *Journal of Economic Perspectives,* vol. 12 (1998), pp. 115–32; Candice Prendergast, "The Provision of Incentives in Firms," *Journal of Economic Literature,* vol. 37, no. 1 (1999), pp. 7–63.

6. Edward P. Lazear, "Performance, Pay, and Productivity," *American Economic Review,* vol. 90, no. 5 (2000), pp. 1346–61.

7. For a critical summary of Lazear's study, showing what in the analysis is transferable to other kinds of work and what is not, see James N. Baron and David M. Kreps, *Strategic Human Resources: Frameworks for General Managers* (Wiley, 1999), pp. 243–44.

8. Iris Bohnet and Felix Oberholzer-Gee, "Pay-for-Performance: Motivation and Selection Effects," in Bruno S. Frey and Margit Osterloh, eds., *Successful Management by Motivation: Balancing Extrinsic and Intrinsic Incentives* (Berlin: Springer, 2001), pp. 119–39.

9. One Next Steps Initiative executive said that "the crispness of the targets, the discipline it exerts on us, the clarity of accountability, the focus on customers, are all good for us. . . . I can tell you from personal experience it is certainly very real and marked. It does make a difference." Roberts, "Performance-Based Organizations," p. 471.

10. Ibid., p. 467.

11. Alan S. Blinder, *Paying for Productivity: A Look at the Evidence* (Brookings, 1990), p. 3.

12. Bengt Holmstrom and Paul Milgrom, "Multi-task Principal-Agent Analysis: Incentive Contracts, Asset Ownership, and Job Design," *Journal of Law, Economics, and Organization,* vol. 7 (1991), pp. 24–52.

13. Charles Brown, "Firms: Choice of Method of Pay," *Industrial and Labor Relations Review,* vol. 43 (February 1990), pp. 165S–82S.

14. James Q. Wilson, *Bureaucracy: What Government Agencies Do and Why They Do It* (Basic Books, 1989), p. 42.

15. Max Stier and the Partnership for Public Service, "Performance-Oriented Pay in the Federal Government," paper prepared for Kennedy School of Government Executive Session, Future of Public Service, Washington, April 29, 2002.

16. Brian Hall and Jeffrey B. Liebman, "Are CEOs Really Paid Like Bureaucrats?" *Quarterly Journal of Economics,* vol. 113, no. 3 (1998), pp. 653–92; Kevin J. Murphy, "Executive Compensation," in Orley Ashenfelter and David Card, eds., *Handbook of Labor Economics,* vol. 3 (Amsterdam: Elsevier, 1999), pp. 2485–63; Cynthia G. Wagner, "Soaring CEO Salaries," *The Futurist,* vol. 33, no. 9 (1999), pp. 9–10.

17. Marianne Bertrand and Sendhil Mullainathan, "Are CEOs Rewarded for Luck? The Ones without Principles Are," *Quarterly Journal of Economics*, vol. 116, no. 3 (2001), pp. 901–32.

18. Joseph Newhouse, "The Economics of Group Practice," *Journal of Human Resources*, vol. 8, no. 1 (1973), pp. 37–56.

19. Daniel Hansen, "Worker Performance and Group Incentives: A Case Study," *Industrial and Labor Relations Review*, vol. 51 (1997), pp. 37–49.

20. Ruth Wageman, "Interdependence and Group Effectiveness," *Administrative Science Quarterly*, vol. 40 (March 1995), pp. 145–80.

21. For additional discussion, see J. Richard Hackman, *Leading Teams: Setting the Stage for Great Performances* (Harvard Business School Press, 2002).

22. Hal G. Rainey, *Understanding and Managing Public Organizations*, 2d ed. (Jossey-Bass, 1997), p. 213.

23. John P. Meyer and Natalie J. Allen, *Commitment in the Workplace: Theory, Research, and Application* (Thousand Oaks, Calif.: Sage, 1997).

24. Douglas McGregor, "Theory X: The Traditional View of Direction and Control," and "Theory Y: The Integration of Individual and Organizational Goals," in *The Human Side of Enterprise* (McGraw-Hill, 1960), pp. 33–57.

25. William Ouchi, *Theory Z: How American Business Can Meet the Japanese Challenge* (Addison-Wesley, 1981).

26. Clayton Alderfer, *Existence, Relatedness, and Growth* (Free Press, 1972).

27. For an extensive survey of psychological studies, see E. L. Deci, R. Koestner, and R. M. Ryan, "A Meta-Analytic Review of Experiments Examining the Effects of Extrinsic Rewards on Intrinsic Motivation," *Psychological Bulletin*, vol. 125, no. 3 (1999), pp. 627–68. For an application to management, see Frey and Osterloh, *Successful Management*. Kenneth Arrow in *The Limits of Organization* (Norton, 1974) was among the first economists to point out that financial incentives can disrupt "implicit agreements" in organizations. Teresa M. Amabile, "How to Kill Creativity," *Harvard Business Review* (September–October 1998), pp. 77–87, shows that pay for performance can decrease creativity.

28. Frederick Herzberg, "One More Time: How Do You Motivate Employees?" *Harvard Business Review*, vol. 65, no. 5 (1987), pp. 109–20.

29. Alfie Kohn, *Punished by Rewards* (Houghton-Mifflin, 1993), p. 36.

30. Rainey, *Understanding and Managing Public Organizations*, p. 215.

31. For a summary, see Carole L. Jurkiewicz, Tom K. Massey Jr., and Roger G. Brown, "Motivation in Public and Private Organizations," *Public Productivity and Management Review*, vol. 21, no. 3 (March 1998), pp. 230–50; they also report that some studies have found fewer differences between the private and the public sector.

32. Katherine C. Naff and John Crum, "Working for America: Does Public Service Motivation Make a Difference?" *Review of Public Personnel Administration*, vol. 19, no. 4 (Fall 1999), pp. 5–16; J. L. Perry, "Antecedents of Public Service Motivation," *Journal of Public Administration and Research*, vol. 7, no. 2 (1997), pp. 181–97.

33. James J. Heckman, Jeffrey A. Smith, and Christopher Tabor, "What Do Bureaucrats Do? The Effects of Performance Standards and Bureaucratic Preferences on Acceptance into the JTBA Program," *Advances in the Study of Entrepreneurship, Innovation, and Growth*, vol. 7 (1996), pp. 191–217.

34. Daniel Kahneman and Amos Tversky, "Prospect Theory: An Analysis of Decisions under Risk," *Econometrics,* vol. 47 (1979), pp. 263–91.

35. Truman F. Bewley, *Why Don't Wages Fall during a Recession* (Harvard University Press, 1999).

36. Baron and Kreps, *Strategic Human Resources.*

37. Robert Behn, "Measuring Performance against the 80-30 Syndrome," *Governing* (June 1993), p. 70.

38. V. H. Medvec, S. F. Madey, and T. Gilovich, "When Less Is More: Counterfactual Thinking and Satisfaction among Olympic Medalists," *Journal of Personality and Social Psychology,* vol. 69, no. 4 (October 1995), p. 603.

39. Personal communication, January 28, 2003. See also Robert D. Behn, "A Personnel System That Motivates," *Governing* (May 1995), p. 78.

40. Harry Levinson, *The Great Jackass Fallacy* (Harvard Business School Press, 1973).

41. Roberts, "Performance-Based Organizations," p. 474.

42. Ibid., p. 471.

43. Al Gore, "Governing in a Balanced Budget World," speech at the National Press Club, Washington, March 4, 1996 (http//: govinfo.library.unt.edu/npr/library/speeches/272e.html [February 11, 2003]).

44. James R. Thompson, "Devising Administrative Reform That Works: The Example of the Reinvention Lab Program," *Public Administration Review,* vol. 59, no. 4 (1999), pp. 283–93. Research laboratories are technical agencies relatively close to the ideal (a clear line of accountability avoids multiprincipal problems, and user fees mean that the goods the agencies provide are not public). They collect or disseminate information, expedite work processes, automate cash transactions, and so forth.

45. See Baron and Kreps, *Strategic Human Resources,* pp. 189–210, or any good human resources management text for a series of examples.

14

DEREK BOK

Government Personnel Policy
in Comparative Perspective

I MAGINE RUNNING A large conglomerate, such as General Electric, with the following personnel practices. The top eight to ten levels of corporate executives, from chief executive officer to associate deputy assistant vice president, are almost all filled by people recruited from outside the company. Their average term in office is approximately two years. Most of them have prior business experience, but many have never been employed by this particular firm, and few have ever served in the same division in which they now work. Because the hiring process is agonizingly slow, with much checking and rechecking by other offices in the company, many key positions are unfilled at any point in time, adding further to the confusion caused by the constant turnover within the ranks of higher management.

In contrast to the upper-echelon executives, the rest of the company's management and professional staff are mainly permanent employees, most of whom have served for a decade or more. Their CEO regularly refers to them dismissively as "the bureaucracy." They are a badly paid lot, by and large, with salaries that are often well below average for persons holding comparable jobs in private industry. The company is hardly an aggressive recruiter; campus visits are erratic, hiring procedures are cumbersome, and job offers are typically made months after other companies have snapped up the most talented prospects. Opportunities for advancement are limited, of course, since almost all the jobs with real power and responsibility are held by managers recruited from elsewhere. Training is far less extensive than what one normally finds in large corporations. Under these conditions it is hardly surprising that recent college surveys have found that seniors give high ratings to working for the conglomerate only for its job security and fringe benefits, two of the items that other surveys have shown to be among the least important factors to graduating students choosing jobs. In more important respects, such as opportunities for advancement, the chance to do challenging work, and levels of compensation, the company ranks so low as to be virtually off the charts.

Judging by this account, almost anyone would conclude that the prospects for the conglomerate are exceedingly bleak. How could any company operated in this fashion hope to survive? Why would it even try? Odd as it may seem, however, this corporation is run almost exactly like the executive branch of the United States government.

Consider now another large, diversified company. In this firm only the top two or three tiers of officers are appointed from outside, and almost all of these have extensive firsthand experience with the external environment in which the company operates. The rest of the professional and management staff are long-term employees of the firm. Most of them were recruited based on merit from the country's leading universities, where they compiled strong academic records. They receive excellent on-the-job training and can realistically aspire to jobs of great influence if they perform well. (Even those who retire or leave the firm often go on to hold important jobs in industry or political life.) Many observers say that the long-term staff virtually run the business, while the top officials brought in from outside occupy themselves chiefly with representing the firm to important external audiences and aligning its policies with major needs and opportunities emerging from this larger environment.

In contrast to the first company, this corporation seems to be organized along quite rational lines. Its officials seem far more qualified by ability and experience to operate a highly complicated organization in a complex, constantly changing environment. The second company, of course, is managed much like the governments of most other advanced democracies, such as Japan, Britain, France, Germany, and Canada.

Our normal sense of what it takes to run an organization effectively tells us that the second company must be functioning much better than the first. This sobering thought has not escaped notice. The handicaps under which our government operates have been described with much clarity and with a wealth of detail by a succession of blue-ribbon commissions formed from time to time over the past several decades to study the operation of the executive branch. Again and again these distinguished panels have advised the government to improve its recruiting procedures, lift its pay scales, increase its training efforts, streamline its personnel procedures, and cut back severely on the number of political appointees, in order to give career civil servants a better chance of holding important, challenging jobs. These recommendations regularly meet with approval by knowledgeable audiences. Yet just as regularly, once the dust has cleared, the previous problems reappear virtually intact, allowing the old methods of operation to continue much as before.

The author of this chapter served as a member of the so-called Volcker Commission, which conducted an extensive review of government personnel policies in the late 1980s in response to wide public comment on a "quiet crisis" of morale within the federal civil service. The commission's final report repeated most of the familiar nostrums for improving the federal bureaucracy—more aggressive recruiting, better training, greater exposure to general management experience, higher salaries, performance-based compensation, simplified hiring procedures, and a one-third reduction in the number of political appointees in order to increase opportunities for civil servants to rise to positions of real responsibility.[1] The commission's proposals were greeted with the usual approbation from seasoned government-watchers. Yet ten years later, a well-known scholar, Paul Light, included the following words in a book about the "new" public service:

> There can be little doubt that the quiet crisis continues. . . . The federal government's . . . hiring system for recruiting talent, top to bottom, underwhelms at almost every task it undertakes. It is slow in the hiring, almost useless in the firing, overly permissive in the promoting, penurious in the training, and utterly absent in the managing of a vast and hidden work force of contractors and consultants. . . . Sad to say, when young Americans are asked to picture themselves in public service careers, particularly at the federal level, they picture themselves in dead-end jobs where seniority, not performance, rules.[2]

Obstacles to Reforming Government Service

What accounts for this stubborn reluctance to change? Why have a succession of commissions offering suggestions that seem so obvious met with such strikingly meager results? Government officials offer various explanations. They insist that corrective changes are already under way, or they blame the neglect on a previous administration, or they plead the distractions of other pressing problems. But these are rationalizations. The fact is that reforming the civil service has rarely seemed important enough to merit high-level attention, and the changes that do get made often erode over time, leaving the original state of affairs more or less intact. The incentives facing political leaders and high-level administrative officials—coupled with simple human nature—have much to do with this inertia. In brief, when government leaders think about implementing civil service reform, the benefits seem speculative and long-term, whereas the costs are all too tangible and immediate.

Expanded training and larger recruiting budgets are ideas attractive in principle but easily discarded when it becomes clear that paying for such steps would require cutting back other programs or jeopardizing new initiatives by which political appointees hope to make their mark. After all, what will better training actually accomplish? And when will the results begin to show? For a harried agency head, how can such intangible, long-run benefits outweigh the immediate cost and disruption of paying valued employees to leave work and study for a year in Harvard's midcareer program or Princeton's Woodrow Wilson School?

Top officials find reducing the number of political appointees an even less appetizing prospect. American presidents relish the fact that they can place many more individuals of their choosing in high policymaking jobs than heads of government in other leading democracies. Such appointments help the White House see to it that its policies are faithfully carried out. What is more, they provide the means to exercise control over the bureaucracy, award patronage, counter the influence of congressional committees over important federal agencies, and gain the services of able people from the private sector. Why should a president trade these immediate advantages for the distant possibility that expanded opportunities for career officials will someday improve the quality of the civil service?

Politicians regard pay increases for top civil servants as almost equally unappetizing. Such raises are not popular with ordinary citizens, who look upon career bureaucrats as lazier and less competent than employees in the private sector. Closing the gap with private sector salaries costs a tidy sum, never a happy prospect during times when budget cutting is in favor. And what will the benefits be? Higher morale? Lower turnover? Better quality of new recruits? At best, these are all intangible gains that can usually be postponed for another year or two until the effects of further delay become obvious enough to force a major readjustment.

Lest one criticize political leaders too harshly for their shortsightedness, it is only fair to acknowledge that the benefits of civil service reform are speculative. No conceivable pay increase will make top government posts financially competitive with the private sector jobs open to graduates of leading schools of law and business. No amount of aggressive recruiting can fully overcome a culture in America that has traditionally held government bureaucrats in low esteem. As for increasing the challenge of civil service positions, even the one-third reduction in political appointments urged by the Volcker Commission would still leave all the truly attractive policymaking jobs in the hands of short-term recruits from outside the government. Besides, has not real success in attracting good people always depended on conditions beyond any politician's control—notably, a widely shared enthusiasm for social reform, such as existed in the 1930s and early 1960s—when public service was imbued with an excitement and meaning largely absent at times like the present, when government is widely looked upon with cynicism and distrust?

How Ineffective Is Our Bureaucracy?

This line of reasoning leads naturally to a second question. How much of a price do we pay for continuing to operate our executive branch in ways so easily criticized? How much more effective are government agencies in Britain, France, Japan, and other countries that seem to attract and retain such able people for their civil service?

For many years the verdict seemed to be that our federal government must be losing a great deal. That is clearly the result one would infer from the praise that many English-speaking writers traditionally gave to the civil servants of other advanced democracies. As T. J. Pempel said of Japan, "There is no denying that many of Japan's public policies have been highly efficient, both in the instrumental sense of achieving targeted goals and in objective comparisons with other industrialized countries. . . . Much of this political success can be attributed to the country's national bureaucracy."[3] Commentators on postwar France also gave high marks to the French civil service for providing efficient administration and much-needed stability amid the kaleidoscope of multiple parties and repeated cabinet shifts that characterized French politics during much of the period.[4] British civil servants likewise received a generous measure of praise. In the words of Lord Hailsham, who served a total of nineteen years in the cabinet, the British civil service was "surely one of the most talented bodies of men ever to be engaged in the art and science of civil government, recruited from the cream of the universities, selected by examination and interview, trained in political impartiality and secretiveness, rewarded for industry far beyond the calls of duty, advanced for efficiency, and gaining during the experience of a working lifetime more than the most able and experienced minister can summon to his task."[5]

During the past twenty-five years, however, these favorable impressions have been overtaken by a tidal wave of criticism. In every advanced democracy, faced with looming deficits, slowing economic growth, and the emergence of a "new" conservatism, the civil service and the entire administrative state have come under sharp, wide-ranging attack. In the words of Patricia Ingraham, a veteran civil service watcher, "As we approach the end of the twentieth century, there is no region of the world whose nations express satisfaction with public bureaucracies and civil service systems."[6] Almost everywhere the criticisms have been the same. Government officials have been accused of being too remote, too inattentive to the citizens they serve, too slow to adapt to basic changes in the surrounding society, too preoccupied with policy, and too little concerned with the need for efficient administration.[7]

The language used in commenting on the official bureaucracy seems quite different in the past quarter century from what it was in earlier times. In speaking of Great Britain, Stephen Taylor, an experienced consultant to the government, describes the civil service as "closed, secretive, defensive, overconcerned with traditional precedent, still too preoccupied with advising ministers on policy . . . still insufficiently seized of the crucial importance of managing people and money, and nothing like as good as it should be, given the proportion of prime British brainpower it possesses, at confronting hard long-term problems by thinking forward systematically and strategically."[8] Adds Gerald Caiden, writing in 1991 to describe the situation in Japan: "The Japanese administrative elite was [even] more elitist than Whitehall, probably more 'closed, secretive, defensive, overconcerned with tradition and precedent' than its British counterpart. It was not as good as it should have been given its talent, and it was a drag on the private sector with its excessive formalism and bureaucratism."[9]

Peter Drucker is even more scathing in discussing Japan's elite civil service in 1998: "The bureaucracy's record is dismal. It reeled from one failure after another for the past twenty-five years. It failed miserably to pick the winners in the late 1960s and early 1970s, choosing instead such losers as the mainframe computer. . . . The bureaucracy failed again in the 1980s. Panicked by a mild recession, it plunged Japan into the wild excess of the speculative fiscal bubble and with it into the present financial crisis. . . . Since then, the bureaucracy has been revealed to be riddled with corruption, even prestigious agencies such as the Bank of Japan or the Ministry of Finance. This has cost the bureaucrats their claim to moral leadership. Even the bureaucracy's staunchest supporters, the big companies, have turned against it."[10]

Commentators in other countries have harped on similar themes. As Ezra Suleiman has acknowledged, "The institution in France that today bears the brunt of attacks from the entire range of the political, economic, and social spectrum is the French administration and the state bureaucracy."[11] The well-known French social analyst Michel Crozier has accused the administrative elite of imposing a stifling conformity on all branches of government that makes genuine adaptation and reform extremely difficult.[12] In Canada former prime minister Brian Mulroney remarked that "since coming to Ottawa, I have been appalled by the waste of time and talent in government," adding that civil servants under his administration could expect to receive "pink slips and running shoes."[13] In Sweden Professor Petersson has struck a similar note, observing that "expansion of the public sector has produced a large bureaucracy, which becomes ever more intractable and unmanageable."[14] Increasingly Swedes have accused public officials of being too inflexible, too insistent on following the rules, too obsessed by procedural details.

America's bureaucracy, of course, has not escaped harsh treatment from both sides of the political aisle. Jimmy Carter was an outspoken critic. So was Ronald Reagan. Al Gore also spoke loudly of the need for thoroughgoing reform, although he took pains to point out that civil servants themselves were not the problem; it was the system they worked in that caused all the difficulties.[15] Significantly, like White House critics before him, Gore paid no attention in his voluminous report to the role of political appointees. Apparently they were not part of the problem, as officially defined.

Unfortunately we cannot reliably determine whether the executive branch of the United States works better or worse than its counterparts abroad. There is no way of measuring overall success or failure, let alone figuring out what portion of any good or bad results can be fairly ascribed to the work of the bureaucracy. Moreover, the responsibilities of executives and bureaucrats differ so greatly from one country to another—as do the powers they are allowed to exercise and the constraints imposed upon them by their respective constitutional systems—that any attempt at precise comparison would be virtually impossible.

What does seem clear is that recent criticism of government administration in other advanced democracies is no less harsh than the assessments we are used to hearing in the United States. Other straws in the wind likewise suggest that our executive branch may not fare as badly, comparatively speaking, as the analysis at the beginning of this chapter might lead one to believe. In contrast to countries such as Japan and France, corruption in our federal bureaucracy is generally thought to be quite rare. Federal bureaucrats are not only much more trusted (by a rate of five to one) than members of Congress; in surveys of public opinion in Britain, France, Germany, and the United States toward a long list of occupational groups, civil servants commanded greater trust in America than in any of the other three countries.[16] Recent polls by the University of Michigan also suggest that Americans do not regard most federal agencies as notably less responsive or less efficient than most of the private companies with which they come in contact.[17]

Why Does Our Executive Branch Compare As Well As It Does?

Although these bits and scraps of information prove nothing, they at least raise the possibility that our peculiar way of organizing the executive branch may not work as badly, relative to more conventional systems, as first impressions could lead one to believe. How could this be? What conceivable cause might allow our executive branch to compare reasonably well with that of other leading democracies?

Is it simply that our executive branch has taken on fewer tasks and has delegated more of its work to outside organizations than most other advanced democratic governments? Compared to their counterparts in Europe, our government leaders have clearly been much less inclined to try to operate banks, railroads, television, health services, steel mills, and other major enterprises. At the same time our executive branch has also been noteworthy for its willingness to contract out the bulk of its administrative tasks to state and local governments, nonprofit organizations, and corporations. Analysts estimate that only 15 percent of the services for which the federal government is responsible are actually performed directly by federal employees. With so few functions to perform, perhaps it is not surprising that the executive branch performs as well as it does.

While there is something to this point, it falls far short of explaining why the government might not perform too badly, compared with other leading democracies, in carrying out the nation's programs. True, our government has taken on fewer functions than most other industrialized countries, but our officials have had to administer programs covering a much larger and more diverse nation. Moreover, delegating work to other organizations may relieve the government of some responsibilities, but it imposes others, notably selecting and overseeing those who do the work of administering public programs. These monitoring tasks can be quite manageable where the work involved is simple and straightforward, as in repairing roads or removing garbage. But supervising nursing homes or the contracting out of complex weapons systems can be extremely difficult if officials are to succeed in holding waste, fraud, and abuse to a minimum. Up to a point the government can rely on market forces to help attain reasonable levels of efficiency, but competition does not work equally well in all situations, and even where it does, it gives rise to added incentives to cheat and evade the law that impose further burdens on federal overseers.

To fully explain why other governments might not perform demonstrably better than our own, we should consider another possibility that may cause discomfort in some academic circles. If bureaucracies such as those in Japan and France have run into trouble, it just might be that recruiting "the best and the brightest" does not work as well in practice as many of us in leading universities would like to think. There are several reasons why this could be so. Academic success does not correlate especially well with leadership ability, administrative judgment, or managerial skill (which may explain why grades seem to count for a lot less in business school than they do in law school). Instead academic proficiency may lead civil servants to emphasize policy analysis more than administration, a common complaint about government bureaucracies around the world. Worse yet, success at school may breed a kind of intellectual smugness that causes civil servants to pay too little attention to the views of their political superiors, on the one hand, or the desires of the citizenry, on the other. Such attitudes could be reinforced by the fact that the best and the brightest in most advanced democracies tend to come predominantly from upper-middle-class backgrounds and hence to be largely unrepresentative of most people they serve.

The recruitment and personnel practices common to many advanced democracies may also impair the performance of public bureaucracies in other ways. The fact that many civil servants spend their entire career in the government, or even in a single government agency, may build relevant knowledge and skills, but it can also contribute to a certain insularity, a lack of sensitivity to the needs, problems, and feelings of people and organizations affected by the government's decisions. When ordinary citizens become more independent and resentful of paternalistic governments, as they have come to be in most advanced democracies, elite bureaucracies may be slow to adapt and give the public greater freedom of choice.

The long service of so many senior career officials could likewise contribute to a certain inertia—an exaggerated fondness for established procedures, familiar policies, accustomed routines—for which bureaucrats everywhere are famous. The dominance of a certain type of education, no matter how dazzling, must add even more to a tendency toward conformity, insularity, and resistance to change. Recruiting generalists from Oxford and Cambridge may have served Britain well in some respects, but it could have severe disadvantages now that governments confront an array of problems that are increasingly technical and specialized. The tendency in much of continental Europe to choose civil servants from backgrounds in law could well dispose bureaucracies to be too rigidly preoccupied with observing "correct" procedures and scrupulously following the rules. Similarly, taking the cream of the nation's youth from a single source, such as the École Nationale d'Administration or the Law Faculty of Tokyo University, may produce an intellectually distinguished civil service, but it may also yield an approach too rigid and uniform to cope effectively with all the different kinds of political and social problems on a modern government's agenda. The narrow training received by such bureaucratic elites may create even greater difficulties in countries where many top civil servants extend their influence more widely over national affairs by retiring early to assume high political posts and leadership jobs in large corporations and other major institutions throughout the society[18]

With these potential drawbacks in mind, one can more easily perceive the advantages of the distinctive American practice of relying heavily on short-term political appointees.[19] The constant infusion of new blood from outside the government virtually guarantees fresh ideas and greater sensitivity to other groups and sectors of society, thus effectively counteracting the insularity exhibited by many foreign bureaucracies. Political appointees may likewise bring exceptional energy and zeal to their brief periods of public service that are hard for long-service bureaucrats to match. For obvious reasons political appointees tend to have views similar to those of the regime in power, and hence are more likely to avoid the policy conflicts that sometimes occur between top civil servants and cabinet ministers in other advanced democracies. Finally the very presence of so many outside appointees makes it unlikely that the civil service will ever dominate political leaders and obstruct efforts to reform the government in the ways some critics have ascribed to French and Japanese career bureaucrats.[20]

Of course none of these advantages would outweigh the disadvantages if political leaders in the United States made extensive use of their appointive powers to reward political supporters of indifferent ability. Appointments of this kind have become relatively rare, however, except in a few limited areas of government. Among political appointees as a whole, the levels of education and government experience have gradually risen to quite impressive levels. In the current administration a remarkable 55 percent of President Bush's political appointees have spent more than half of their prior careers in government service.[21] By now almost all such officials have graduated from college, and 75 percent have Ph.D.s or professional degrees. The tendency to seek highly educated appointees has survived even the most ideological presidencies. For example, it is a little-known fact that Ronald Reagan appointed more than three times as many Harvard faculty members to government positions than did John F. Kennedy.[22]

In sum, the practice of having each new administration appoint several thousand officials from outside the government, bizarre as it may seem on first impression, turns out to have some marked advantages. It counteracts inertia, ensures an influx of new ideas, and keeps the government in touch with a variety of interested groups and constituencies. It also allows a steady infusion of talent that is possibly greater, and certainly more diverse, than a country such as ours could hope to achieve by trying to create an elite form of career civil service.

To be sure, none of these advantages can overcome the flaws in the current system. Such heavy use of outside appointments cannot help but make the civil service less attractive to talented, ambitious young people. For all the ability and prior government experience of the "in-and-outers," their brief terms of service—less than two years on average—must interfere with orderly administration and lend an excessively short-term view to the work of many agencies. Even with so many political appointees having prior terms in government, their lack of experience in the offices where they currently work—a handicap exacerbated by their short periods of service—presumably takes a further toll on the quality of their performance.

What comparative analysis suggests, therefore, is not that the American system approaches perfection, but that every system has substantial weaknesses. It is this conclusion that best explains why our executive branch, with all its problems, may still not perform as badly as one might expect, compared with the record of other advanced democracies. There are doubtless ways to improve upon our current record. Probably our executive branch could function somewhat better if political leaders were willing to take such measures as more vigorous recruitment, higher salaries, better training, and perhaps a modest reduction in the number of political appointees. But even if leaders felt impelled to make such reforms, perfection would almost certainly remain beyond their grasp, as it seems to in every other nation, if only because the various goals of an ideal civil service are not fully compatible with one another.

Implications for Schools of Public Policy and Administration

The preceding discussion has several implications for schools of policy and administration in planning their educational strategy. Eight points seem particularly apposite.

—Professional schools in major universities hope to educate the future leaders in their chosen field of activity. Accordingly leading schools of policy and administration seek to prepare students who will go on to assume positions of high responsibility in government. With this aim in mind, it may seem frustrating that so few master's degree students go directly into government service following graduation. Even so, it is well worth maintaining an active master's program for recent college graduates. The most revealing indicator for a leading school of policy and administration is not the percentage of master's students who go to work for the government immediately after graduation; rather, it is more important to observe what happens to these students over a ten-to-fifteen-year period and how many of them eventually become appointed and elected officials. Most high-level officials will begin their careers outside of government. Although relatively few of them have MPA or MPP degrees today, one should not regard current career patterns as permanent. After all, an MBA did not count for very much in business for many decades. As late as the 1960s more Harvard Law graduates were CEOs of large companies than Harvard MBAs, although the business school was graduating 50 percent more students every year. The percentage of federal political appointees with MPA or MPP degrees, though still small, has been increasing steadily in the past few decades and should continue to rise in the future.

—Faculties of public policy and administration should consider expanding the size of their joint-degree programs with law schools and business schools. (It is not necessary that joint programs be developed exclusively with law and business schools in the same university.) Most political appointees come from law or business backgrounds. Even among political appointees with an MPA or MPP degree, a large proportion also have degrees in law or business. Small wonder. Since most political appointees go in and out of government, it is only prudent to take another professional degree along with the MPA or MPP. Hence, if schools of public policy and administration hope to educate a larger share of the most influential government officials, they need to seek out talented students and offer them a joint program that allows them to earn two degrees in as efficient a manner as possible. (For much the same reason, these schools would also be well advised to offer courses that prepare their MPP and MPA students to take responsible positions in nonprofit organizations.)

—In addition it might be useful to ask law schools to consider developing a minor (say, a three-course cluster) in public policy and administration for law students. The standard law school curriculum has a lot of slack, especially in the third year. Although it could take time to develop a group of courses that would attract substantial numbers of law students, the prevalence of lawyers in politics and government service renders such a venture well worth the effort.

—Another possibility to consider is the creation of one or more joint courses for law, business, and MPP and MPA students. At present America suffers from an abrasive interface among lawyers, business executives, and public officials that makes fruitful cooperation more difficult than it should be. Each profession is prone to look at the others with suspicion or even disdain. The best place to counteract such prejudices (as well as to reach law and business students with some policy analysis) would be in classes made up of students from all three professions. Such courses could take up any of several subjects—the environment, energy policy, labor relations, and so forth—where law, business, and government converge. Classes would be taught by the discussion method using cases or problems, and participants would be encouraged to form study groups consisting of at least one student from each of the three schools. The experience could broaden the horizons of the participants and teach them at an early age that each profession has something of genuine value to bring to the table. Such an experience could be especially valuable for those students who later become in-and-outers by combining a private profession with periods of public service.

—Schools of public policy and management should also show initiative in urging college faculties to take more responsibility for the civic education of their students. The need for civic education is barely recognized today on college campuses, even though interest in politics and rates of voting are lower today among undergraduates than they have ever been since people began paying attention in the 1960s. It is true that more college students are participating in various forms of community service, but polls show that such activity is generally regarded on campus as an alternative rather than a stepping stone to involvement in government and politics. The inability of college students to perceive the ties linking public policy and politics with the problems they encounter working in housing projects and homeless shelters is symptomatic of a much larger failing on the part of undergraduate faculties. Although civic involvement has been a primary aim of education since the time of Plato and Aristotle, most colleges today are no longer paying explicit attention to this responsibility. Schools of policy and administration are the most natural source within the university to recognize this problem and try to do something about it, since they are the first to feel the consequences.

—Executive programs will continue to be of special importance for schools of policy and administration, since it is most unlikely in the foreseeable future that the majority of political appointees will have completed an MPP or MPA program. Nevertheless, since executive programs are brief, and busy professionals have limited time to spend on campus, it stands to reason that schools of policy and administration should take a special interest in experimenting with ways to educate government officials at their place of work. Already business schools are reaching high-level executives with audiotapes that can be listened to on airplanes or driving to work, decision books that give managers instant computer access to articles and other readings relevant to important decisions they face, and advanced courses that combine brief periods on campus with extensive problem-oriented work carried out at home or at work via the Internet. Schools of policy and administration would do well to experiment along similar lines.

—Insofar as other priorities permit, schools of public policy and administration might also consider doing more to help other countries develop schools of public service for their own citizens. To a surprising degree (at least to this writer) American public policy curricula seem to have great appeal to students from other countries, even though these students come from nations with very different systems and institutions of government. Conceivably therefore schools of policy and administration might have their greatest impact through efforts to build similar programs overseas, much as business faculties influenced management education everywhere in the 1960s by helping to develop business schools in other countries around the world.

—Finally, by capitalizing on their appeal to foreign students, schools of policy and administration might do a lot to help build a cadre of genuinely cosmopolitan civil servants who could collaborate more effectively in future years in resolving a variety of international problems. The point is not that such students would all learn to love America through their period of study in this country. Rather the hope would be that the common language and common educational experience derived from study in the United States would help in countless unanticipated ways to promote greater understanding and more effective international problem-solving in years to come. To fulfill this hope, however, will require greater efforts than are currently being made on most campuses to recruit promising students from abroad and integrate them fully into classroom discussions and extracurricular life in the university.

The Road Ahead

Those who toil in schools of public policy and administration are used to hearing gloomy talk about the prospects for the profession they serve. Many Americans look upon government as clumsy, ineffective, and unresponsive to their needs. Bureaucrats are widely considered to be a lazy, unimaginative lot. Few able young people are interested in public service, preferring the headier, more remunerative world of business, investment banking, and corporate law. Never, it seems, will the United States rival other leading democracies in luring the best and brightest into public service.

While there is some truth to this account, it is vastly overstated. In fact the quality of people electing to work for the government is not nearly as depressing as the conventional wisdom would have one believe. Although able students may not be much attracted to lifetime careers in the civil service, many highly talented and successful individuals go to great lengths to wangle appointments for themselves in Republican and Democratic administrations. Members of Congress have never been as highly educated as they are today, and the quality of people being recruited to policy positions in state and big city administrations is clearly better than it was fifty years ago.

In short, there are plenty of able, highly educated Americans spending substantial portions of their careers in important government jobs. Unlike their counterparts in other advanced democracies, however, such people do not necessarily begin their working lives in government, nor do they remain toiling permanently in government bureaucracies. Instead they move in and out of government in a manner that has obvious disadvantages but also has many benefits that are often overlooked.

For American schools of public policy, these career patterns present a challenge much greater than anything facing schools of law, business, and medicine. Future leaders in government do not pass uniformly through a single educational point of entry, as they do in the major private professions. Thus it is hard to reach them through a traditional entry-level professional education. Still, the problem is far from hopeless. With a growing acceptance of the need for midcareer education and the rapid development of new technologies for training professionals in their homes and places of work, the opportunities for educating leaders in government have never been as great as they are at present.

In addition, for whatever reason, American schools of public policy and administration are widely regarded by interested students abroad as the best of their kind in the world. They are almost certainly the destination of choice for talented people overseas who are committed to careers in public service and want to have a year or two of education in another country. This preferred position creates another set of important opportunities for faculties of policy and administration.

The outlook for such schools, therefore, is actually much brighter than much of the current talk about government might have one believe. The question before these faculties is not whether there are any exciting possibilities for them at a time when people seem so cynical and distrustful of government. Rather the true question is whether such schools can summon enough imagination to take full advantage of the important opportunities they already possess.

Notes

1. National Commission on the Public Service, *Leadership for America: Rebuilding the Public Service* (Government Printing Office, 1989).

2. Paul C. Light, *The New Public Service* (Brookings, 1999), pp. 2, 4.

3. T. J. Pempel, "Organizing for Efficiency: The Higher Civil Service in Japan," in Ezra N. Suleiman, ed., *Bureaucrats and Policy Making: A Comparative Overview* (New York: Holmes and Meier, 1985), pp. 72–107. See also Takeshi Ishido and Ellis S. Krauss, eds., *Democracy in Japan* (Pittsburgh University Press, 1989), p. 35.

4. See Ezra N. Suleiman, *Politics, Power, and Bureaucracy in France: The Administrative Elite* (Princeton University Press, 1974).

5. Quoted in Peter Hennessy, *Whitehall* (Simon and Schuster, 1989), p. 686. When the author of this chapter went to see that long-time veteran of foreign affairs and defense policy Paul Nitze, in the early 1970s, to ask support for the new and struggling Kennedy School, Nitze replied that, in his experienced view, recruiting top students with a good general education, in the manner of the British civil service, was clearly far superior to trying to train students in a professional school of public policy.

6. Patricia W. Ingraham, "The Reform Agenda for National Civil Service Systems: External Stress and Internal Strains," in Hans A. G. M. Bekke, James L. Perry, and Theo A. J. Toomen, eds., *Civil Service Systems in Comparative Perspective* (Indiana University Press, 1996), p. 247.

7. See, for example, Gerald E. Caiden, *Administrative Reform Comes of Age* (New York: Walter de Gruyter Press, 1991); B. Guy Peters and Donald J. Savoie, *Governance in a Changing Environment* (McGill-Queen's University Press, 1995).

8. Hennessy, *Whitehall*, p. 686.

9. Caiden, *Administrative Reform*, p. 233.

10. Peter F. Drucker, "In Defense of Japanese Bureaucracy," *Foreign Affairs*, vol. 77 (September–October, 1998), p. 68.

11. Suleiman, *Politics, Power, and Bureaucracy*, p. 30.

12. Michel Crozier, *Crise de l'Intelligence: Essai sur l'Impuissance des Élites a se Reformer* (Paris: InterEditions, 1995).

13. Quoted in Donald J. Savoie, *Thatcher, Reagan, Mulroney: In Search of a New Bureaucracy* (University of Pittsburgh Press, 1994), p. 91.

14. O. Petersson, "Democracy and Power in Sweden," *Scandinavian Political Studies*, vol. 14 (1991), p. 173.

15. Al Gore, *From Red Tape to Results: Creating a Government That Works Better & Costs Less, A Report of the National Performance Review* (1993) (http://govinfo.library.unt.edu/npr/whoweare/historypart1.html [October 1, 2002]).

16. Hal G. Rainey, "Public Opinion toward the Civil Service," in Bekke, Perry, and Toomen, *Civil Service Systems*, p. 180.

17. Robert Kuttner, "Government's Happy Customers," *Boston Globe*, December 19, 1999, p. C7. More generally, see Daniel Katz and others, *Bureaucratic Encounters* (Washington: Institute for Social Research, 1975).

18. See Crozier, *Crise de l'Intelligence*.

19. For one of the few balanced assessments of America's heavy use of political appointees, see Hugh Heclo, "The In-and-Outer System: A Critical Assessment," *Political Science Quarterly*, vol. 103 (1988), p. 37.

20. Indeed one professor of public administration, Fred Riggs, maintains that America's peculiar mixture of civil servants and political appointees is responsible for the fact that our bureaucracy has not overthrown or dominated the government, as he claims it has in most other presidential (as opposed to parliamentary) systems. Ali Farizmand, ed., *Modern Systems of Government: Exploring the Role of Bureaucrats and Politicians* (Sage, 1997), p. 43.

21. See John D. Donahue, "A Half-Century of In-and-Outers in the Senior Federal Civil Service: Some Data on Career and Educational Backgrounds," paper prepared for Visions of Governance in the Twenty-First Century Faculty Seminar, John F. Kennedy School of Government, Harvard University, January 28, 2002.

22. G. Calvin MacKenzie, *The In-and-Outers: Presidential Appointees and Transient Government in Washington* (Johns Hopkins University Press, 1987).

Contributors

All contributors are at the John F. Kennedy School of Government, Harvard University, unless otherwise indicated.

Robert D. Behn
Visiting Professor and Professor of Public Policy, Duke University

Linda J. Bilmes
Lecturer in Public Policy

Iris Bohnet
Assistant Professor of Public Policy

Derek Bok
Harvard University President Emeritus and the 300th Anniversary University Professor

George J. Borjas
Robert W. Scrivner Professor of Economics and Social Policy

John D. Donahue
Raymond Vernon Lecturer in Public Policy and Director, Weil Program on Collaborative Governance

Susan C. Eaton
Assistant Professor of Public Policy

David Gergen
Professor of Public Service and Director, Center for Public Leadership

Stephen Goldsmith
Professor of the Practice of Public Management and Faculty Director, Institute for Government Innovation

Merilee S. Grindle
*Edward S. Mason Professor of
    International Development*

Elaine Ciulla Kamarck
Lecturer in Public Policy

Barbara Kellerman
*Executive Director, Center for Public
    Leadership*

Alex Keyssar
*Matthew W. Stirling Jr. Professor of
    History and Social Policy*

Ernest R. May
*Charles Warren Professor of
    American History at Harvard*

Jeffrey R. Neal
*Director, Human Resources, Defense
    Logistics Agency*

Pippa Norris
*Paul F. McGuire Lecturer in
    Comparative Politics*

Joseph S. Nye Jr.
*Don K. Price Professor of Public
    Policy and Dean*

Kenneth Winston
Lecturer in Ethics

Index